...rn Ameri

P9-EEQ-776

DATE DUE

WITHDRAWN

MODERN AMERICAN POETRY

MODERN AMERICAN POETRY

edited by
R. W. (Herbie) Butterfield

VISION
and
BARNES & NOBLE

Vision Press Limited
Fulham Wharf
Townmead Road
London SW6 2SB

and

Barnes & Noble Books
81 Adams Drive
Totowa, NJ 07512

ISBN (UK) 0 85478 385 7
ISBN (US) 0 389 20460 9

© 1984 by Vision Press Ltd.
First published in the U.S.A. 1984

All rights reserved

Printed and bound in Great Britain by
Unwin Brothers Ltd.,
Old Woking, Surrey.
Phototypeset by Galleon Photosetting,
Ipswich, Suffolk.
MCMLXXXIV

Contents

Introduction

by R. W. (HERBIE) BUTTERFIELD

Emerson and Poe are the two most influential American poets and poetic theorists to have lived and written before those poets considered in this volume, at whose head stands Whitman, the founding father of modern American poetry, of a poetry both—let the words be spoken slowly and emphatically—modern and American. Emerson's celebrated dictum yoking the expansive American nation with a poetry appropriate to its character is to be found in his essay, 'The Poet' of 1844, where he announces: 'America is a poem in our eyes; its ample geography dazzles the imagination, and it will not wait long for metres.' Some five years later, in the last year of his life, Poe made a statement, equally famous but of utterly different bearing, wherein he devoted himself in principle to a pure poetry, existing in a sphere of technique and artifice alternative to the natural and historical world: 'There neither exists nor *can* exist any work more thoroughly dignified—more supremely noble than this very poem—this poem *per se*—this poem which is a poem and nothing more—this poem written solely for the poem's sake.' At about the same time Whitman was discovering the wider American continent on his journey from New York to New Orleans and back, and was beginning to experiment with the poetic forms that were soon to shape *Leaves of Grass*, the life's work that in 1888 in 'A Backward Glance O'er Travel'd Roads' he termed in retrospect 'an attempt, from first to last, to put a *Person*, a human being (myself, in the latter half of the Nineteenth Century, in America,) freely, fully and truly on record'.

These three remarks from a century and more ago on the nature of an envisaged or an achieved poetry may serve between them to describe the principal concerns of the

7

American poetry that has followed. These are, simply named, America, the poem '*per se*', and the self: America, perceived extensively as a whole or intensively as a region or locus— America, exalted for its extravagant, creative possibility or execrated for its abysmal, destructive actuality; the poem, conceived either as the imagination's subjective haven or as craft's objective structure—the poem, small and accomplished or lifelong and interminable; and the self, in general tendency more isolated from society and the other than its old world counterpart—the self, expressed, explored, incarcerated, liberated, revealed, confessed, indulged, proclaimed. America, the poem, the self; and, of course, these elements conjoined: the American poem, the American self, the American poetic self.

This American poetry that began to come into its own in the mid-nineteenth century through the work in particular of Emerson, Poe and Whitman, has become in the twentieth century one of the great national literary achievements, composing a body of work remarkable on the one hand for its exceptional subtlety, on the other for its extraordinary vitality, and altogether for its amazing variety. American readers do not need an Englishman to tell them this; and English readers should not, although it is to be feared that too many do. (Strange, how little known in England still, outside a very small world of initiates, poets and professional specialists, are all save a handful of Americans: a back-handed tribute perhaps to American poetry's distinctiveness, its foreignness for the English.)

This collection of essays examines the work of some of that art's major practitioners, opening with the two brightest luminaries of the later nineteenth century, Walt Whitman and Emily Dickinson, although Dickinson's light was fated to shine only posthumously. There follow essays on six poets from the great generation of modernists, who came to the fore in the first decades of the century, to work and write, long-lived most of them, through into the 1960s. Ezra Pound, Wallace Stevens and William Carlos Williams are the acknowledged masters here, Marianne Moore and Hart Crane also assured in their standing, with Robinson Jeffers presently somewhat less secure in his reputation, but a poet, for all his eccentricity, his off-centredness, of major stature. The remaining essays concentrate on figures who may have begun to publish volumes in the 1930s but most of whose work has been done since the Second World War and to whom recognition has come in more recent decades. The two, so different New Englanders, Charles Olson and Robert Lowell, here loom largest, in several senses; and the four other poets treated are in turn invigoratingly different from one another, in their casts of mind, their subjects and their forms. How continually entertaining, how broadly instructive is that literary culture which possesses contemporaneous poets as different as J. V. Cunningham from Edward Dorn, as George Oppen from Robert Duncan, or as, a generation previously, Marianne Moore from Hart Crane, or as the ur-examples indeed, Whitman from Dickinson, Emerson from Poe: tokens perhaps of American individualism, triumphs certainly of individuality.

The editor of the collection is a member of the University of Essex Department of Literature, whose first Chairman in the 1960s was Donald Davie, the poet, critic and authority on Ezra Pound, an Englishman of course but one who on leaving Essex was to take up residence chiefly in the United States. At Essex Davie ensured that a major preoccupation of his Department was with the poetry of various linguistic cultures and historical periods, but in particular with modern poetry, and in particular again with American poetry. Early on he invited to the Department the youngest poet considered here, Edward Dorn, who between 1965 and 1975 spent five academic years at Essex. After Davie left, his successor as Chairman, Philip Edwards, invited to the Department another of the poets discussed here, Robert Lowell, who at the time of occupancy of his Essex post from 1970 to 1973 had probably the widest renown of all American poets then living. Two other American poets, Tom Clark and Ted Berrigan, were also associated with the Department, before economic belts began to be worn tightly and bleakness descended. It is in the manner of a small testament to the University of Essex's aesthetic faith in American poetry and to its professional expertise in the subject that all who have been asked and have agreed to contribute to this volume have a close connection with Essex, as teachers or students, present or past, and in one case as the longstanding external examiner of the Essex M.A. in American Poetry.

1

Whitman's Anti-Grammar of the Universe

by JACKIE KAYE

Whitman's essay of 1888, 'A Backward Glance O'er Travel'd Roads', sums up thirty years of constant revision of his radically heterodox poetic sequence *Leaves of Grass*. Whitman describes the poems as his 'carte de visite to the coming generations of the New World',[1] thus quoting and comparing himself with the famous French Egyptologist Champollion. Champollion's *Egyptian Grammar* had for the first time deciphered the markings on the tombs and monuments of the Nile empire and translated them into the language of nineteenth-century France. On his deathbed Champollion had pronounced his *Grammar* to be his 'carte de visite' to the world. He had found that the apparently random designs on ancient Egyptian monuments were based upon a discoverable order; Whitman on the contrary is concerned with a radical disordering of language and events. The language of Whitman's poetry is pragmatic and affective and it exists in a paratactical relationship with the world of objects and actions, neither subordinated to nor subordinating that world. Foucault in *The Order of Things* announces the birth of literature in the dissolution of the link between knowledge and language:

> . . . that reciprocal kinship between knowledge and language. The nineteenth century was to dissolve that link, and to leave

11

behind it, in confrontation, a knowledge closed in upon itself and a pure language that had become in nature and function, enigmatic—something that has been called, since that time, *Literature*.[2]

For Whitman however that reciprocity still exists and his poetry is disturbingly unenigmatic. Like Pound, Whitman writes poetry which is 'a mimesis of some external and consequently verifiable event'[3] and thus, instinctively, he writes the contradiction of all that was written as 'literature' in the last century:

> The Old World has had the poems of myths, fictions, feudalism, conquests, caste, dynasties, wars, and splendid exceptional characters and affairs, which have been great; but the New World needs the poems of realities and science and of the democratic average and basic equality, which shall be greater. In the centre of all, and object of all, stands the Human Being.[4]

Whitman's authority as a poet derives from two sources. There is the historical moment upon which the 1855 Preface relies: 'The American poets are to enclose old and new for America is the race of races.'[5] This is the authority which, when the tension is slackened, gives us 'The Song of the Exposition' and the kind of unrestrained nationalism which disfigures some of the later poems. Yet this kind of authority is a real need in a poet who does not assert himself as the sole composer of his own songs. Whitman's assertion that *Leaves of Grass* would not exist without the war of secession[6] is an acknowledgement of the need for a firm root in the historical event and a sense of being part of the tribe whose moment the poet is living even when that unrestrained lack of humility out of which all individual works of art are created is moving towards a sentence which will announce the 'mortuum est' of history.

So the Preface of 1855 invites a reciprocity from the reader which invokes the context of community and shared culture and validation. The poet is an arranger, a reference point around which the moment coheres, and that moment is specific: the United States of America in the middle of the nineteenth century. If the Civil War gave Whitman a sense of validation, then that validation was double. The *Drum Taps* poems commemorate the feeling of being one of the tribe,[7] but

12

'When Lilacs Last in the Door-yard Bloom'd' is not only a tribute to Lincoln but a closely worked poem celebrating the regenerative powers of artistic creation. Ten years later Whitman wrote 'Passage to India' where the terror of isolation, of being cast out from the pack, is masked by a simultaneous defiant assertion of the sole validity of the mythic consciousness in its celebration of death disguised as a commemoration of technological innovation as the most available form of patriotism. 'A Backward Glance', then, is not a guide to what we can expect to find in the first edition of *Leaves of Grass*. By 1888 Whitman had become far more conscious of the problem of authority, and the essay can be seen in many ways as a post-hoc justificatory exercise. However, it is truthful:

> I had my choice when I commenc'd. I bid neither for soft eulogies, big money returns, nor the approbation of existing schools and conventions. . . . I have had my say entirely my own way.[8]

The ability to speak out of the self is the source of Whitman's power and subversive force. It is true that 'I have had my say . . .' could stand as the epitaph for the most élitist kind of poetry. It all hinges on what is said, the value of the self that is uttered. The self that Whitman speaks is not exclusive, it invites response and identification; yet the power of speech is located in a religious consciousness set against the historical moment. This is the other source of Whitman's double authority. He must speak at one and the same time of the permanent truths he has experienced and the timebound facts through which he has lived, and to do that he has to find a language which can be simultaneously transcendent and contingent and remain authentic.

I have written so far of Whitman's language in terms of speech, the word out loud. And this is the way Whitman himself refers to his poetry; he always talks of saying, singing, chanting. Whitman's poems are uttered not written. They offend the eye as they ramble across the page. They have no metre, no rhyme, no stanzaic form. They remain unpredictable and present real problems of readability as they spurn narrative and indulge in indiscrete and inappropriate use of

13

the written word. These lines mimic speech in that they seek to capture its ephemerality and ability to shift from one plane of experience to another in one breath: 'I concentrate towards them that are nigh, I wait on the doorslab.'[9]

Speech is anarchic, it implies freedom of a radical kind; it is not recoverable, it can never be unsaid. The only arrangement in it is that of the individual lungs and tongue and consciousness. Time and again we find Whitman exhilarating in this multifarious possibility—'Speech is the twin of my vision'—and exhorting himself, 'Walt, you contain enough, why don't you let it out then?'[10] What comes out is not literature, for literature is finite, enclosing, contained; it is the rooms and rows of books on shelves which Whitman invites us to abandon. Yet his long rambling lines are more than a deconstruction of poetic form or even an attempt to find an equivalent for the exciting temporariness of speech. They are a way of locating and justifying the nature of knowledge in a manner that is not predetermined or metaphoric. The core of this attempt is Section 5 of 'Song of Myself', and the experience described there pervades Whitman's poetry. Upon the reading of these lines depends the validity of the whole of *Leaves of Grass* so that if they are read as symbolic or allegorical, then the whole structure fails. This single moment of intense religious illumination has to be heard as something that really happened:

> I believe in you my soul, the other I am must not abase
>   itself to you,
> And you must not be abased to the other.
> Loafe with me on the grass, loose the stop from your throat,
> Not words, not music or rhyme I want, not custom or
>   lecture, not even the best,
> Only the lull I like, the hum of your valvèd voice.
>
> I mind how we lay such a transparent summer morning.
> How you settled your head athwart my hips and gently
>   turn'd over upon me,
> And parted the shirt from my bosom-bone, and plunged
>   your tongue to my bare-stript heart,
> And reach'd till you felt my beard, and reach'd till you held
>   my feet.

Swiftly arose and spread around me the peace and
   knowledge that pass all the argument of the earth,
And I know that the hand of God is the promise of my own,
And I know that the spirit of God is the brother of my own,
And that all the men ever born are also my brothers, and
   the women my sisters and lovers,
And that a kelson of the creation is love,
And limitless are leaves stiff or drooping in the fields,
And brown ants in the little wells beneath them,
And mossy scabs of the worm fence, heap'd stones, elder,
   mullein and poke-weed.[11]

It is out of this experience that the authority to speak arises
in terms of the mythic force of the poem. What is spoken
reconstitutes that individual mystical illumination as uni-
versally available: 'And what I shall assume you shall assume,/
For every atom belonging to me as good belongs to you.'[12]
What is celebrated is the connectedness of life; differentiation
and selection are a kind of impiety. Systems of ordering,
control, containment are discounted:

I harbor for good or bad, I permit to speak at every hazard,
Nature without check with original energy
. . . . .
Through me many long dumb voices,
Voices of interminable generations of prisoners and slaves,
Voices of the diseas'd and despairing and of thieves and
   dwarfs.
. . . . .
Through me forbidden voices,
Voices of sexes and lusts, voices veil'd and I remove the veil,
Voices indecent by me clarified and transfigur'd.[13]

Out of this capacity to transfigure and be transfigured emerges
a self, announced as 'Walt Whitman, a kosmos, of Manhattan
the son'.[14] This self, like those of another epic hero, Odysseus
the man of many turns, is both a guise and a disguise. It is the
product of divine transformations like those undergone by the
Greek hero who, like Whitman, is seldom named but when he
is, it is to great effect. What matters is not the socially bestowed
identity but the capacity to be one with the universe in its
phases and flows and that harmony which is discovered not
ordered.

15

Whitman is composing a kind of anti-grammar of the universe. If we can take the invention of grammar as a system of ordering the disorderly and mysterious power of speech and reducing it to a series of laws, then Whitman's anti-grammar releases once more the flows between speech and the universe: 'To me the converging objects of the universe perpetually flow/ All are written to me, and I must get what the writing means.'[15] What is also unwritten in this process is the individual personality. Life exists to reproduce itself and thus no particular life form can be privileged:

> Urge and urge and urge
> Always the procreant urge of the world
> . . . . .
> To elaborate is no avail
> . . . . .
> Showing the best and dividing it from the worst age vexes
>   age.[16]

Whitman's equation of all beings is sometimes connected to the idea of democracy or 'en-masse', that is, it is linked to the political institutions of the United States. But Whitman the poet is not really concerned with an end to social inequalities, although Whitman the journalist might have been. In 'The Sleepers' master and slave exist in a complementarity which is a product of a different kind of perception than the political. Significantly, however, this poem of the first edition was transposed in the final edition of *Leaves of Grass* to the back of the book along with that other awkward celebration of death, 'Passage to India'. What Whitman celebrates is in fact the explosion and atomization of individual identity into a total sharedness of life. It is true that this freeing of self from form is alibied by Whitman in terms of the hobo-tramp figure. In 'Song of the Open Road' there is a double movement outward. There is the invitation to freedom from social constraint: 'Divesting myself of the holds that would hold me'.[17] Yet there is also that sense of fluid interaction which mocks all distinctions and turns words into objects: 'You objects that call from diffusion my meanings and give them shape!'[18]

Whitman often rejects the inauthentic social self imposed on the fluid contradictoriness of life, the self which is 'not the Me

myself'.[19] In 'Song of the Open Road' he is concerned with the
social form which annihilates the potential of life and forces it
into a bogus identity of 'self':

> Another self, a duplicate of everyone, skulking and hiding it
>   goes.
> Formless and wordless through the streets of the cities,
>   polite and bland in parlors,
> . . . . .
> Smartly attired, countenance smiling, form upright, death
>   under the breast-bones, hell under the skull bones,
> Under the broadcloth and gloves, under the ribbons and
>   artificial flowers,
> Keeping fair with the custom, speaking not a syllable of itself,
> Speaking of anything but never of itself.[20]

It is against this self that Whitman says, 'I nourish active
rebellion.'[21] It is here that the mythic vision even seems to
verge on a programme for action, but the poetry is more
radically subversive than that for Whitman announces the
unity of all life: 'We also ascend dazzling and tremendous as
the sun.'[22] There is no radical disjuncture between the human
and the non-human, which are both formed out of the general
flux of life. This vision when expressed as a desire to live with
animals or addressed as 'I think I have blown with you you
winds'[23] is containable as the kind of pantheistic sensibility
which the bourgeois culture of rooms and books has no
difficulty in appropriating and transforming into sentimentality
and nostalgia. But at other times, especially in those poems
which hinge upon a specific experience like 'Song of Myself',
'Out of the Cradle' and 'Crossing Brooklyn Ferry', Whitman
finds a language which is radically uncontainable:

> I find I incorporate gneiss, long-threaded moss, fruits,
>   grains, esculent roots.
> And am stucco'd with quadrupeds and birds all over,
> And have distanced what is behind me for good reasons,
> But call anything back again when I desire it.[24]

Like the tattoos on Queequeg's body these images are a
product of a pre- or anti-metaphoric mode of consciousness.
Santayana's essay on Whitman takes him at his word and that
word is 'barbaric'.[25] What is barbaric is that which stops at

surfaces which Santayana classifies as 'the most primitive type of perception'.[26] The tattooed body is a thing entirely of surfaces. The tattoo configures on the human body the natural world. In *Moby-Dick* the *Pequod* is tattooed by the whales it has pursued and these tattoos are reproduced on the body of the whale by the scars of harpoons and lances. 'With Whitman the surface is absolutely all'[27] says Santayana, but this does not denote limit, for everything is surface as all life exists on the face of the earth.

By the middle of the nineteenth century the work of geologists and naturalists was moving towards the invention of a system of ordering which would account for life according to fixed laws and towards an exploration of the possibility that these laws would operate invisibly. The focus of this system of ordering was man himself who thus was to become the subject and object of his own contemplations. 'Song of Myself' grows out of these kinds of concerns. Man does appear at certain junctures in the poem as a kind of culmination and he is certainly the object of his own quest for knowledge. But at the same time the poem radically displaces this point of view:

> I am the acme of things accomplish'd, and I am encloser of
>   things to be,
> My feet strike an apex of the apices of the stairs,
> On every step bunches of ages, and larger bunches between
>   the steps.
> All below duly travel'd, and still I mount and mount.
> . . . . .
> All forces have been steadily employ'd to complete and
>   delight me.
> Now on this spot I stand with my robust soul.[28]

The surrealistic reach of Whitman's language transcends the evolutionary interpretation. The experience evoked here is not biological but religious, and it comes out of that instinct which led man to worship his first immediate object—his own body.

Systems of ordering such as produced *Origin of Species* four years after the first edition of *Leaves of Grass* were attempts to turn the apparent chaos of observed life into a meaningful pattern. Whitman, however, allying himself with the spotted hawk, cries 'I too am untranslatable.'[29] The desire to compare, to be concerned with similarities and differences, gives rise not only to the 'laws' of nature but also to metaphor and symbol. If things, including men, are 'untranslatable', then nothing can be turned into anything else. Everything is as it is, both unique and the same as everything else. I said Whitman's poetry is pre- or anti-metaphoric and one could certainly argue that this might represent a more 'primitive' mode of perception or a post-historical one. Whitman himself tempts us to both conclusions by his reference to his 'barbaric yawp'[30] and his assertion that he is writing 'the history of the future'.[31] Such conclusions would merely slot Whitman back into the old cyclical view of life which is a product of the very law-bound mind which the poetry invites us to escape from. *Leaves of Grass* is a radically unhierarchical structure. It suggests that hierarchical thinking results in chaos and pain.

'Crossing Brooklyn Ferry' does not describe the ferry crossing as a metaphor for the continuity of life after death. It describes a real experience which is analogous to or alongside the experience of death. Both the sensuous delight in the river crossing and the apprehension of life as a flux from which the individual briefly takes his identity exist simultaneously in the poem; they do not represent or replace one another. In 'Out of the Cradle' and 'When Lilacs last in the Dooryard Bloom'd' the bird, the sea, the flower and the star are not symbols of some invisible order to which they give clues. They are things seen which construct the mood of the poem and structure Whitman's awareness of death, loss and bereavement. He asserts these thoughts 'are not original with me' and instructs the reader to 'filter them from yourself'.[32] This is a poetic discourse which does not engage in symbolic ordering or give priority to any one consciousness. If Whitman's poetry is pre- or anti-metaphoric, it is also a language which is 'desacrilised', that is, it is no longer at the service of hierarchical thinking:

> The result of the desacrilisation of the word is to destroy the impulse to see eternal hierarchies in the order of things. Once language is freed from representing the world of things, the world of things disposes itself before consciousness as precisely what it was all along: a plenum of *mere* things. No one of which can lay claim to privileged status with respect to any other.[33]

Whitman's language liberates itself from the task of ordering and frees the human from the burden of identity and allows the impulse to celebrate to explode. Unlike the grammarian Champollion, Whitman is not a product of a culture which was to find its twentieth-century parameters in the laws laid down by that necromantic trinity Marx, Darwin and Freud. He is not concerned with predictions of the past or memories of the future; instead he sees the possibility of occupying time and space as fields of simultaneously existing and contradictory possibilities which are liberating and unpredictable. What Whitman calls 'correspondances' between the land and the people are a matter of potentials, of the possibilities inherent in all things, of the glimpse of that earthly paradise captured in the illuminations of Section 5 of 'Song of Myself'. What becomes in some later poems an overtly nationalistic celebration and implicit sanction of geographical expansion should not be read back into the poems where what is being celebrated is a transcendence of form as a way of occupying space without displacing or colonizing. That radical optimism which led Zukofsky to write 'Our world will not stand it/ the implications of a too regular form'[34] is a twentieth-century reworking of Whitman's concern. Revised and redrafted, shuffled so that all continuity and chronology are lost, *Leaves of Grass* remains a fragment expressing the possible simultaneity and contiguity of matter and language.

NOTES

1. 'A Backward Glance O'er Travel'd Roads', *Leaves of Grass*, p. 562. All quotes from Whitman are reprinted by permission of New York University Press from Walt Whitman, *Leaves of Grass, Reader's Comprehensive Edition*, edited by Harold W. Blodgett and Sculley Bradley. Copyright © 1965 by New York University.
2. Michel Foucault, *The Order of Things* (New York, 1970), p. 89.
3. Michael Bernstein, *The Tale of the Tribe* (Princeton, 1980), p. 5.
4. 'A Backward Glance O'er Travel'd Roads', *Leaves of Grass*, p. 568.
5. *Leaves of Grass*, p. 711.
6. 'A Backward Glance O'er Travel'd Roads', *Leaves of Grass*, p. 570.
7. See Bernstein, Introduction, *The Tale of the Tribe*; also Gilles Deleuze and Félix Guattari, 'Un seul ou plusieurs loups', *Mille Plateaux* (Paris, 1980).
8. 'A Backward Glance O'er Travel'd Roads', *Leaves of Grass*, p. 562.

9. 'Song of Myself', l. 1327, *Leaves of Grass*, p. 89.
10. Ibid., ll. 566 and 568, *Leaves of Grass*, p. 55.
11. Ibid., ll. 82–98, *Leaves of Grass*, p. 33.
12. Ibid., ll. 2–3, *Leaves of Grass*, p. 28.
13. Ibid., ll. 12–14 and ll. 508–18, *Leaves of Grass*, p. 29 and pp. 52–3.
14. Ibid., l. 497, *Leaves of Grass*, p. 52.
15. Ibid., ll. 404–5, *Leaves of Grass*, p. 47.
16. Ibid., ll. 43–4, l. 47, l. 55, *Leaves of Grass*, p. 31.
17. 'Song of the Open Road', l. 57, *Leaves of Grass*, p. 151.
18. Ibid., l. 26, *Leaves of Grass*, p. 150.
19. 'Song of Myself', l. 74, *Leaves of Grass*, p. 32.
20. 'Song of the Open Road', ll. 198–205, *Leaves of Grass*, p. 158.
21. Ibid., l. 211, *Leaves of Grass*, p. 54.
22. 'Song of Myself', l. 526, *Leaves of Grass*, p. 54.
23. 'Salut au Monde!' l. 216, *Leaves of Grass*, p. 148.
24. 'Song of Myself', ll. 670–73, *Leaves of Grass*, p. 59.
25. George Santayana, 'The poetry of Barbarism', *Interpretations of Poetry and Religion*, republished in *Walt Whitman: A Critical Anthology*, edited by Francis Murphy (London, 1969).
26. Ibid., p. 161.
27. Ibid., p. 162.
28. 'Song of Myself', ll. 1148–169, *Leaves of Grass*, pp. 80–1.
29. Ibid., l. 1333, *Leaves of Grass*, p. 89.
30. Ibid., l. 1334, *Leaves of Grass*, p. 89.
31. 'To a Historian', l. 7, *Leaves of Grass*, p. 4.
32. 'Song of Myself', l. 355, and l. 37, *Leaves of Grass*, p. 45 and p. 30.
33. Hayden White, 'Foucault Decoded', *Tropics of Discourse* (Johns Hopkins Press, 1978), p. 250.
34. Louis Zukofsky, 'Mantis', *All the collected short poems 1923–1938* (London, 1966), p. 77.

2

Emily Dickinson: The Regulation of Belief

by JOSEPH ALLARD

1

Emily Dickinson's poetry is amongst the purest in the language. Traditional critical approaches that consider the poet in relation to her historical period, or that focus upon her particular and peculiar biography or upon her chronological development, yield in her case especially arid and unhelpful results. Her often enigmatic, ambiguous and epigrammatic poems seem to have more to do with poetry itself, its possibilities and parameters, than with external matters, personal or public. Read one by one, the poems burn with an intensity that springs from fully felt individual experience but that, at the same time, transcends the individual. The best of the poems reveal to us a symbolic realm of spiritual 'truth' which is predicated upon the material world but which escapes the mutable. This is made possible in the poems by Dickinson's total and humble dedication to poetry, by her belief that symbolizing and metaphorizing are mankind's highest 'natural' activities. Whatever external subject she addresses, be it love, the seasons, religion, or death, becomes both fixed and vibrant in accord with her own profound sensibility and awe in the presence of incomprehensible externality. It is fixed because of her mastery of the craft; and vibrant because of the multiplicity of meanings and levels of

22

perception and sensation evoked in her dense and often daring figures.

Again, almost as fruitless a task as the discussion of the life and times is the classification of themes in her poetry. Inder Kher's recent sympathetic study begins with this observation:

> In an organic sense, Dickinson's poetry can be regarded as one long poem of multidimensional reality, each dimension presenting a certain deep and penetrating mood, a certain phase, a certain stage of that reality, and yet the whole of reality. It is unwise to assume an easy distribution of Dickinson's poems into various thematic concerns, because her themes invariably overlap and eventually merge with the fundamental concern for existence itself as seen through the power of the creative imagination.[1]

Our responsibility as readers is to study the individual poems in their own terms—to extract as much as possible from each—but with the intention, as well, of approaching the poet's larger universe: the circumference of her imagination.

Dickinson's biography is curiously unhelpful in revealing much about the main-springs of her work. The notion of the 'Amherst nun', the Connecticut Valley reclusive spinster, white clad and misanthropic, repels rather than explains. Discussions of her forbidding, neurotically private father, or of her crisis with and rejection of late Valley Calvinism during the recurrent awakenings of the period, make for interesting biography but could arise, no doubt, from events in the biographies of numerous nineteenth-century New Englanders. The workaday New England mind has always had a strong streak of eccentricity. A character with the external manifestation of Emily Dickinson would be at home in one of Hawthorne's *Twice-Told Tales* or a Frost narrative poem.

No, Dickinson compels by her ability to forge poems that succeed in their attempt to capture a moment in the experience of one who believed sincerely that the moment was all. Unable to accept fully, or to internalize New England Calvinist belief in Election, Dickinson, like other modern pessimists, was left isolated, futureless, in the present and past. For if in the future was no guarantee, at least in the present was the possibility of electrifying sensation. Others in the Valley, most of her family included, accepted a vision of futurity which culminated after death in a Christian translation to 'heaven'. But Dickinson was stunned to awe in death's presence—stopped still. For her there was no penetrating that mysterious seeming-finality. What abided after death abided with the living:

> Each that we lose takes part of us;
> A crescent still abides,
> Which like the moon, some turbid night,
> Is summoned by the tides.

(1605)[2]

Death, God, Love, Life even, were, strictly speaking, incomprehensible for Dickinson. Her neighbours might 'know'; she could only know that she could not know. And her felt uncertainties about existence were expressed in subtly intricate, often ambiguous metaphors.

According to the occasion of the sermon, the Congregational Meeting House Master was either Jehovah or Christ, who was to be met, after death, at Judgement. But Dickinson's God was not this post-mortem presence, awaiting her in heaven. God for her was immanent in nature here and now. This was not an uncommon notion in nineteenth-century New England; it was the common property, for instance, of the Transcendentalist tribe. Emerson's 'Oversoul' removed the Calvinist sense of a threatening nature, whilst in another essay's alarmingly awful metaphor Emerson becomes

> a transparent eyeball; I am nothing; I see all; the currents of the Universal Being circulate through me; I am part or parcel of God. . . . In the wilderness, I find something more dear and connate than in streets or villages. In the tranquil landscape, and especially in the distant line of the horizon, man beholds somewhat as beautiful as his own nature.[3]

As distinct from the Concordians, however, Dickinson lacked self-assurance. She also lacked bland optimism. God *was* immanent in nature, but God and nature could be apocalyptically terrible, as well as cheerful. Divinity was the source of the incredible beauty in life and nature, but Dickinson was aware, at the same time, that there was much that was inexplicably terrible, and unjust. 'God is indeed a jealous God' (1719) who might at times be 'a distant, stately lover' (357), or even implicated in what might seem natural evils. An almost sinister indifference is apprehended here:

> Apparently with no surprise
> To any happy Flower
> The Frost beheads it at its play—
> In accidental power—
> The blonde Assassin passes on—
> The Sun proceeds unmoved
> To measure off another Day
> For an Approving God.
>
> (1624)

The Calvinist Jehovah, as represented in the Old Testament in particular, gained her contempt:

> So I pull my Stockings off
> Wading in the Water
> For the Disobedience' Sake
> Boy that lived for "or'ter"
>
> Went to Heaven perhaps at Death
> And perhaps he didn't
> Moses wasn't fairly used—
> Ananias wasn't—
>
> (1201)

At his worst God was little better than an unpredictable beast:

> Abraham to kill him
> Was distinctly told—
> Isaac was an Urchin—
> Abraham was old—
>
> Not a hesitation—
> Abraham complied—
> Flattered by Obeisance
> Tyranny demurred—
>
> Isaac—to his children
> Lived to tell the tale—
> Moral—with a Mastiff
> Manners may prevail.
>
> (1317)

One might observe that Dickinson is objecting chiefly to aspects of the God celebrated by her neighbours, and that it was specifically with local Calvinist doctrine in mind that she wrote 'The Bible is an antique Volume—/ Written by faded Men' and

> Had but the Tale a warbling Teller—
> All the Boys would come—
> Orpheus' Sermon captivated—
> It did not condemn—
>
> (1545)

This is certainly true; and yet her sense of the malevolent side of God's nature coincides with her sense of the malign in external Nature. There is an awareness throughout her poems dealing with nature that, like life, it could be alternately glorious and destructive. It could, of course, also be drab:

> The Sky is low—the Clouds are mean.
> A Travelling Flake of Snow
> Across a Barn or through a Rut
> Debates if it will go—
>
> A Narrow Wind complains all Day
> How some one treated him
> Nature, like Us is sometimes caught
> Without her Diadem.
>
> (1075)

The key to much of her best verse is her courageous, often martyr-like willingness to confront the whole of life and feeling and sensibility with all her faculties alert and aware. Her sensibility was profound. Her reactions were frankly, sometimes starkly honest. Kenneth Rexroth puts it succinctly when he observes:

> Emily Dickinson's nunlike life and ascetic verse protect a sensibility so fragile and so sharp that life out in the world, struggling with the flesh and the devil, would have destroyed it instantly, and what little of the world did penetrate in the cloister wounded, crippled and eventually destroyed her.[4]

2

Throughout the canon is evidence of Dickinson's utter dedication to poetry. It was through poetry alone that she could feel herself break through her existential isolation, write her 'letter to the world', and tell 'The simple News that Nature told—/ With tender Majesty' (441). Poetry for her was a divine act, coeval with natural creation. Genuine poetry was coeternal with God, Nature and Love:

> I reckon—when I count at all—
> First—Poets—Then the Sun—
> Then Summer—Then the Heaven of God—
> And then—the List is done—
>
> But, looking back—the First so seems
> To Comprehend the Whole—
> The Others look a needless Show—
> So I write—Poets—All—
>
> Their Summer—lasts a Solid Year—
> They can afford a Sun
> The East—would deem extravagant—
> And if the Further Heaven—
>
> Be Beautiful as they prepare
> For Those who worship Them—
> It is too difficult a Grace—
> To justify the Dream—
>
> (569)

The most pointed comment about poetry's awesome power is in one of the almost epigrammatic, tightly compressed late poems, written about 1873:

> To pile like Thunder to its close
> Then crumble grand away
> While Everything created hid
> This—would be Poetry—
>
> Or Love—the two coeval come—
> We both and neither prove—
> Experience either and consume—
> For None see God and live—
>
> (1247)

And it's Amherst thunder—summer thunder. Just as to know the Yorkshire Moors illuminates our response to the Brontës, so to know New England, especially its larger-than-European

27

storms, makes us further aware of what Dickinson meant in
her many awestruck references to her natural surroundings,
references such as 'To pile like Thunder to its close/ Then
crumble grand away.' The New England climate is more
dramatic than many others, and more various, and responses
to it in her poetry range from apprehension of its peculiar
beauties, to terror at its vast majesty and potential for
destruction. The reality of the Connecticut Valley and its
climate in the 1850s, '60s and '70s was deeply moving to
her. Parts of the Valley are still majestically Edenic (against
the odds, and going quickly); what it must have been like
then for *her*. Her equation between Nature and Poetry in
terms of her surroundings indicates her religious regard for
both.

If we accept this religous regard for poetry as sincere, and,
of course, we must, then the next question is the central one.
How do the most successful lyrics operate? From where does
the power spring? What qualities of thought, emotion and
technique force us to share in her faith that poetry has a
power equivalent to God's and Nature's, transcending,
indeed obliterating the individual? Dickinson's intense
'aloneness' in relation to both other people and the natural
world is a regular subject in her poetry. The only way for her
to forge any relation whatever with the other is through
poetry, through metaphor in particular. Only in this way can
she convey the intensity of her own experience and, at the
same time, because poetic creation is, she feels, the highest
level of natural human activity, become part of Nature
through the activity. 'A Bird came down the Walk—' (328) is
a conscious statement of the problem, and an example of the
resolution.

As she stands an unobserved onlooker she can relate her
observations in a child-like fashion which borders, purpose-
fully, on the sentimental. The rhythms and rhymes in the
first two stanzas are unusually exact for her, as are the
end-stopped lines:

> A Bird came down the Walk—
> He did not know I saw—
> He bit an Angleworm in halves
> And ate the fellow, raw,

> And then he drank a Dew
> From a convenient Grass—
> And then hopped sidewise to the Wall
> To let a Beetle pass—

The verse and action are mechanical and decorous; birds and worms and beetles behave as in a Victorian children's story. The gulf between the worlds of poet and of nature is impassibly wide. The natural process carries on as it does precisely because the bird 'did not know' the poet was there.

In the third stanza the poet begins her gesture of communion; the bird becomes aware of an alien presence.

> He glanced with rapid eyes
> That hurried all around—
> They looked like frightened Beads, I thought—
> He stirred his Velvet Head

The prosody alters markedly. The poet shifts to self-conscious figuration: 'They looked *like* frightened Beads, *I thought*—.' It is the fear that she inspires in the bird that appals her. And the exact rhymes of stanzas one and two (saw-raw, Grass-pass) disappear in this moment of shock (around-Head). So, too, vanish the end-stopped lines, the clarity, and the simplicity. The poem becomes ambiguous in syntax and meaning in the fourth stanza:

> He stirred his Velvet Head
>
> Like one in danger, Cautious,
> I offered him a Crumb
> And he unrolled his feathers
> And rowed him softer home—[5]

Both poet and bird are in danger; both, for an instant, are cautious. The brilliance of Dickinson's punctuation is that at the moment of most importance in the gesture of communion, the 'me' and the 'not me' are mutually aware: on the verge, possibly, of important discovery. The poem is powerful because it charts a failed (and, we discover, futile) attempt by the poet to approach a seemingly simple mystery of nature, to participate in 'otherness'. The poem's power and meaning have little to do with birds or works or beetles; all one can say about them is said in the sentimentally childish first and second stanzas. From the moment of shocked, and shocking, failure in the middle of the poem she realizes yet again (and this is not an unusual motif in her poetry) that the only way for the human being to participate in nature is through the natural process of metaphor. The final six lines of the poem present a breathtaking impacting of images that aspire to be as beautiful and rich as the object/experience they describe:

> And he unrolled his feathers
> And rowed him softer home—
>
> Than Oars divide the Ocean,
> Too silver for a seam—
> Or Butterflies, off Banks of Noon
> Leap, plashless as they swim.

These six lines provide a good example of Dickinson's poetic method. The bird's flight is seen first in a mixed nautical image which includes both sailing and rowing ('and he unrolled . . . and rowed him'). She then shifts from the metaphor of bird-boat into an expanded figure which is intensified by a simile: 'Than Oars divide the Ocean'. The bird's flight metaphorized as a boat is softer *than* Oars dividing an ocean. And that ocean, which we have only just been given, is further described as 'too silver for a seam'. We have made the leap, suddenly, from a failed attempt at objective description and communication to a realm of figurative description and imagination that transcends rational language. The final touch,

> Or Butterflies, off Banks of Noon
> Leap, plashless as they swim.

lays yet another complex of figures on the initial ones. The boating images are invoked particularly to convey, to capture, the 'softer'-ness of the bird's flight. Air becomes ocean. Butterflies flying in summer air (but air that is 'Banks of Noon') leap into the so-silver ocean. And they leap 'plashless'. Metaphors are impacted, words are forged, meanings are stretched to capture, to freeze, a particular, in this case sorry, reality of experience. Nature is beautiful but foreign, so foreign that it is always impossible to join it, to feel a secure part of it, and *almost* never possible not to feel deeply its beauty.

Our total alienation from beautiful but foreign and inaccessible nature is poignantly commented upon in 348. April is a far crueller month for Dickinson than for Eliot. The pain experienced during the returning spring derives from a sense of almost overwhelming beauty combined with the awareness that the poet is different from those beautiful elements to which she responds so unavoidably, and with the knowledge that her own march through ever-returning springs is a march, alone of necessity, to death.

> I dreaded that first Robin, so,
> But He is mastered, now,
> I'm some accustomed to Him grown,
> He hurts a little, though—
>
> I thought if I could only live
> Till that first Shout got by—
> Not all Pianos in the Woods
> Had power to mangle me—
>
> I dared not meet the Daffodils—
> For fear their Yellow Gown
> Would pierce me with a fashion
> So foreign to my own—

The daffodil's fashion is not hers; the grass, the bees, have 'no word' for her. She longs to be quit of it all. It crucifies her year after year. However, nature, gently indifferent in this instance, has no truck with her suffering.

> They're here, though; not a creature failed—
> No blossom stayed away
> In gentle deference to me—
> The Queen of Calvary—

And Queen of Calvary she is, because she knows of her poet's god-like ability to create, her Christ-like otherness from nature, her inevitable crucifixion by life. Any hope for response from nature, for acknowledgement, for 'gentle deference' is a sentimental futility. She is but one more creature of nature, but with the tragic difference of an awareness of self and of passing. The poem ends with a death-march:

31

Each one salutes me, as he goes,
And I, my childish Plumes,
Lift, in bereaved acknowledgment
Of their unthinking Drums—

It is clearly the reality of death that gives such poignancy and urgency to life. Because of our seeming extinction at that mysterious and impenetrable barrier, life's 'natural' pains and contradictions and tragedies are rendered even more painful, contradictory and tragic. Every syllable of her neighbours' creed dictated that death, for the saved, was a glorious beginning. To accept and take comfort from such a faith, however, meant adhering rigorously to the Congregational system of belief. This Dickinson could not do. But her poems about death, either her own or others', avoid a cosmic pessimism. There is never a sense of total extermination; always a sense that something abides. In her total honesty to herself, however, she could seldom posit traditional 'heavens'. 'Eternity' often occurs as a concept to express 'after-death-ness':

The Bustle in a House
The Morning after Death
Is solemnest of industries
Enacted upon Earth—

The Sweeping up the Heart
And putting Love away
We shall not want to use again
Until Eternity.

(1078)

But such references to 'Eternity', and they are regular, seem to be more a convenient way for her to admit her inability to pierce death's mask, to speculate beyond the death throe, than anything else.

Poems dealing with her own death often invoke 'Eternity' but seldom leave the here and now except in fantasy. In 'Because I could not stop for Death—' (712) death is personified as a decorous, polite and stately gentleman, but the final carriage ride to the tomb involves a reflection upon life, rather than any commentary on what happens after death, as is often assumed.

We passed the School, where Children strove
At Recess—in the Ring—
We passed the Fields of Gazing Grain—
We passed the Setting Sun—
. . .
We paused before a House that seemed.
A Swelling of the Ground—
The Roof was scarcely visible—
The Cornice—in the Ground—

The carriage ride *leads to* the grave but cannot go beyond it.
The final stanza invokes 'Eternity'. It seems to comment upon
some quality of life after death

Since then—'tis Centuries—and yet
Feels shorter than the Day
I first surmised the Horses' Heads
Were toward Eternity—

but must surely be a comment about life after the *discovery* of
death, rather than a Sunday School bit of comfort for children.
The centuries since death allowed the poet into His carriage
feel shorter than the day of realization of death's inevitability.
Rather than an allegory of her own death the stopping of
Death in the poem surely represents her first intimation of
mortality and her entrance into History. The 'Centuries' in
the final stanza are all of the past—and all of her life—rather
than anything to do with the future. She is alone in the
carriage with 'Immortality' but the end deposits her in the
grave. For the intents and purposes of the living poet the grave
was the end of the only life she knew. That the spirit was not
extinguished at death was an article of her faith generally, but
not one that could be written about directly because so utterly
beyond experience.

Her poems that imagine her own death-bed are focused in a
way that supports my argument. The reality of the death
chamber is precise and articulated:

I heard a Fly buzz—when I died—
The Stillness in the Room
Was like the Stillness in the Air—
Between the Heaves of Storm—

33

The Eyes around—had wrung them dry—
And Breaths were gathering firm
For that last Onset—when the King
Be witnessed—in the Room—

I willed my Keepsakes—Signed away
What portion of me be
Assignable—and then it was
There interposed a Fly—

With Blue—uncertain stumbling Buzz—
Between the light—and me—
And then the Windows failed—and then
I could not see to see—

(465)

Death has occurred by the end of the poem. The body has
expired but the 'I' resides; it 'could not see to see—'. The force of
the poem is not to do with futurity or immortality so much as
with the final moments of life. The moment of death itself was the
most profound she could imagine. It was the inscrutable unalter-
able that made life what it was—both wonderful and terrible.
The moment of focus is 'when the King/ Be witnessed—in the
Room—'; the king is death, and death comes, or rather the
reality of death comes, in calm, after 'The Eyes around—had
wrung them dry—'. In the presence of finality the most mun-
dane, finite activity, like the buzzing of a fly, can become the
focus of attention because, in death's presence all else, especially
egotistical aspiration, is rendered totally insignificant. Although
there is an intimation that something called 'I' survives death's
coming, the moment is one of uncomprehending awe.

This moment of death is treated from the point of view of
the friends in attendance in another poem:

The last Night that She lived
It was a Common Night
Except the Dying—this to Us
Made Nature different

We noticed smallest things—
Things overlooked before
By this great light upon our Minds
Italicized—as 'twere.

(1100)

There is no record here of the thoughts of the dying woman, of her consciousness. All is centred upon the others in the room, on their thoughts and feelings. And those thoughts and feelings are curiously elusive—a combination of guilt and jealousy, of belief that her death is not her end, and that she must 'finish quite'. This confusion of sense, thought and sentiment in the mourners is entirely credible:

> As we went out and in
> Between Her final Room
> And Rooms where Those to be alive
> Tomorrow were, in Blame
>
> That Others could exist
> While She must finish quite
> A Jealousy for Her arose
> So nearly infinite—

It is the 'narrow time' of the passage that informs this one. Much of the awesomeness of life for Dickinson was isolate in its passing:

> We waited while She passed—
> It was a narrow time—
> Too jostled were Our Souls to speak
> At length the notice came.
>
> She mentioned, and forgot—
> Then lightly as a Reed
> Bent to the Water, struggled scarce—
> Consented, and was dead—
>
> And We—We placed the Hair—
> And drew the Head erect—
> And then an awful leisure was
> Belief to regulate—

(1100)

One might use Dickinson's own expression, 'Belief to regulate', as a signpost towards the understanding of her poems about death, and as a focus for most of the others since her sense of death's awesome significance was basic to her poetic position and imagination. The regulation of belief, and of unbelief, in the presence of something so completely beyond our ken and so completely in power over us: this is the challenge, with the willingness, perhaps necessity, of trying to come to terms with it, of not ignoring it, of facing the seeming oblivion that comes to each and all. Not just to do this, but to write about it, and to give it a form that was indelible in an otherwise constantly fading existence: this was her triumph and her epitaph.

Dickinson's use of the dash rather than the full-stop or the semi-colon, which seemed so odd to Higginson, is actually one key to the intensity of her best lyrics. In many instances the dash heightens the significance of a recorded sensation because sensation itself, comprising sense, emotion, intellect and so on, does not have full-stops or semi-colons. The dash makes us pause, but does not make a full break from one thought or image to the next. As in the line from the last poem 'And We—We placed the Hair—' the dash functions as an interrogative, a sign of the hopelessness of their grief and, from the preceding line, a point of relation between the dead woman and the living: 'Consented, and was dead—/ And We—We . . .'. With careful use of dashes Dickinson can strike a mood at the start of a poem which will remain actively in both emotional and syntactic control. Because an early theme isn't punctuated to a firm conclusion with a full-stop or semi-colon, the theme resides through the poem and can give it far great homogeneity and texture than it would otherwise have. At its best, the technique can push poetry closer to a state of music.

'I should not dare to leave my friend', is a prime example of the mechanism Dickinson employs to capture the intensity of feeling in death's presence:

> I should not dare to leave my friend,
> Because—because if he should die
> While I was gone—and I—too late—
> Should reach the Heart that wanted me—

The poem is driven by the question as to why she will remain at a friend's death-bed. The work is shaped by both grief and guilt; but it is an imagined guilt. The friend has not yet expired; the poet has not left, and will not leave. The tone is one of breathless intensity, trying hard, especially with its

36

repetitions, to make verbal the overwhelming awe in the combined presence of friend and death. The dash joining 'Because' and 'because', like the dash between 'We' and 'we' in the preceding poem, acts as interrogative as well as a means of expressing intense feeling, of conveying urgency, breathlessness and, ultimately, the inability to speak meaningfully at a moment like the one she is dealing with. The answer to the first 'Because'—'because if he should die/ While I was gone— and I—too late—/ Should reach the Heart that wanted me—' bursts out with great fluency, but is starkly incomplete.

The next two stanzas are conditional:

> If I should disappoint the eyes
> That hunted—hunted so—to see—
> And could not bear to shut until
> They "noticed" me—they noticed me—
>
> If I should stab the patient faith
> So sure I'd come—so sure I'd come—
> It *listening*—listening—went to sleep—
> Telling my tardy name—

Neither stanza yet answers the question of why she dares not leave her friend. Like the first stanza both rely on the dash and upon repetition to heighten the intensity of the moment, to reveal the real and deep anguish she suffers. Since there is no final punctuation in the first three stanzas the initial statement 'I should not dare to leave my friend/ Because . . .' remains in full control of each succeeding thought or image. The building of intensity that results is, as I've said, musical, and leads in the last stanza to a climax and resolution of heightened power:

> My Heart would wish it broke before—
> Since breaking then—since breaking then—
> Were useless as next morning's sun—
> Where midnight frosts—had lain!

(205)

The poem ends with a simile of natural devastation which rounds out our own awareness of the real tragedy in the poem about both death and friendship, the certain knowledge that her heart is going to break one way or another and that the pain she feels, and will feel on the morrow, and will always feel, is an inevitable and inescapable part of real life. The intense, almost neurotic questioning of the impossible, 'What if my friend were to die with me absent?', and the convolutions of seeming guilt that that notion inspires, are no more than a blind, or an attempt to blind her soul's eye and heart from the awful reality she faces. Her friend is dying. Her heart is breaking. All she can do is accompany the friend to death's portal, be present when death arrives. The only safe way to pass this crisis is to have her heart break in company with her friend's death. The other option is complicating the heart-break with guilt by not being present; hence wishing her heart had 'broke before'. But break it will. Break it must.

3

I would like to close with a remark by Charles R. Anderson that pinpoints both the importance of Dickinson and the responsibility that faces us all:

> To give her poetry the serious attention it deserves is the real task that remains. To study it intensively, to stare at a hole in the page until these apparently cryptic notations yield their full meanings—this is the great challenge to modern readers.[6]

I have centred my consideration of Dickinson's poetry in this essay on only a few of her abiding themes—God, Nature and Death—and on the more pessimistic, darker side of these. This is in no way intended to give the impression of a uniformity of gloom in the entire opus. Careful readers of Dickinson know that she is fully capable of enthusiasm, of good cheer, of wonder, of wit, of wisdom, of irony, of joy. My emphasis has been such as it is because I believe that any sunlight and joy in her work could only be generated against the background of the darkness and void signalled by extinction.

Her choice of an almost monastic life dedicated to poetry might be seen as a life dedicated to her own spirit and sensibility, to a belief born from her awareness of inevitable, existential 'apartness' from others. Only by keeping herself to herself could she explore her own depth of significant truth, and give that truth an enduring form in the art she knew to be divine, more divine, indeed, than the shared faith and rituals of her neighbours. She was like her neighbours in the sense that each Calvinist was involved in a personal query with God about the state of his or her soul. But she was radically different in her awareness, or suspicion, that the trappings of religion—the heavens, and saints, and futures, and gods— were, in themselves, only convenient images and symbols and time-denying answers for questions that were asked in, and demanded by, the immediate state of the self in the moment. To have chosen any other course in life would have destroyed her utterly. But to choose her course meant to deny a realm of social experience she would have loved and respected more than most of us. The painful dilemma was genuine. That she chose the road she did has given us an incomparable body of work that pointedly addresses questions of life, sensation and death that most of us prefer not to think about because they *are* so important, so necessary, and so painful.

Basic to all of her poetry is the self. That self is vibrantly alive in the moment, but alienated, finally, from everything else. Each poem, each fragment, resides on the border between self and other. Dickinson chose to dedicate her life to the transmission of articulated truth from inner to outer, to make manifest and objective in poetry her sometimes painful, always profound discoveries about the only world to which she had real access—the world of her own soul. Her task was complete when the words were committed to paper. She never spoke to us; she wrote us 'letters'. The task that remains for us is to read those letters. It is the careful and serious reading of them that can give us entrance into the poet's own realm of imagination, of reality, and of life. And this journey is, of course, an internalizing one for us. We gain access into the mind and heart and soul of Dickinson by taking the poems she offered us into ourselves. This process is the final and awesome mystery of the art of poetry at its most profound. It is the awareness that by serious and sympathetic reading—listening—we break out of our own isolation. We participate in genuine communion. And that Mass we celebrate can devastate as well as uplift:

Could mortal lip divine
The undeveloped Freight
Of a delivered syllable
'Twould crumble with the weight.

(1409)

NOTES

1. Inder Nath Kher, *The Landscape of Absence: Emily Dickinson's Poetry* (New Haven, 1974), p. 2.
2. The numbers in brackets refer to the numbered poems in *The Complete Poems of Emily Dickinson*, ed. Thomas H. Johnson, based on the 1955 variorum text of *The Poems of Emily Dickinson* (London, 1975).
3. Ralph Waldo Emerson, 'Nature', 1836. *The Complete Works of Ralph Waldo Emerson*, Vol. I, Centenary Edition (Boston and New York, 1903), p. 10.
4. Kenneth Rexroth, *American Poetry in the Twentieth Century* (New York, 1971), p. 69.
5. This poem is a good example of Thomas Wentworth Higginson's butchery through re-punctuation. He adds a semi-colon after 'danger', ie. 'Like one in danger; cautious,'. This, of course, restricts 'danger' to the bird. That Dickinson meant to include herself as in danger must be beyond argument.
6. Cited in Kher, *The Landscape of Absence*, p. 1.

Quotations are reprinted by permission of the publishers and trustees of Amherst College from *The Poems of Emily Dickinson*, edited by Thomas H. Johnson, Cambridge, Massachusetts; the Belknap Press of Harvard University Press, copyright © 1951, 1955, 1979 by the President and Fellows of Harvard College; and from *The Complete Poems of Emily Dickinson*, edited by Thomas H. Johnson, copyright © 1914, 1929 by Martha D. Bianchi, copyright © renewed 1942 by Martha D. Bianchi, copyright © 1957 by Mary L. Hampson, reprinted by permission of Little, Brown and Co.

3

Poetry and the Subject of the Poem: Wallace Stevens

by RICHARD GRAY

'Poetry is the subject of the poem', wrote Wallace Stevens in 'The Man with the Blue Guitar'. 'From this the poem issues and/ To this returns.'[1] Characteristically, Stevens meant a number of things by this, if only because as he saw it and expressed it in his 'Adagia', 'Poetry and materia poetica are interchangeable terms.'[2] 'Poetry' for him included 'that/ Irrational moment' when the mind feels reconciled, at one with its surroundings as well as 'the gaiety . . . of language' or indeed any other means the mind might employ to achieve this feeling. On a more elementary level, however, by 'poetry' Stevens also meant the poetry of other people, or statements made about poetry by other people with whom, perhaps, he felt he had some kind of intellectual *rapport*. For like many artists in different fields during this century—like Joyce, for instance, or Picasso or Stravinsky—Stevens was fascinated by the nature of his own art, and felt compelled to explore its possibilities and limitations. His work is nothing if not self-conscious. It almost asks us to look for contents and ante-cedents; it virtually obliges us to see it, and its creator, in terms of a particular time and place. In seeing things in this way, of course, there is the danger of becoming the kind of reader that

Stevens deplored in one of his letters, 'who spends his time dissecting what he reads for echoes, imitations, influences, as if no one was ever simply himself but is always compounded of a lot of other people'.[3] Not to do so, though, or rather not to look for signs of *kinship*, of spiritual resemblance rather than influence, would be to ignore Stevens's centrality and, quite possibly, under-estimate his importance. Stevens was a great original, certainly: as indeed anyone who believes that 'All poetry is experimental poetry'[4] must be. But he was a great original precisely because he could absorb and cope with so much pressure—because he could gather up so many different threads and out of them weave something entirely personal, coherent and new.

The first and probably most obvious sign of kinship is to be found in Stevens's 'final belief', the impulse that shapes and gives life to all of his work, and which marks him as a true heir of the Romantics. 'I do very much have a dislike of disorder', he admitted once, 'One of the first things I do when I get home at night is to make people take things off radiator tops.'[5] Put in a characteristically self-mocking way, this sums up the nature of the impulse: a 'rage for order', for form and a sense of meaning recovered, however temporarily, from the essential chaos of life. For Stevens, in fact, as for most of the great Romantic poets and philosophers, reality is not something given to us, which our minds receive passively, but is on the contrary something made, the product of an interchange, an interplay or dialectic between our minds and our given circumstances. We, or more accurately our consciousnesses, are not simply blank pieces of paper, Stevens felt, on which the world writes its messages, not just mirrors that reflect our environment; rather, they are lamps, active, creative things which illuminate that environment, helping to give it shape and perspective and so making it adequate, even if only momentarily, to ordinary human desires. 'The imagination', declared Stevens echoing Blake and Coleridge, 'is the power of the mind over the possibilities of things'; 'like light, it adds nothing, except itself.'[6]

Stevens was sometimes irritated by references to the Romantics. 'The past is my own', he insisted in one of his letters, 'not something marked Coleridge, Wordsworth etc. I know of no one who has been particularly important to me.'[7] Nevertheless, when one looks in detail at what Stevens terms his 'reality-imagination complex', it is not difficult to see several correspondences. 'Conceptions are artificial',[8] Stevens argued; our world is always, in a sense, an imagined one, because as soon as we begin to think about it we begin to structure it according to some law—such as the scientific law of cause and effect. We begin, in effect, to 'read' and interpret it in the same way that, instinctively, we read and interpret a written text. On this level, the mind or imagination, as Stevens described it, broadly corresponds to what Coleridge, in *Biographia Literaria* called the primary imagination: 'the living power and prime agent of all human perception, and . . . a repetition in the finite mind of the eternal act of creation in the infinite I AM.'[9] Much more important for Stevens, though, were those acts of the mind which made it correspond with what Coleridge termed the secondary imagination; that is to say, those acts whereby man attempts quite consciously to give significance to his life—to devise some moral or aesthetic order, however fragile or provisional, which can give coherence and a sense of purpose to things. This kind of order was what Stevens called a 'supreme fiction'; and for him, as for Coleridge, the prime creator of such fictions was the poet. The poet, according to Stevens, strives for a 'precise equilibrium' between the mind and its environment at any given moment in time; and then creates a fiction which is at once true to our experience of the world and true to his and our need for value and meaning.

It is worth emphasizing that Stevens was no different from Coleridge and other Romantics, either, in insisting on the fact of change. We are always altering, Stevens believed, our given circumstances alter too, and the fictive world created out of the synthesis or union of the two must invariably respond to this. We must be reassessing our personal needs and given circumstances continually so as to devise new ideas which do full justice to the dynamic nature of both mind and world; and the poet, in turn, must be writing new poems, new fictions all the time so as to pay his tribute to the metamorphic nature of things. Stevens's favourite metaphor for this was the seasons, with winter seen as the bare, icy reality void of all fictive covering; spring as the moment when the imagination and the world come together and embrace; summer as the period of fruition, when the marriage between the desires of the mind and the things of the world is complete and harmonious; and autumn as the moment when the fiction no longer suffices because the imagination that created it, and the world it was created for, have altered, requiring new fictions, fresh identities and relationships. As this rather bare outline indicates, perhaps, the imagery of sexual congress and conflict mingles with that of natural growth and decay to describe what Stevens, in one of his poems, termed the imagination's 'ancient cycle'; and in this respect, again, he was not so very different from a writer like Coleridge. Consider, for example, these two brief passages, one from 'Dejection: An Ode' and the other from *Notes Toward a Supreme Fiction*:

> O Lady! we receive but what we give
> And in our life alone does Nature live. . . .
>
> Joy, Lady! is the spirit and the power
> Which wedding Nature to us gives in dower
>   A new Earth and a new Heaven. . . .
>   *   *   *
> Two things of opposite natures seem to depend
> On one another, as a man depends
> On a woman, day on night, the imagined
>
> On the real. This is the origin of change.
> Winter and spring, cold copulars, embrace
> And forth the particulars of rapture come.[10]

Mind and world, night and day, male and female: both writers see life here as a marriage of opposites. Joy, or a sense of meaning, is the offspring of this marriage. And what Coleridge called dejection, a sense of melancholy and futility, comes when the marriage fails; when, for example, the world is too much with us and the mind becomes a passive instrument— or, alternatively, when the mind escapes from the pressures of the world completely and withdraws into solipsism and day-dreaming.

'A poet looks at the world as a man looks at a woman.'[11] This, from the 'Adagia', offers a variation on the sexual metaphor: and it is also a reminder of just how seductive, for Stevens, was the figure of the poet. For Stevens was no less of a Romantic in this, his tendency to see the fabulator, the maker of poems, as a latter-day prophet: someone who creates the myths that give meaning to people's lives and so enables them to survive—and who also offers an example to his audience, by showing them how to devise their own myths as well as listen to his. Stevens was quite categorical about this. For, whenever he discussed the task or function of the poet, the thrust of his argument was invariably the same. 'I think', he would say,

> . . . that he fulfills himself only as he sees his imagination become the light in the minds of others. His rôle, in short, is to help people to live their lives.[12]

In effect, Stevens returned the poet to his ancient rôle of bard or myth-maker, offering purpose and a sense of meaning to his tribe. And to this he added another, more peculiarly Romantic and American, dimension: which was that of hero. For the poet, Stevens suggested, is his own hero because his mind, his representative imagination, is the catalyst of events. Instead of a third person protagonist, the poet, the 'I' of the poem, occupies the centre of the stage; there, 'like an insatiable actor, slowly and/ with meditation', he speaks words and acts out a drama to which

> an invisible audience listens,
> Not to the play, but to itself, expressed
> In an emotion as of two people, as of two
> Emotions becoming one.[13]

To the extent that Stevens did attribute such an extra-ordinarily powerful and central rôle to the poet, he was of course revealing a kinship with some of the later poets and philosophers in the Romantic tradition, like Matthew Arnold, Henri Bergson—and, above all, George Santayana. While he was still a student at Harvard, Stevens became acquainted with Santayana and was often invited to visit him; he read the older man some of his early poetry and then, much later, addressed one of his finest poems, 'To an Old Philosopher in Rome', to him. In a way, Stevens seems to have regarded

Santayana as a saint—a type, anyway, of the imaginative man, who can use his mind to redeem the essential poverty of life—and Santayana's ideas served as a lamp and guide to the poet throughout his career, illuminating his way, his various poetic voyages, and giving him some hazy sense of a possible destination. This famous passage from the 'Adagia', for example, recalls Santayana's suggestion that 'religion and poetry are identical in essence', since both, ignoring 'matters of fact', 'repair to the material of existence . . . and then out of that . . . material . . . build new structures, richer, finer, fitted to the primary tendencies of our nature':

> The final belief is to believe in a fiction, which you know to be a fiction, there being nothing else. The exquisite truth is to know that it is a fiction and that you believe in it willingly.[14]

'Poetry', said Stevens elsewhere, in 'The Man with the Blue Guitar', '. . . must take the place/ Of empty heaven and its hymns.'[15] For him, as for Santayana, the old religious myths had crumbled and poetry had now to act as a means of redemption. The poet had to replace the priest (or, alternatively, the priest had to accept the rôle of poet). Art had to replace the liturgy of the church. Imaginative belief, or what Coleridge called 'a willing suspension of disbelief', had to replace religious faith. And a possible earthly paradise, created here and now out of the marriage between mind and world, had to replace the vision of a heavenly paradise situated in some great hereafter. Beginning with an essentially Romantic belief in 'The imagination, the one reality/ In this imagined world',[16] and building slowly and meditatively on this, Stevens ended in fact with another centrally Romantic notion—that (to quote from the 'Adagia' again)

> in the absence of a belief in God, the mind turns to its own creations and examines them, not alone from the aesthetic point of view, but for what they reveal, for what they validate and invalidate, for the support they give.[17]

To dwell on Stevens's Romanticism, however, to the exclusion of other aspects of his poetic character would be to forget how very important to him both the French poets— and, in particular, the Symbolistes, their immediate precursors and successors—and his own American background were. The kinship with the French was undoubtedly less crucial than is often supposed; many commentators have exaggerated it, perhaps because it is fairly obvious—a matter, more often than not, of vocabulary and idiom. Nevertheless, it proved useful to Stevens in several respects, and not least in his efforts to distinguish himself from the English tradition. 'Nothing could be more inappropriate to American literature than its English source', he once declared, 'since the Americans are not British in sensibility.'[18] And one way he chose to underline this in his early work was by adopting, on occasion, a self-consciously Gallic tone, with phrases from the French, a smattering of French words—or that demureness of statement combined with elegance of manner and the kind of sonorous, precious and witty language that is often associated with such poets of the late nineteenth century as Verlaine and Laforgue. In turn, the later work often recalls more recent French poets like Valéry, in its openly philosophical approach, its confident use of large abstractions, and its extraordinarily complex network of figurative reference.

Perhaps the French poet with whom Stevens shared most, however, was not Verlaine, Laforgue, or even Valéry, but Baudelaire because, in this case at least, the sense of kinship operated on a rather deeper level. Certainly, the parallels in technique are evident here as well. Both Baudelaire and Stevens manage, for instance, to combine rule and misrule in their poems. Their rhythms are elegantly exact; the movement of each line is measured and poised; and the structure of each of their longer pieces seems to be premeditated, precise, a matter of inherited rather than imitative form. And yet, on the other hand, their language can be bizarre; their imagery gaudy, intentionally startling; and, on closer inspection, it seems that their longer poems do not so much progress as stand still or go round in a circle—existing in space, really, rather than time. As several critics have observed, Baudelaire was at once a Romantic writer and a Classical one, which is perhaps one of the reasons why he described the right to be inconsistent as 'a right in which everyone is interested'.[19] Exactly the same could be said of Stevens, who openly admitted to a correspondent that he liked to move 'in many

directions at once'. 'No man of imagination is prim', he added
defiantly, 'the thing is a contradiction in terms.'[20]

'May it be', asked Stevens half-seriously when he was just
26, 'that I am only a New Jersey Epicurean?'[21] That question
leads indirectly to the other, deeper level on which Baudelaire
and Stevens meet: which is their shared insistence on the
artificial, figurative nature of their poetic worlds. Very often,
this insistence led them to play the literary dandy. Even if it
did not, however, even when the tone was more agonized or
philosophical, there was invariably this emphasis on the poet
as maker, inventing a world rather than simply reporting
one—and, in doing so, uncovering a possibility available to
everyone. One of the most vivid and memorable descriptions
of this activity—of the mind giving life whatever savour or
meaning it possesses—occurs in 'The Idea of Order at Key
West'. In it, the poet describes a woman whom he once heard
singing by the sea (a traditional figure for raw experience),
who becomes identified for him with the 'blessed rage for
order', the need that singer, poet, and all of us must feel to
discover form and significance in our lives. 'When she sang',
the poet declares,

> the sea
> Whatever self it had, became the self
> That was her song, for she was the maker. Then we,
> As we beheld her striding there alone,
> Knew that there never was a world for her
> Except the one she sang and, singing, made.[22]

The stress on that final 'made' is enormous, reminding us of
the infinite series of makings that add up to the experience of
the poem: the woman 'makes' or interprets the sea, the poet
'makes' or interprets the scene, and in turn each reader, each
time he reads the piece, 'makes' or interprets what he sees and
hears.

It may be worth pointing out that, in reminding us
constantly of the figurative nature of poetic truth and the
fictive nature of poetry, Stevens is (as so often) poised between
paradoxes. The world the poem creates is real, Stevens seems
to be saying, because the material for it is discovered *in* reality;
and yet it is unreal, a fiction in a way, because it depends on

the mind then reshaping that material. It is true in the sense that it reproduces a true—that is to say, a true Romantic-Symboliste—version of things; but it is untrue in that it does not reflect 'the first idea', pure, unadorned fact. Above all, it is perfect and complete in so far as it represents a perfect marriage, a complete synthesis of mind and circumstance; and yet it is imperfect, incomplete to the extent that, as mind and circumstance change, the poet must go on to devise new marriages, new syntheses, and so in effect new poems. Of course, Stevens never tried to achieve a logical reconciliation of these opposites because, like so many writers since the Romantic revolution, he realized that his beliefs stemmed from a profound illogic, a deep unreason. 'The poem', Stevens suggested, 'reveals itself only to the ignorant man'[23] for the simple reason that it depends on contradictions which can never be explained or argued away—but which can perhaps be reconciled with the help, and under the 'miraculous influence', of the imagination.

'Do I contradict myself?/ Very well then I contradict myself,/ (I am large, I contain multitudes)'.[24] That would be one way of dismissing any objections Stevens's paradoxes might raise: the lofty gesture of a poet like Walt Whitman who insists that his self-contradictions are part of his representative nature, his attempt to register the variety of his homeplace. Which leads me, inevitably, to the native context; for all his kinship with the English Romantics and poets like Baudelaire, Stevens was nothing if not an American writer—and someone who believed that (to quote one of his very last poems) 'a mythology reflects its region'.[25] 'The gods of China', Stevens declared, 'are always Chinese'[26]; that is, the world the imagination embraces is always a specific, local one and the fictions created out of that embrace must bear the stamp of their locality. 'One turns with something like ferocity toward a land that one loves', he said elsewhere, in a revealing discussion of another poet, John Crowe Ransom, '. . . to demand that it surrender, reveal, that in itself which one loves.'[27] As Stevens saw it, this consummation devoutly to be wished, this marriage between a particular person and place, was 'a vital affair, not an affair of the heart . . ., but an affair of the whole being, a fundamental affair of life'.[28] It was not simply a

49

matter of idiom and gesture, in other words, but of identity and vision. Of course, the paraphernalia of American culture is there in Stevens's poems—things like coffee, saxophones and large sombreros—and, like Whitman, Stevens shows that he has fallen in love with American names. But these things matter less, as a mark of origin, than the fact that Stevens chose as his starting-point what he called 'human loneliness/ A part of space and solitude'[29]; like every great American poet, in fact, he began with the isolated consciousness—Whitman's 'essential Me'—and then progressed from there to the new dimensions, the moments of self-assertion or communion, which that consciousness struggles gamely to create.

Here, however, we are confronted with another paradox in Stevens's work. Like so many American writers, Stevens began with the isolated self, the separate mind and its world; unlike most of them, though, he then moved in two quite different directions, which could perhaps be termed *centripetal* and *centrifugal*. The centripetal movement recalls that arch-egotist and solipsist, Edgar Allen Poe; and, to some extent, Stevens does sound very much like Poe. The self, he insists, creates its own world, and the poem presents us with a supreme version of that world—which is self-contained, fixed and (in a sense, as I have already suggested) perfect. The centrifugal movement, in turn, recalls Emily Dickinson. For Stevens can be quite as insistent as Dickinson was that the self is fragile, evanescent, dwarfed by its surroundings, and that the world it creates must—due to the limitations of its creator—be provisional and incomplete. In some respects, Stevens's poems resemble Poe's in that they drive inwards upon what Poe, in one of his reviews, called 'the circumscribed Eden' of the poet's dream. 'Pure' or 'closed' poems in a way, they are as autonomous and intangible as the worlds they describe; they exist in their own special dimension, or, as Stevens himself put it once, 'beyond the compass of change/ Perceived in a final atmosphere'.[30] In other respects, though, Stevens's poems seem far more like Dickinson's, edging out tentatively as they do towards the boundaries of perception. 'Open' poems of a kind, they tend to emphasize their arbitrariness, to offer themselves up to reinterpretation and re-invention—and so to remind us that they are (to quote

Stevens again) 'inconstant objects of inconstant cause/ In a universe of inconstancy'.[31]

Just how Stevens manages to walk this tightrope between 'open' and 'closed' structures is beautifully illustrated by one of his most famous earlier pieces, 'Anecdote of the Jar'. The animating conception in this poem is very simple: the jar serves as a point which orders all that surrounds it. It performs the function of the imagination just as its surroundings, organized for a moment into a series of significant relationships, perform the function of reality. What complicates things, however, and gives an additional dimension to the poem is its form, the way in which Stevens chooses to flesh out this conception. 'Anecdote of the Jar' begins with a series of unrhymed couplets, continues with them until the eighth line, and then suddenly presents the reader with two end-stopped lines, set off for the first time by rhyme:

> It took dominion everywhere.
> The jar was gray and bare.

It sounds for a moment as if the argument is completed, the poem rounded off. But then, it turns out, it is not; and the premature finality of the lines I have quoted gives an air of *un*finality to the two lines which follow, and which form yet another unrhymed couplet. Even this, the feeling that things have not quite been rounded off, is not left unqualified, however, because the last line returns us to a word used in the first line: 'Tennessee'. Joining the end to the beginning, the poet still seems to be trying to round the poem off, to seal it; and we, the readers, cannot really be sure that he has failed. So we are made to feel that the work is at once complete *and* incomplete, that the argument has been concluded and yet that something has been missed out, left hanging loose. 'Anecdote of the Jar' is, in effect, made to imitate in its form (as well as describe in its content) the continuing act of the imagination, by which worlds are created that are complete in themselves and yet subject to alteration. The mind behind the poem has apparently composed things for a moment, achieved an order 'beyond the compass of change'; and yet it intimates that it must give that order up soon and—casting aside 'the rotted names',[32] obsolete forms and vocabulary—submit itself to 'a universe of inconstancy'.

'Anecdote of the Jar' is exemplary in several ways. The same essential structure, for instance, is used with a difference in 'Thirteen Ways of Looking at a Blackbird'. Here, a blackbird serves as a focal point, a means of bringing out the significance of the context in which it is involved. The meaning of the bird depends on each context, just as the meaning of the context depends on it, with the result that there is exactly the same condition of interdependence between the bird and each of its settings as there is between the jar and its surroundings: a condition which (it need hardly be added) Stevens felt to be characteristic of the relationship between the imagination and its surroundings. In the first section of the poem, for example, the blackbird provides a focal point for the landscape it composes in the same way that a compositional centre composes a landscape painting; and, in doing so, it provides a paradigm of the way the mind orders reality by discovering significant relations in it.

> Among twenty snowy mountains,
> The only moving thing
> Was the eye of the blackbird.

In this case, the snowy surroundings are static, and the eye/I of the blackbird offers the only motion. By contrast, in the final section the terms are reversed:

> It was evening all afternoon.
> It was snowing
> And it was going to snow.
> The blackbird sat
> In the cedar-limbs.

Now the blackbird is motionless in a world of swirling, snowy movement. The bird has become a still point; the imagination is, apparently, at rest; and the poet, making the last lines echo the first, seems to be bringing things full circle, rounding them off. Everything appears to be completed; that is, until we are reminded that, for Stevens, winter was a beginning as well as an end. This section concludes 'Thirteen Ways', certainly; but by reminding us of the process of decreation—what Stevens called 'getting rid of the paint to get at the world itself'[33]—it also acts as a prelude to further imaginative activity, an opening to poems as yet to be written. Once again, things are complete and yet somehow incomplete, closed and at the same time open.

Quite apart from the structure, the tone and idiom of 'Anecdote of the Jar' are also characteristic. The tone is serio-comic as with so many of Stevens's poems, especially the earlier ones; here as in, say, 'Bantams in Pinewoods' or 'Le Monocle de Mon Oncle' the poet uses wit and irony to qualify and complicate matters further, and so prevent the reader from coming to too simple or final a conclusion. And the idiom, in turn, is characterized by repetition and echo ('round . . . Surround . . . around . . . round . . . ground'), a series of significant if often subterranean connections. This repetitive pattern becomes far more elaborate in some of the longer pieces, with the result that poems like (for example) 'Sunday Morning' or 'The Idea of Order at Key West' resemble mosaics, in which the poet seems to be trying to construct his own personal version of the imaginative fictions he celebrates. Complex designs of word, sound and image, they offer the reader a special world, in this case a verbal one, which may be abstracted from and so depend upon our given surroundings— but which has its own innate structure and system of cross-reference.

It would be wrong, however, to dwell on 'Anecdote of the Jar' as if it summed up the whole of Stevens's work, even in its paradoxes and ambiguities. No one poem can do that; and not merely because the later poetry is, on the whole, less spry and balletic than the earlier—more meditative and austere, more discursive and openly philosophical. It is also because Stevens rarely allowed himself to be contained by a particular idiom even within the space of one poem. Each of his pieces is complexly layered, moving almost casually and quite unpredictably between high rhetoric and the colloquial, bookwords, foreign borrowings, and native slang. As a result, each seems unique in a way, with its own particular rhythms and adjustments—its own special way of turning the world into words. Of modern poetry, Stevens once said,

> It is like the voice of . . . some . . . figure concealed. . . . There is no accompaniment. If occasionally the poet touches the triangle or one of the cymbals, he does it only because he feels

like doing it. Instead of a musician we have an orator whose speech sometimes resembles music.[34]

This passage, from the poem that concludes the third section of *Notes Toward a Supreme Fiction*, suggests something of what he meant. The poem is a hymn to the earth, which Stevens describes as a 'fat girl' and addresses in exactly the same way that earlier poets addressed God or their mistress. Like God, the poet suggests, the earth is mysterious, hidden, infinite in its surprises; like the traditional notion of the mistress she is also enticing but elusive, given to radically varying changes of mood. More important, perhaps: like both, she can only be understood through an act of the imagination, a poem or fiction of some kind—something in which her changeableness, her extraordinary vitality and variety, can be caught for a moment in a single, crystalline image.

> Fat girl, terrestrial, my summer, my night
> How is it I find you in difference, see you there
> In a moving contour, a change not quite completed?
>
> . . . . .
> Even so when I think of you as strong or tired.
>
> Bent over work, anxious, content, alone,
> You remain the more than natural figure. You
> Become the soft-footed phantom, the irrational
>
> Distortion, however fragrant, however dear.
> That's it: the more than rational distortion,
> The fiction that results from feeling. Yes, that.
>
> They will get it straight one day at the Sorbonne.
> We shall return at twilight from the lecture
> Pleased that the irrational is rational.
>
> Until flicked by feeling, in a gildered street,
> I call you by name, my green, my fluent mundo.
> You will have stopped revolving except in crystal.[35]

The image of the revolving crystal is, of course, an image of an image: a fictional embodiment of the kind of imaginative fiction that can at once recover the world about us, in all its brightness, plenitude, and vitality, and raise it to a higher power, a superior dimension of reality. And with this image we are back, really, where we began, at the centre of the Romantic-Symbolist tradition, which is the great tradition in modern poetry; since the forms of knowledge and vision that Stevens celebrates here are no different from those celebrated by the great Romantic poets and their successors when they have talked, for example, about the truth of the imagination, the power and suggestiveness of the deep image, or described the world as a forest of symbols. In its own way, the crystal corresponds to—which is to say, has the same basic significance and performs the same symbolic function as— Coleridge's moon imagery, Keats's nightingale and urn, or the memorable allusion to the dancer that concludes Yeats's 'Among School Children'. For it summarizes in the only way possible for Stevens (that is, in an imaginative way) what was for him the central fact of life: the ability of the mind to achieve a kind of redemption—by working *with* the world to abstract something of value out of that world, and so (as Stevens himself put it once) build a bridge between fact and miracle.

'Why do poets in particular resent the attribution of the influence of other poets?' asked Stevens in a letter to Richard Eberhart. 'It seems to me that the true answer is that with a true poet his poetry is the same thing as his vital self. It is not possible for anyone else to touch it.'[36] This necessarily brief essay has been in no sense an attempt to deny the simple fact that Stevens states here; like every 'true poet', Stevens declared his own unique being in his work—developed his own personal sense of things, and of himself, using his own characteristic voice. Despite what some critics may assert, however, Stevens was not a solipsist, any more than he was an aesthete or a hedonist; he was 'a man speaking to men' (to borrow a familiar but nevertheless useful phrase from Wordsworth) preoccupied with 'what will suffice' and enable us all to live our lives. 'We can never have great poetry', Stevens insisted in one of his very last speeches, 'unless we believe that poetry serves great ends';[37] and, in pursuit of those ends, he willingly absorbed the best that had been thought and said by other writers—other people who had tried to make their imagination the light in the minds of their readers—to absorb it and then make it a part of his own meditations. He was a solitary poet, of course, and something of an eccentric visionary—aware, even while he sought knowledge, that 'always there is another life/ A life beyond this present knowing'.[38] But his very solitude made him an heir of the Romantics, as well as a kinsman of Poe, Dickinson and Whitman; while his visions were shared ones, their eccentricity deriving not from any personal idiosyncrasies but from the fact that, in an age of disbelief, the truth can only be arrived at, he felt, by the most circuitous and stony of routes. The figure of Santayana perhaps best sums up this central paradox, of being apart from and yet a part of things. For in describing his former mentor, in 'To an Old Philosopher in Rome', Stevens seems to be describing himself—or, to be more accurate, his own particular choices and best possibilities. 'Be orator', he implores Santayana,

> but with an accurate tongue
> And without eloquence . . .

> So that we feel, in this illumined large,
> The veritable small, so that each of us
> Beholds himself in you, and hears his voice
> In yours, master and commiserable man. . . .[39]

Throughout his life, Stevens sought exactly the kind of dual rôle, of 'master and commiserable man', that he asks Santayana to assume here: which is why, in the end, his poetry bears so many signs of kinship with others, living and dead, while remaining utterly and unmistakably his own.

NOTES

1. *The Collected Poems of Wallace Stevens* (London, 1955), p. 176. The quotations from *The Collected Poems of Wallace Stevens, Opus Posthumous, The Necessary Angel* and *Letters of Wallace Stevens* are reproduced by kind permission of Faber and Faber Ltd., and Alfred Knopf, Inc., copyright © 1954, 1957, 1960, 1966.
2. *Opus Posthumous*, ed. Samuel French Morse (London, 1957), p. 159.

3. *Letters of Wallace Stevens*, ed. Holly Stevens (London, 1967), p. 813.
4. 'Adagia', *Opus Posthumous*, p. 161.
5. *Letters*, p. 300.
6. 'Imagination as Value', in *The Necessary Angel: Essays on Reality and the Imagination* (London, 1960), p. 136; 'The Figure of the Youth as Virile Poet', ibid., p. 37.
7. *Letters*, p. 792.
8. 'Adagia', *Opus Posthumous*, p. 164.
9. *Biographia Literaria* (1817), Chapter XIII.
10. *Collected Poems*, p. 392.
11. *Opus Posthumous*, p. 165.
12. 'Noble Rider and the Sound of Words', *Necessary Angel*, p. 29.
13. 'Of Modern Poetry', *Collected Poems*, p. 239.
14. 'Adagia', *Opus Posthumous*, p. 163.
15. *Collected Poems*, p. 167.
16. 'Another Weeping Woman', *Collected Poems*, p. 25.
17. *Opus Posthumous*, p. 159.
18. 'Adagia', *Opus Posthumous*, p. 176.
19. Cited in Michael Hamburger, *The Truth of Poetry* (London, 1969), p. 3.
20. *Letters*, p. 300.
21. Ibid., p. 87.
22. *Collected Poems*, pp. 129–30.
23. 'Adagia', *Opus Posthumous*, p. 160.
24. 'Song of Myself', section 51.
25. 'A Mythology Reflects its Religion', *Opus Posthumous*, p. 118.
26. 'Two or Three Ideas', *Opus Posthumous*, p. 211.
27. 'John Crowe Ransom: Tennessean', *Opus Posthumous*, p. 211.
28. Ibid.
29. 'The Sail of Ulysses', *Opus Posthumous*, p. 100.
30. 'The Man with the Blue Guitar', *Collected Poems*, p. 168.
31. *Notes Toward a Supreme Fiction*, *Collected Poems*, p. 389.
32. 'The Man with the Blue Guitar', *Collected Poems*, p. 183.
33. *Letters*, p. 402.
34. 'Effects of Analogy', *Necessary Angel*, pp. 125–26.
35. *Collected Poems*, pp. 406–7.
36. *Letters*, p. 815.
37. 'Honors and Acts', *Opus Posthumous*, pp. 245–46.
38. 'The Sail of Ulysses', ibid., p. 101.
39. *Collected Poems*, p. 509.

4

William Carlos Williams: Value and Form

by JIM PHILIP

Everything rests, so far as I can see, on a condition, obvious to the eye, which may be called, if one cares to, the pluralism of experience. And, obviously, no 'law' or abstract summary can include this since in itself it stands outside a generalization, it is plural concretely and in fact.

This has not been sufficiently realized in thought: it is crudely stated in the multiples of Pagan mythology, in the politics of 'Democracy' and in such inborn feelings as nationalism, 'states' rights', etc., etc.

Its present use to me—

It offers this release—life, continued productivity not only in fish eggs but thought.

It is opposed by the pinching academy which tries to relegate it to paleontology, to the 'crude beginnings,' to an earlier condition. But it is as new—so new, that it will shortly be the newest, most pregant motivation of thought in the world.

It is decentralizing in effect as opposed to the merely opportunistic tendencies (due to the surrounding barbarism of the world) of centralization—in the sciences, arts, etc.[1]

A man who, in the course of his medical practice, attended the delivery of one thousand babies might well be expected to have a particular view on 'the pluralism of experience'. Williams's faith in the capacity of individuals to originate structure and meaning in their own lives shines through this passage as it does through the rest of his writings. It is, however, this quality that has led sometimes to the labelling of his work as yet another example of American naïvety, as a continuation of that Adamic myth by means of which real history is evaded. But such is hardly the case, here or elsewhere. The passage above, like many of Williams's texts, has its roots in a deeply felt personal occasion. It comes from one of that group of essays, not published in his own lifetime, that he wrote around his fortieth year, and that carry the dedication 'TO MY BOYS—Wishing them luck'.[2] As such it stands not only as a declaration of faith, but also as an attempt to alert a rising generation to the major pitfalls and dilemmas of the society that surrounds them and that will play its part in the construction of their own lives. What is most interesting, though, is that this review is conducted not only at the level of institutions, but also at the level of discourse. Williams points to the dangers of massive and centralized power structures, but also to the failings of those languages that play their part in the propagation and maintenance of them. The proposals of 'Democracy' in their immediate forms he elsewhere describes as 'tough, universal—a magic lining between men everywhere and their desire'.[3] The language of science, of 'abstract summary', is also questioned in the light of its pervasive effects. What he calls for here is not only the 'decentralizing' of political and cultural life, but also, by implication, the 'release' of new languages more adequate in the expression of human presence and human need. It should be more widely recognized, then, that it is this condition of anxiety and challenge across a wide field that constitutes the true nature of Williams's Americanism. Moreover it should be possible on these grounds also to rebut another familiar criticism of his writings, namely that they are more remarkable for experiment than for insight, that the restless inventions of form are undertaken more for display and subversion than for revealing inquiry. There is certainly an element of nervous showmanship, particularly in the earlier work, but this is a minor matter. In the main, Williams's structures emerge as they do because of the intensity of that underlying debate that he conducts with his own culture. There is, or so this essay proposes, a continual and active relation between value and form.

Between 1946 and 1951 Williams produced his long poem

Paterson, and it is in relation to that major text that any arguments about his work must finally be deployed.[4] The groundwork, however, lies much earlier, in the poems of *Al Que Quiere* (1917), and in the essays that he wrote in that period, particularly for the magazine *Contact* that he co-edited with Robert McAlmon. The title word is one that recurs many times in his writings of that time, and a good way to see what he means by it is to examine some of the editorial statements that he wrote for the magazine. In one of them he declares that

> we have said simply and as frequently as possible and with as many apt illustrations as we could muster that contact with experience is essential to good writing or, let us say, to literature. We have said this in the conviction that contact always implies a local definition of effort with a consequent taking on of certain color from the locality by experience, and these colors or sensual values of whatever sort are the only realities in writing or, as may be said, the essential quality of literature.[5]

Contact is here defined as 'contact with experience'. Good writing, he suggests, should be a record of actual relationship; it should deal with 'colors' and with 'sensual values', that is to say with the concreteness of particular things and people, and the drama of their actual impression on the experiencing subject. Notable also is that the concept of localism has already entered his thinking. The new writing will only emerge, he suggests, as the result of a 'local definition of effort', and it is clear that, in his own mind, a commitment to reality has already become synonymous with a commitment in the first instance to the detailed life of a particular community. His words gain extra weight when we remember that by the time he wrote them he was already in the tenth year of his settlement at Rutherford, New Jersey, close to Paterson, and his own lifelong commitment, both as doctor and as writer, to the cities of the Passaic region.

It is in the poems of *Al Que Quiere* that we can see the first fruits of Williams's responses to his chosen world. The subjects of these short pieces are all moments: of relationship, of release, of recreation. As we read them we feel the pressure of a contrary experience, which, even as it renders them more intense, makes more uncertain the possibility of connection

between them. One does not have to look far through the book
to discover that one of the recurring sources of fascination for
Williams was that natural world that continued to assert itself
in the interstices of the industrial and suburban scene. We
may begin by examining one of the several poems which have
as their subject an experience of this kind. It is the first of a
pair of poems entitled 'Chicory and Daisies'.

> Lift your flowers
> on bitter stems
> chicory!
> Lift them up
> out of the scorched ground!
> Bear no foliage
> but give yourself
> wholly to that!
> Strain under them
> you bitter stems
> that no beast eats—
> and scorn greyness!
> Into the heat with them:
> cool!
> luxuriant! sky blue!
> The earth cracks and
> is shrivelled up:
> the wind moans piteously:
> the sky goes out
> if you should fail.[6]

However many times one reads this one cannot help being
surprised afresh by the accuracy with which the natural form
is perceived. Its shape, its colour, its stance, even its taste, are
there for us to enjoy over and over again. But the structure of
the poem is such that we cannot divorce Williams's appreciation
of the form from his fascination with the energy that suffuses it.
In the opening lines we can see how his first recognition is that
of the thrusting force of the plant as it defies the power of
gravity; it is only when this has been established that the
conventional name of 'chicory' is allowed to take its place. The
point has been made that what we are witnessing is an event
as much as it is an object. The dramatic force of the first word
is recalled in the repeated 'lift', and the echoing 'strain' of later

lines. Indeed we may say that these three energetic verbs act as the introductory signals to three developing sections of the poem, and that what happens in these sections is that the forces at work in the plant are seen in a progressively more complex way. Thus, despite its brevity, the poem does have a definite and interesting plot; contact with the simplest realities is revealed as a continuing voyage of discovery.

One of Williams's closest collaborators on the early issues of *Contact* was the critic, Kenneth Burke. It was he who, in an article written after the poet's death, had the following to say about the work of his friend.

> I feel sure that . . . its essence resides in a kind of physicality imposed upon his poetry by the nature of his work as a physician. Thus . . . my understanding of his slogan (Contact) took a noticeable step forward when, sometime after giving up his practice, he said explosively that he missed the opportunity to get his hands on things. . . .[7]

It is obvious that the practice of medicine is one that must lead to a heightened sensitivity to the drama of physical life, to the organic complexity of the human body and the rôle that it has to play in the creation and expression of personality. For Williams, as we can see from the comment above, this awareness was not a matter simply of professional knowledge; the need for closer contact, to have 'his hands on things', was a personal and continuing one. If we look again at the poem 'Chicory' we can see how it also depends for its precision upon an alert sense of the human body and its co-ordinated functions. What is being celebrated is not simply the plant itself, but also the act of perceiving it; the eyes, hands and muscles that each play their related part in the recognition and enjoyment of it.

We should not be doing the poem justice, however, if we were not to acknowledge those elements of exaggeration and self-parody that are also inscribed in it. The plant is not only appreciated in its separate particularity, it is also imbued with a heroic 'personality'. The repeated apostrophes suggest the longing to transform the non-human into the human, and, in the last lines, a supportive community is invoked that verges on the absurd. Moreover, stripped of their human feeling, these final images present a collapse of natural force into entropy that contrasts paradoxically with the energies of endurance and creativity, that have previously been celebrated. We are made acutely aware, then, of the ways in which recognition and misrecognition are bound together. In this alert poetry of relationship the world is approached not only with wonder and care, but also with confusion and need, and the teasing consciousness of these.

Although it is important to see the roots of such poems as 'Chicory' in Williams's own circumstances, it would be wrong to suggest that the elements of feeling contained in them are a matter only of personal idiosyncrasy. There is much evidence to suggest that, at the time he was writing the poems in *Al Que Quiere*, he felt his own work to be part of a larger artistic revolution that had as one of its motive forces a shared appreciation of the contemporary French painting that had first been seen in America in the Armory Show of 1913. The extent of Williams's admiration of this work can be gauged by examining a short piece that he wrote for the second issue of *Contact* entitled 'A Matisse'.

> On the french grass, in that room on Fifth Ave., lay that woman who had never seen my own poor land. The dust and noise of Paris had fallen from her with the dress and underwear and shoes and stockings which she had just put aside to lie bathing in the sun. . . . Bare as was his mind in anything save the fulness of his knowledge into which her simple body entered as into the eye of the sun himself, so he painted her. So she came to America. No man in my country has seen a woman naked and painted her as if he knew anything except that she was naked. No woman in my country is naked except at night.
>
> In the french sun, on the french grass in a room on Fifth Ave., a french girl lies and smiles at the sun without seeing us.[8]

Here the sensory and emotional immediacy that Williams admires in the painting, and that he seeks to express in his own work, is revealed in its full context. It is experienced as a direct challenge to that repressive Puritanism that is felt to be a still potent influence upon the American character. There is moreover an implicit contrast between the aggressive assault upon the natural world that underlies the commercial power of Fifth Avenue, and that reverent attention to particulars that characterizes the painting. We can understand, then, the excitement that attends this piece as it does Williams's other writings of the period. What began as a personal need has assumed a larger context: at once a radical criticism of the American character, and an attempt to find a new basis for it.

Williams was not the only American to respond with such vigour to the Armory Show and the exhibition that followed it. His taste was in fact guided and confirmed by a number of American painters, including Marsden Hartley, John Marin and Georgia O'Keefe, whose work was exhibited primarily by the photographer Alfred Stieglitz in his New York galleries '291' and 'An American Place'. There is no doubt that it is in their paintings that the American landscape lives for the first time as a vibrant presence. It is a sign, though, of the richness of Williams's response that, while appreciating this work, he was not led by it into the simplifications that it implied. It is clear that he viewed a restored contact with the natural world as an urgent necessity, but this was neither the sole nor the exclusive basis of his criticism. What he sought was not simply an evasion of the American social world, but rather the reinvigoration of it; to achieve this one had to live within it, and to experience to the full both its contradictions and its possibilities.

An interesting poem to examine in this context is the one called 'Portrait of a Woman in Bed'. From the title, and from the opening four lines, one might well surmise that this is yet another piece that displays the influence of the painters. The sense of a particular physical occasion is quickly and economically established:

> There's my things
> drying in the corner:
> that blue skirt
> joined to the grey shirt—[9]

However as the poem progresses it becomes clear that Williams's concern is not simply to isolate and celebrate the woman's physical presence, but rather to approach her in the full complexity of her personal and social life. The poem develops into a moving appraisal of her situation as she struggles against the facts of poverty and isolation. In living alone with her two sons, in refusing to work, and in squatting in empty property, she has flouted the unwritten laws of middle-class respectability. The righteous citizens of Ruther-ford have responded with a cold and self-regarding charity that she is forced to accept even as she reviles it. Her isolation has had its effects in forming within her a combination of fierce loyalty to her sons, aggressive wariness towards strangers, and an underlying desperation:

> My two boys?
> —they're keen!
> Let the rich lady
> care for them—
> they'll beat the school
> or
> let them go to the gutter—
> that ends trouble.
>
> This house is empty
> isn't it?
> Then it's mine
> because I need it.
> Oh, I won't starve
> while there's the bible
> to make them feed me.
>
> Try to help me
> if you want trouble
> or leave me alone—
> that ends trouble.[10]

What is remarkable about this is not simply the accurate recording of complex feeling, but also the manner in which the structure is controlled by the tones and habits of the woman's own speech. The questions, assertions and disruptions are all signs of her disturbed and defiant emotional presence. We can see, then, that in the terms of this poem the process of contact has an added dimension. What is attempted is a complete embodiment of the woman's condition, a knowledge that includes and relates wide aspects of her life, from the gestures of the body and the habits of speech to the tensions of economic and social survival. Moreover, it is clear that this sympathetic response to individual life is one that has to be fought for piecemeal against the effects of social prejudice and moral dogmatism. Indeed we may say that this poem also is one that ends in paradox. Williams's absence, his presence only as listener and observer, lends a fragility to the occasion that cannot be ignored. The moment is one of appeal and recognition, rather than achieved relationship. We are left to speculate on what kind of response it will be possible for the doctor or the man to make from his separate position.

Perhaps enough has been said to suggest that close connection that exists in these poems between value and form. Their structures and their rhetorical devices, their manipulations of movement and tone all contribute to the exploration of human presence and relationship. Williams's disruption of conventional modes is liberating and instructive. Also evident is that the poems, despite their immediacy and brevity, do offer an engagement with what are taken to be some of the most limiting and distorting forces of American life. Williams's poetry of the '20s and '30s is in fact surrounded by those prose texts in which he takes on directly the institutions around him, and in which he seeks with great energy to re-write conventional versions of American history, social analysis and literary criticism. And we should note also that he offered to the public several volumes in which all are included, in which prose passages mediate and extend the immediate recognitions of the poems. That Williams wanted his work to be read in this co-ordinated way is a fact often overlooked. One striking example is that much discussed and much anthologized poem 'The Red Wheelbarrow'. In its original setting in *Spring and All* it is followed by one of several passages in which Williams seeks to wrest from conventional criticism and adapt to his own purposes the crucial term 'the imagination'.[11] An intended and important relation between the poem and the prose is established. Indeed, with their multiple materials, and with their attempts to engage the reader in various kinds of discourse and the relations between them, *Spring and All* and other such works as 'The Descent of Winter' should really be seen as forerunners for the more extended efforts of *Paterson*.

Some familiar criticisms of the nature of Williams' long

poem must briefly be dealt with. Those who complain of the prose sections as 'interruptions' have really missed the point of a good deal of his earlier work, and in particular the argument that the poet, the worker in words, has as much to do in listening to the language of others as in developing new formations of his own. Williams's recognition that the impasse of his own culture is partly one of language becomes one of the structural principles of the work. In the context of his own efforts we are offered a variety of other American languages, varying from local histories to political tracts to personal letters, and we are asked implicitly to measure their effects, of evasion, of partial expression, of unexpected revelation. Other readers, coming to *Paterson* from the long poems of the nineteenth century, have found themselves disturbed by the absence of a controlling and consistent meditative voice. But against this we must set Williams's own conviction that 'a man is indeed a city',[12] that he exists in the network of his relations with the world around him, and nowhere else; that his subjectivity is liable to effacement, contradiction and change. But if *Paterson* does not have a transcendent authorial presence, that is not to say that it lacks coherence or organization. Williams's dictum 'no ideas but in things'[13] has been taken by some to be an excuse for mere randomness, but its real meaning is very different. What he is interested in, and what he seeks to elucidate, are those ideas that have survived the battery of a lifetime's daily experience and that persist as deep and powerful categories of explanation. In the following paragraphs an attempt will be made, all too brief, to suggest something of that underlying structure and of the way that Williams deploys it amidst the manifold of events.

We have already seen the stress that Williams lays upon the need for a careful and considered relationship between men and the natural world in which their lives are set. From the start of *Paterson* it becomes clear that one of his major concerns is that of rebuilding, under the local conditions, the possibilities of such closeness. The most striking natural feature of Paterson is the Falls of the Passaic river, and it is in relation to these that Williams conducts the major part of his re-exploration:

And the air lying over the water
lifts the ripples, brother
to brother, touching as the mind touches,
counter-current, upstream
brings in the fields, hot and cold
parallel but never mingling, one that whirls
backward at the brink and curls invisibly
upward, fills the hollow, whirling,
an accompaniment—but apart, observant of
the distress, sweeps down or up clearing
the spray—[14]

Here Williams celebrates first of all the diversity of the natural order, the wealth of phenomena, each distinct in form and function, 'parallel but never mingling'. However, what he also seeks to draw our attention to is the ceaseless process of interaction in which those separate entities are involved. The rock affects the wind, the wind the water; even the wind itself has its origins in the variation of temperature, the 'hot and cold' of the surrounding land-mass. Williams's depiction of the non-human world reaches in such passages its final fruition. That appreciation of precise form that has always been a part of his work is here enlarged by a further awareness of the intricate life of one place. If the effect of the former was to destroy forever the conventions of nineteenth-century landscape description, then the effect of the latter is to reconstruct the natural scene as a rich process of inter-related events.

Williams also records a series of other meetings with the falls that he has culled from local records. There is the case of Mrs. Cumming, the minister's wife, who, in 1812, here plunged mysteriously to her death. He suggests that for her the falls constituted

A false language, A true. A false language pouring—a language (misunderstood) pouring (misinterpreted) without dignity, without minister, . . .[15]

She is, literally, caught between two worlds, unable to decide which is the 'false language', and which the true: the rigid institutional life embodied by her husband, or the profuse non-human energy by which she is confronted. Unable to relate one to the other, or to live contentedly with either, she is moved to destroy herself in a moment of panic and loneliness. Williams also records the visit to Paterson of Alexander Hamilton who 'looked (at the falls!) and kept his counsel'.[16] Throughout the poem Hamilton is used as an early example of that kind of American in whom the drive towards wealth and power has become a dominant obsession. Out of this meeting there emerges no vivid sense of a particular place, but rather the plan for a 'great manufacturing center'[17] powered by the falls, that might become the hub of the new nation's commercial life. In both these cases there has been a failure of felt connection: an act of settlement has not occurred. These are local examples, but what Williams is suggesting is that it is the reduplication of such disruption that is one of the major causes of restlessness and dissatisfaction in American life.

While it is centred in issues of this kind, Book One also introduces some of these themes that are to assume the foreground later on. The effects of Paterson's past are measured in the lives of some of its present citizens, and, in the last section, Williams, still using concrete examples, offers a wider review of his own project in relation to the efforts of other Americans of his own generation. Books Two and Three, though, are the heartland of the poem, in which Williams struggles with the flow of daily experience as he has encountered it in the Passaic region. In his search for the renewal of a purposive local community he is sometimes encouraged, sometimes repulsed, and sometimes directly accused. The scene is set by the long opening section that dramatizes the events of one Sunday afternoon in Garrett Mountain Park, a preserved open space above the city. Williams records the movements and sounds about him, and he suggests further that they are the signs of a latent but unfulfilled energy. As he presents it, the occasion is one that is perceived by all to be separate from, indeed contradictory to, the weekday routines of the industrial city. One man, lying beside his partner, is described as he

> Sees, alive (asleep)
>   —the fall's roar entering
> his sleep (to be fulfilled)

>   reborn
> in his sleep—scattered over the mountain
> severally.
>   by which he woos her, severally.
>
> And the amnesic crowd (the scattered),
> called about—strains
> to catch the movement of one voice.
>
>   hears
>   Pleasure! Pleasure!
>
>   —feels,
>
> half dismayed, the afternoon of complex
> voices its own—
>   and is relieved
>   (relived)[18]

Here, against the pressures of exhaustion, there are linked processes of recovery. An intrinsic sociality, however tenuous, has reasserted itself, and it is in the context of this that revival becomes possible, both of personal identity and personal relationship. And it is, of course, the 'voices' that are the crucial factor, the achievement of language being seen as the first stage in a wider articulation of meaning and choice. It is in this section of the poem that we can see most clearly both the strengths and the weaknesses of Williams's approach to the 'people' of his chosen city. There is, on the one hand, the longing for an accuracy of encounter, for the precise registration of perceptions and intuitions. There are, on the other hand, undeniable elements of sentimentality. For Williams his fellow beings live most fully in their moments of recreation, of escape. Neither here nor elsewhere in the poem is there any full engagement with their working lives and the struggles that they may contain. In a strange way they are seen both as victims and as heroes, condemned to a barren wasteland that the text excludes, but rescued in other moments as the agents of significant change. But there is little indication of how 'Sunday' is to re-occupy the weekday world, of how spontaneous feeling is to transform the economic and political process.

We should not forget, however, that it is in part due to Williams himself that we are moved to make these criticisms. At the end of Book Two there occurs that extraordinary moment when the poem is given over for the space of six pages to an exterior and questioning voice, that of Marcia Nardi, alias 'Cress', an impoverished woman writer of Williams's acquaintance. Her attacks are of such a kind as to threaten to demolish the whole project. She suggests that Williams's class and professional background are such as to prohibit any full understanding of 'life in the raw'.[19] The notion of the poem as a significant form of social action is also dismissed with the mocking comment that it offers 'the insight and humanity of words on paper only'.[20] Cress's extreme views are partly the product of an evident personal bitterness and cannot be wholly accepted. But we should not under-estimate the literary radicalism of this moment. What other works, before or since, offer as deliberately a position from which the deconstruction of their sustaining assumptions is possible? The reader is forced to pause, to re-examine all that has gone before, and to wonder how the poem can continue on the new and deepened ground that is now revealed. Once this debate has been opened, it can never fully be closed, and it is clearly not Williams's intention that it should be. The determination remains, however, that, so far as possible, opposition should be turned into opportunity, for revaluation, for clarification of purpose. Book Three sets out to demonstrate these processes in action. It is in many ways the most introspective and embattled part of the poem as Williams seeks to redefine his own positions while at the same time admitting their potential limitations. As his assaults on the sterilities of the 'Library'[21] suggest, the search for a new literary practice is still felt to be an urgent and necessary one. But there is an admittance of the threatening impotence that this brings with it in the absence of other initiatives. In his writing about the black girl he reaches out to other centres of consciousness, while accepting that this process is one that may involve distortion and wish-fulfilment.[22] As the book progresses there is the rising of an apocalyptic despair, presented in images of fire and flood, that is only just held at bay by Williams's commitment to his own more patient processes of renewal.

In Book Four the poem does, as Williams put it in a letter
to Horace Gregory, 'definitely break out into the world at
large'.[23] Like many other liberals of the period, Williams saw
the greatest danger to a vigorous democratic culture as lying
in the growing metropolis with its combination of economic
power and spectacular allurement. It is to these issues that
he turns as he examines the experience of a young nurse who
makes the move from Paterson to Manhattan. Significantly
the form shifts into the dramatic mode as Williams stands
back from a world in relation to which he is observer rather
than participant. The girl is hired by a rich and lonely older
woman but soon finds herself required to play the rôle of
'Phyllis' in an elaborate pastoral fantasy, and to listen, in the
absence of any other audience, to the 'poem' that her
employer is composing. Williams seeks to suggest the atrophy
and perversion of the imagination under metropolitan con-
ditions. Art has become style, pervaded by a self-conscious
cynicism, and an ultimate acceptance of the cash nexus as
the arbiter of human relations. The wider effect is to justify
what has come before. For all its inarticulacy and its atmos-
phere of divorce, Paterson does offer those residual elements
of human community out of which an indigenous culture
may be constructed.

The book continues in what seems a perplexing way, its
central subject becoming the research work of Madame Curie
that led eventually to the discovery of radium. It becomes
clear, though, that Williams is attempting an analogy between
the work of the scientists and the proposed advance that he
envisages for his own society. What he admires most about
Curie's work is her heroic attention to detail, the persistence
with which the original eight tons of pitchblende ore were
slowly broken down until they yielded one decigramme of the
potent new metal. He is also impressed by her questioning of
scientific authority, her determination that the theories should
be revised to take account of the new facts. What the analogy
involves is the emergence in the social sphere of a spirit of
inquiry as rigorous as this. There must be a challenging of the
present centres of control, of the financial and cultural
domination of the metropolis. There must be a reappraisal of
particular communities that is as precise in its attention as was

Marie Curie's research. As an example of the kind of local experiment that he has in mind he brings forward his own faith in the potential of social credit schemes. It may be said that Williams here approaches the economic and political dimensions of his vision, but he does so by characteristically concrete means, resisting the temptation towards slogans and panaceas. If there is to be a new political practice it must be original in its methods, human in its scale, and precise in its objectives. Williams's anxieties are as evident here as his faith that such a transformation is possible. Indeed the poem ends on this combined note of underlying conviction and strategic doubt. The final emblematic figure is that of the man who, with his dog, turns back from the shore, back towards Paterson, and the limited but real possibilities of the known world.

Such an abbreviated view of the poem inevitably overlooks much of its detailed texture. It does, however, have the advantage of allowing us to see the considerable coherence of its form, and the ways in which this gives voice to a continuing and deepening debate. It should be evident also that Williams's positions are not those of an eccentric localist but rather the most complex expression of contemporary liberal faiths both deeply and widely held. His interest, for instance, in the social philosophy of John Dewey is well known, and has been recorded by a number of critics.[24] In his book *The Public and its Problems* the latter declares his own views in familiar and relatable terms:

> The Great Community, in the sense of full and free inter-communication, is conceivable. But it can never possess all the qualities which mark a local community. It will do its final work in ordering the relations and enriching the experience of local associations. The invasion and partial destruction of the life of the latter by outside uncontrolled agencies is the immediate source of the instability, disintegration and restlessness which characterise the present epoch.[25]

The ultimate effect, though, of such comparisons must surely be to impress upon us the greater scope and originality of Williams's text. The life of the poem lies not only in its latent organizing view, but also in the way that this is challenged and extended in a larger creative process. *Paterson* is remarkable not only for its recording of obstructions and oppositions in actual experience, but also for its acknowledgement of the doubts and fears that accompany them. We are aware at all points, then, not of a secure network of belief, but of an exploratory faith that is subject to invasions and reversals, and that has to be redefined in each particular encounter. As the poem progresses we are witnesses to a living process that is both inspiring in its honesty and moving in its persistence.

The most comparable attempts in the pre-war period to forge the long poem into an expression of American renewal are, of course, Ezra Pound's *Cantos*, and Hart Crane's *The Bridge*. In *Paterson*, implicitly and at points explicitly, Williams defends his own intentions against the procedures of the former.[26] By the end of the work it is clear that, despite their friendship, there is a deep division between the intelligences of the two men: between the lover of order with his wholesale rejection of the American masses, and the instinctive democrat, carving a possible future out of an uncertain present. However, the poem can be understood as an implicit response also to the methods of Crane's opus and the attitudes that sustain it. Williams's patient attention to particulars is one that contrasts strongly with the vaulting and self-destructive ambition of the latter.

Viewed in this light, then, *Paterson* assumes a centrality and a sanity that it is hard to grant to many other texts. Moreover, if we consider it in relation to some of the characteristic achievements of the post-war period, this impression can only be strengthened. One of the remarkable features of the poem is the way in which it contains within itself a number of those responses that, in their separate forms, can be seen to predominate in the writing of the last thirty years. We have noticed that Williams' patient confidence is often interrupted by a negative mode that includes both frustration and self-doubt. It would be fair to say that it is a similar disillusionment that underlies much of the poetry of the post-war academic tradition. It is a spirit that finds its most complex expression in Robert Lowell's investigations of a reduced and guilt-ridden personal life lived in the presence of a public world that is felt as both threatening and impenetrable. Moreover, Williams's admittance of an extreme apocalyptic

74

vision is one that prefigures much of the underground writing of the '50s and '60s. And we should recall finally that alert humility before the details of the natural world that is as much a part of *Paterson* as it is of Williams's other writings. In the poetry of Charles Olson, Gary Snyder and others we can observe the extension of this awareness as yet another ground on which to oppose the predominant reality. Yet the essential point to make is that in Williams's text these elements of feeling do not exist in separate and exclusive forms, but occur in implicit relationship both with each other and with that more complete vision of a revived democratic community that is the poem's main organizing feature. We may make the claim then, that *Paterson* remains a work of contemporary importance. It may yet bear out Williams's own conviction that 'the art forms of today open the way to the intelligence of tomorrow.'[27]

NOTES

1. William Carlos Williams, *The Embodiment of Knowledge* (New York, 1977), p. 149. Extracts from Williams's texts are included by kind permission of Penguin Books, McGibbon and Kee, and New Directions Publishing Corporation.
2. Ibid., p. 148.
3. Ibid., p. 27.
4. For the purposes of this essay *Paterson* is deemed to conclude at the end of Book IV. There has been no space to discuss the status of the later Books V & VI.
5. William Carlos Williams, *Selected Essays* (New York, 1969), p. 32.
6. William Carlos Williams, *Collected Earlier Poems* (London, 1967), p. 122.
7. Kenneth Burke, 'William Carlos Williams, 1883–1963' in *William Carlos Williams, A Collection of Critical Essays*, ed. J. Hillis Miller (Englewood Cliffs, 1966), p. 52.
8. *Selected Essays*, pp. 30–1.
9. *Collected Earlier Poems*, p. 150.
10. Ibid., p. 152.
11. William Carlos Williams, *Imaginations* (New York, 1971), pp. 138–39.
12. *The Autobiography of William Carlos Williams* (New York, 1967), p. 390.
13. William Carlos Williams, *Paterson* (Harmondsworth, 1983), p. 6.
14. *Paterson*, p. 25.
15. Ibid., p. 15.
16. Ibid., p. 10.
17. Ibid., p. 69.

18. Ibid., p. 60.
19. Ibid., p. 64.
20. Ibid.
21. Ibid., p. 100.
22. See particularly *Paterson*, pp. 104–5.
23. The Selected Letters of William Carlos Williams, edited by J. C. Thirwall (New York, 1957): letter to Horace Gregory, 1948.
24. See particularly the comments of Michael Weaver on p. 34 of *William Carlos Williams: The American Background* (Cambridge, 1971).
25. John Dewey, *The Public and its Problems*, Henry Holt and Co. (New York, 1927), p. 211.
26. See *Paterson*, pp. 37–8.
27. *Selected Essays*, p. 212.

5

'Man Under Fortune': Bases for Ezra Pound's Poetry

by ERIC MOTTRAM

> This is not a work of fiction/nor yet of one man.
>
> (Canto XCIX)

Pound's decision to retrace and possibly regain the bases of a viable culture by living and working in Europe is traditional to that educated section of American society which has ambivalently sought its values in what Hawthorne called 'Our Old Home'. The pattern is there, too, in *The Marble Faun* (1860), with materials Pound gathered in a manner peculiar to himself. Hawthorne's Rome is a centre of mainly concealed autocratic rule, hierarchically religious and usurious, drawing the vulnerable into its labyrinth. The Fortunate Fall from American relative innocence to European experience is instigated and enacted in the presence of social and personal functions of beneficent and malign art, the dark and fair ladies who play archetypal rôles of creation and imitation, risk and safety, and the figure of a faun whose move from nature and agrarian society to love and art (both erotically and in the form of a sculpture), and from pastoral innocence to urban guilt, arouses ambiguous forces the Mediterranean world still represents under the signification of Dionysus. Pound, however, extends his search to ancient China, for a greater extent than Emerson and Thoreau, and, through a reading of Frobenius, to Australia and Africa, although in a limited way.

The *Cantos* opens in 1925 (with drafts a decade or more earlier) with a forcible raising of the dead in their violent pasts by Odysseus as part of his *periplum* voyage without charts, a transit, in so far as he is a persona for the poet, not to home but to the incomplete *Drafts and Fragments of Cantos CX–CXVII* of 1968 (unofficially CX to CXVII appeared in 1967). In the opening poem of *Hugh Selwyn Mauberley (Life and Contacts)* of 1920, Odysseus survives the Sirens and the Wandering Rocks not for Penelope so much as for Flaubert and Circe, as the European image of the man who exemplifies meticulous and impersonalized verbal explorations in art, and survives, too, the erotic ambivalences of a female demi-urge capable of malign arts. Troy gives rise to the voyage, and the fourth section of 'E.P. Ode Pour L'Election De Son Sepulchre' takes off from Arthur Clough's 'Amours de Voyage' in prosody, critical feeling and tonal level to expose the sacrificial wastes in Horace's scurrilous ode expounding war as opportunity for patriotic glory. Clough writes:

> *Dulce* it is and *decorum*, no doubt, for the country to fall—to
> Offer one's blood an oblation to Freedom, and die for the
>   Cause; yet
> Still, individual culture is also something. . . .

Pound, using a common method in his work, tightens the implications, and in ways which will be found throughout the *Cantos*:

> non 'dulce' non 'et decor' . . .

> walked eye-deep in hell
> believing in old men's lies, then unbelieving
> came home, home to a lie . . .
> usury age-old and age-thick
> and liars in public places.

In Canto I Odysseus sacrifices, 'dark blood flowed in the fosse', the dead emerge, and Tiresias gives unwanted and terrible advice, 'Odysseus/ Shalt return through spiteful Neptune, over dark seas,/ Lose all companions', an appalling prophecy for the poet, as it turned out. The passage leaps to Circe, who compels worship, the Latin says, and to Aphrodite, the archetype of love and wisdom, whose gold is not usurious, but purely of the earth and light. She bears the wand of Hermes Psychopompos, the branch which represents solar vitality penetrating the earth for generative prospects. As William Carlos Williams wrote in 1931: 'The thing that is felt is that the quick are moving among the dead. . . . It is the gone world of history.'[1] Chthonic roots have to be examined, not accepted. The nature of gods and religion has to be considered if they are to be used ('Religio', 1918; *The Spirit of Romance*, 1910), and the Great Bass ascertained, if indeed it is there and not in itself an invention.

Pound's work operates between experiential belief, inheritance, and the existential need for guidance from power which he hopes embodies wisdom—just as Odysseus does. He wrote to Herbert Creekmore in 1939, 'I haven't an Aquinas-map; Aquinas *not* valid now'[2]: the implication is—unlike Dante in *his* epic. In 'A Visiting Card' (1942) he refers to 'the Aquinian universe' and then writes:

> the laws of material science presuppose uniformity throughout the cosmos, but they do not offer an hierarchy of anything like the earlier coherence. Call it an hierarchy of evaluation.

And that is a main search in his writings. As a poet, he 'articulates the journey' through a rhythm.[3] His prosody liberates from both the weak mathematics and the flaccid *vers libre* of nineteenth-century decadence, and particularly from the presupposed iambic supremacy. In the introduction to his Cavalcanti translations (1910) he writes:

> I believe in an ultimate and absolute rhythm as I believe in an absolute symbol or metaphor. The perception of the intellect is given in the word, that of the emotions in the cadence. . . . Rhythm is perhaps the most primal of all things known to us. . . . When we know more of overtones we will see that the tempo of every masterpiece is absolute, and is exactly set by some further law of rhythmic accord.[4]

This can certainly be perceived in reading the *Cantos*, and especially in listening to Pound's recorded performances—that 'absolute rhythm' which, he wrote in 'Prolegomena' (1912), corresponds exactly to the emotion or shade of emotion to be expressed. A man's rhythm must be interpretative, it will be, therefore, in the end, his own uncounterfeiting, uncounterfeitable.

Schafer's compilation and commentary on the Great Bass[5] supplies the basis needed to grasp Pound's inferences. Fundamentally, it is a prosodic method to ensure that the three kinds of poetry given in 'How to read' (1927–28) are not separated or ruined by metric fixations: *melopoeia* (words 'charged . . . with some musical property'), *phanopoeia* ('a casting of images upon the visual imagination'), and *logopoeia* ('the dance of the intellect among words', using 'habits of usage', expected contexts and concomitants). A further main guide to controls appears in 'A Retrospect' (1913–18), in advice to score by musical phrase rather than metronomic rigidities, and to abjure iambic pentameters as some supposed natural English beat. Rhythm extends throughout the connotative and denotative meanings and the strongly visual lay-out of the pages (a design force some of whose features derive from Pound's sense of the Chinese ideogram, and which Charles Olson will incorporate into 'Projective Verse' in 1950[6]). Rhythm is 'inner form' in poetic design. Fixed metrics operate as a drug working from outside on 'the nerves and sensorium of the self', whereas

> in the affairs of tempo the *beat* is a knife-edge and *not* the surface of a rolling-pin. . . . Measured time is only one form of rhythm; but a true rhythm sense assimilates all sorts of uneven pieces of time. . . . Constantly varying phrase-length and rhythm-length is a freedom from fixed lengths. . . . A rhythmic unit is a shape, it exists like the keel-line of a yacht, or the lines of an automobile engine, for a definite purpose. . . . To compose in the sequence of the musical phrase, not the sequence of a metronome. Rhythm is a form cut into TIME, as a design is determined SPACE. . . . Most arts attain their effects by using a fixed element and a variable.[7]

These controls are exercised with masterly authority right through to the final cantos, in astonishing alertness and invention. (Another major working-out is the translations of *The Classic Anthology Defined by Confucius*, 1955.) Characteristically, Pound is ambivalent about the term 'absolute'. He could grasp what he required from Cavalcanti and Bartok, and he could claim a spatial effect in poetry derived from music—'some minds take pleasure in counterpoint' (Canto LXXIX)—and the spatial musical performances of the Renaissance associated with San Marco in Venice. But whether keel, engine or score design, it is this which enables the voyage and journey to take place—and, further, the idea of *periplum* is continually challenged by notions of totality, and the concept of play between fixed and variable is thereby interfered with. A key case is within *Antheil and the Treatise on Harmony* (1924) where Pound praises precise notation and a performance obedient to it, but also needs 'a still deeper basis; giving the main form to the sound', so that 'rhythm is nothing but the division of frequency plus an emphasis or phrasing of that division.' He dates his effective discovery to 1910, when he moved from 'working with monolinear verbal rhythm' to rhythms 'in musical structure, even with other dimensions'— what he later calls 'proportional sensitivity' or 'having a musical ear'.

By 1938, in Chapter 7 of *Guide to Kulchur*, Pound could sum up his main practice as 'Great Bass' within an over-all harmony, an 'ideogram' which puts together Leibnitz's 'unsquashable monad', Scotus Erigena's authority of right reason (which emerges so magnificently in the first *Pisan Canto* in 1948), and the nature of Gaudier-Brzeska's sculpture, given in Chapter 6: 'It is the VORTEX of will, of decision, that begins. . . . I shall present my emotions by the arrangement of my surfaces, the planes and lines by which they are defined.' The ideogrammatic prosody of the *Cantos* is not reductive, therefore, but combinatory, or, in Georges Bataille's sense, heterogeneous rather than homogeneous. Relatively static Imagism had to be developed, through Vorticism, towards a narrative of ideograms in designs of incremental feedback, transformations and multiple rhymes of motif, cadence and idea.[8] The *Cantos* exfoliate events, relationships and recurrences along the Great Bass. Ernest Fenollosa's verse 'written in terms of visible hieroglyphics' is aerated from the principles of 'How to Read', towards a non-lineal continuity, an epic. Selective power politics, economics, law, art theories and global myths are to flow without losing too much of the speed of thinking and feeling, without dispersing energy into discursive argument or lyrical ego display:

> ALL typographic disposition, placing of words *on* the page, is intended to facilitate the reader's intonation, whether he be reading silently to self or aloud to friends. . . . There is *no intentional obscurity*. There is condensation to maximum obtainable. It is impossible to make the deep as quickly comprehensible as the shallow.[9]

It follows that the range of information in the Cantos may not overlap that of the reader at every point and that therefore *A Companion to the Cantos of Ezra Pound* is a necessary text-in-aid.[10] Chapter 31 of *Guide to Kulchur* connects this to the Great Bass: 'This sense of time-division and/or duration. . . . We Never know enough. The good artist . . . is oppressed by his own ignorance.'

The *Cantos* therefore tacitly recognizes its absences, gaps and lacks. Pound's Heracles cries out in the translation of Sophocles' *Women of Trachis*, 'SPLENDOUR, IT ALL COHERES',[11] but at the end of his life—and it is Pound who says 'there is no substitute for a life-time'—he knows that total coherence is hubris, a state of blind paranoia. In Canto CXVI he brings to bear 'mind leaping/ like dolphins', and 'concepts the human mind has attained/ To make Cosmos', with Mussolini 'wrecked for an error'—with reference back to Odysseus, to the Sophocles (the Nessus shirt and Heracles as Solar Vitality), then to the structure of palimpsest and 'a little light in great darkness' (recurrent in the poem), to the business of laws (Justinian's 'tangle of works unfinished'), to the recurrences of 'the great ball of crystal' and 'the great acorn of light' (Cantos LXXVI and CVI), and finally a withdrawal from hubris, 'I cannot make it cohere'—with emphasis on *make*. He then leads through Ariadne's thread, Walt Disney, Laforgue, Linnaeus and the *Paradiso*—with a glance back to the Provencal Mont Segur as *Mons Veneris*—to the fact that any earthly paradise falls short. 'To "see again",/ the verb is "see", not "walk on"' recalls the end of 'Provincia Deserta' in 1912: 'I have walked over these roads;/ I have thought of them living.' So that Pound can state firmly, 'it coheres all right/ even if my notes do not cohere', recalling

Canto XXV: 'and saw the waves taking form as crystal, as facets of air,/ and the wind there, before them, moving,/ so that notes needed not move'; and then seal in a last confiding in a possible reader: 'A little light, like a rushlight/ to lead back to splendour'. Heracles is confirmed.

But without an Aquinas-map, Pound had to investigate the possibility of laws to stabilize the Great Bass, the process of coherence through the personal creation of 'a poem containing history'. His 1935 letter to Bunting stresses the need to define until 'the detail of surface is in accord with the root in justice':

> poetry does not consist of the cowardice which refuses to analyze the transient, which refuses to see it. The specialized thinking has to be done or literature dies and stinks.[12]

Detail must include law, the morality of money in the issues of banks and usury, and the nature of supreme leaders. During his first visits to Europe, it is through exploration of the meaning of Provence in the history of cultures that he begins to ascertain the poet's social function: the historical geography of a point of intersection for Mediterranean cultures Pound needed to found himself within—the conjunction of female love and inspiration, aristocratic nobility, poets of extreme virtuosity in *motz el son* (the music of words in rhythm), and the sublime vestiges of Eleusinian cults of light and revelation. In 1910, in his culminatory book *The Spirit of Romance* he is able to write confidently 'all ages are contemporaneous.' In Canto XXIII the destruction of Mont Segur, the Cathar centre, exemplifes dogma destroying creative love, art and rite. For Pound, as Peter Makin's book makes clear,[13] Hellenism survived destructive Christianity in Provence, and had to be made to survive into his own time. Mont Segur is the safe citadel to whose altar the poet as state-adviser must move for his and world health. The benevolent female powers of the *Cantos* represent love as a perception of form, of which art is a crucial definition. Light and form become—and most intensely in *Rock-Drill* and *Thrones*—deeply connected to the bases of law, and, throughout the poem, to the sign of Ming, the total light process (enlightenment in both the Eleusinian and the more intellectual Confucian senses). And these processes in turn relate to *virtu* (defined in the Cavalcanti essay and in the translations of Confucius).[14] While working on *Three Cantos* (the 'ur-cantos' in *Poetry* Vol. X, 3–5, Summer 1917, composed c. 1912–15), Pound composed 'Provincia Deserta' (1915) and 'Near Perigord' (1915), a combined exploration of ways of presenting historical figures as poetic personae for a larger scheme, 'a poem containing history'.[15]

Growing up in a century haunted by the theory and presence of dominant leaders as saviours, and reading Dante on the Fate of dominant men and women, Pound takes part in the search for instances—in Renaissance Italy, ancient China and the early American republic—of governmental control through enlightened if dictatorial leadership from Confucian emperors to Mussolini. But, out of the faun-controlled landscape of Provence and its *kalendar maya* traditions, displayed in *A Lume Spento* (1908), emerges Dionysus, the figure of chthonic and cosmic energies which are never under total control for human benefit. Only his myth coheres the radically uncontrollable. The *Cantos* becomes therefore a major twentieth-century work exploring the inflections of social control and erotic, a-moral forces, including the cult of authoritarian leadership and the irrationalities of racism. Dionysus enters in Canto XI captured on his way to Naxos, his cult centre, by sailors hoping for 'a little slave-money' (the types of money criminals throughout), but comes to in time to propel the Pentheus narrative, the wine cult, the ambivalent energizing of the state he stands for, accompanied by the feral smells of his various wildcats. As he takes his ecstatic form of Lycaeus, Pound links him to another metamorphic figure, Proteus, a sea-god of great knowledge and prophetic powers, referred to in a text which deeply influenced him and for which he wrote a 'Postscript', De Gourmont's *The Natural Philosophy of Love* (1922). De Gourmont's 'new forms assumed by the inexhaustible Proteus' move towards the needs for a Dionysian 'centre of life, with multiple lives diverging from it', rather than an evolutionary model. 'Instinct and intelligence' are inseparable, and 'the sexual act is the most important of all acts.'[16] Therefore, Dionysus appears crucially throughout to the poet's remorseful conclusion that he has not obeyed the god sufficiently ('Notes for Canto CXVII et seq.'), and 'an altar to Zagreus' (Dionysus forms as Zagreus, Bacchus,

Lycaeus, Iacchus, Bromios and Pan) refers back to Canto XC, and in turn to Canto XI: 'the great cats approaching. . . . oi chthonoi [gods of the underworld] myrrh and olibanum on the altar stone. . . . bright flame/ now on the altar/ the crystal funnel of air'. In conclusion, the Dionysian remedy is re-stated:

> Trees die and the dream remains
> > Not love but that love flows from it
> > ex animo
> > & cannot ergo delight in itself
> > but only in love flowing from it.
> UBI AMOR IBI OCULUS EST

Through Richard de St. Victor's maxim—'where love is there is the eye'—Dionysian erotics *may* be diverted from the tyrannies of war, economics and politics in our time. Canto XVII is a praise to the generative, a little paradise in which, after the appearance of Zagreus, gold is not an excuse for usury but a form of energy which gathers energy—gold gathering light.

These notions inform the roots of Pound's anti-semitic moments—points at which not only the Christian but the Hebrew corrupt the Eleusinian:

> hebrew scriptures . . . [are] the annals of a servile and nomadic tribe. . . . Jehovah is a semitic cuckoo's egg laid in the European nest. He has no connection with Dante's god. That later concept of supreme Love and Intelligence is certainly not derived from the Old Testament.[17]

Moreover, the phallic, chthonic leader has to emerge from a wandering race. And the leader is male. The female is conservative, an inheritor, practical and clever but not inventive although 'the enemy of the dead or laborious form of compilation, abstraction'.[18] In *Jefferson and/or Mussolini* (1935) Pound converts this to the required man of action, Mussolini, as 'passion for construction', 'the artist', concerned with 'Italy organic', artifax against abstraction. Jews come to stand for money abstraction together with the principle of denationalization, part of the antagonism of bankers versus producers that Pound found in Brooks Adams' *Law of Civilization and Decay* (1895). Culture should be determined by martial, imaginative men with a sense of agrarian productivity bankers (usurers) cannot conceive—instinctive rather than calculating, a form of the toughening of the gentle Confucian leader of Canto XIII into the leader against evil in Canto LIII. This movement is part of Pound's increased inclination for the melodrama of deterministic beliefs in European, political thought of which fascist leadership is one indication. The instance of ancient Chinese rule through hierarchy, agriculture and Confucian principle resulting in 'a great sensibility' (Canto LXXXV) needs the mysticism of the Dionysian 'phallic heart' in Canto XCIX: 'The Sage Emperor's heart is our heart,/ His government is our government'; '. . . that man's phallic heart is from heaven/ a clear spring of rightness'; 'the State is corporate/ as with pulse in its body.' Law lies with the 'reciprocity' these tenets imply.

In 1918 Pound wrote that 'the undeniable tradition of metamorphosis teaches us that things do not remain always the same.' But there is a Great Bass and it does have laws. Pound dreamed that out of Bacchic energy must be produced the totalitarian man of laws without totalitarian tyranny, the common paradise dream of inter-war men and women, and most of the Modernists in the West. Not for nothing does his Dolmetsch essay of 1918 begin:

> I have seen the God Pan. . . . I heard a bewildering and pervasive music moving from precision to precision within itself. Then I heard a different music, hollow and laughing.

The *Cantos*, Pound told his *Paris Review* interviewer, were to be 'a verbal formula to combat the rise of brutality—the principle of order versus the split atom'.[19] But in Canto XVII, Zagreus appears in violent generation first—and *then* architecture appears as harmony of thought, art and nature, and the forms of love and creativity are born from sea, cave and shell.

In the *Pisan Cantos* Pound appeals, imprisoned for treason, to the Algonquin energy spirit as well as the 'god of lynxes' in 'the close garden of Venus', with Priapus, the phallic, and a variety of female and male generatives, in a moving prayer for creative power and clarity which is both erotic and intellectual. The puma of Hermes, who charmed Apollo with his lyre, appears, and above all Aphrodite, 'terrible in resistance'. Together with passages in the *Drafts and Fragments*, these changes justify Wendy Stallard Flory's understanding that the poet

> has begun to consider his relationships with women he loves from their point of view and to appreciate the different ways in which they have suffered on his account.[20]

The Lady returns from Provence in forms far less domineering, far more paradisal.

But it is doubtful if Pound's 'strong leaning towards the paradisal or untrammelled-beauty aspects of life'[21] could ever be more than a dream. As early as the second section of 'Mauberley' (1920) Anangke (necessity) ends Arcadia. The *Cantos* raises altars and receives partial gifts from the chthonic and divine, but 'the city of Dioce' (the Medean Ecbatan in the 6th century B.C.) remains as remote as Mt. Taishan (the shrine mountain in West Shantung associated in Canto LXXIV with the Emperor Shun, a noted governor, astronomer and regulator of order and ceremony). But Pound clings to his expectation of benevolent despots (rather than democracy or communism), to the possibilities in Sigismundo Malatesta who ruled, *and* built the Rimini *Tempio*. His access to the necessities of science and technology within politics, law and economics is, to say the least, elementary. For Pound, as for Schoenberg (whom he barely recognized), the order of art had to be the key representation of some 'paradigmatic solution within the realm of music or poetry to the general process of disorder, collapse and attempted reconstruction' in the first half of the twentieth century.[22] But money as a major measure of value—without which the poet could not function as state adviser—had to be included in the epic paradigm, since it is the vehicle of the control of stored energy. The state has a duty to stabilize the wage-price relationship, and up to Canto LII (1940) Pound believed his kind of work could contribute to such social responsibility.

Canto LI ends the Fifth Decad which places the Rational Credit system of seventeenth-century Siena, and the reforms of Leopold II of Austria, with the matter of Pound's *Social Credit, an Impact* (1935):

> Credit rests *in ultimate* on the abundance of nature, on the growing grass that can nourish the living sheep. And the moral

is in the intention. It was not for the conqueror's immediate short-sighted profit, but to restart life and productivity in Siena, that the bank was contrived [that is, after the Florentine conquest: Canto LIII—'thus BANK of the grassland was raised in Seignery'].

Canto XLV explodes against usury with its criteria of surplus for immediate hierarchical satisfaction, dedication to crude pleasure, the relegation of craftsmanship, and the postponement of the new paideuma and potential for paradise. The Dantean figure of Geryon presides: 'Geryon is biform. He takes you lower down.'[23] Attempts to legislate controls of money, purchase and goods from a wide range of sources, in Canto XLVI, as an essential basis for culture, are paralleled in the 'Cavalcanti' essay's passages summarizing arts-economics relationships resulting in decay: 'historic method' replaces the merits of 'a modern aesthetic purist' (already the matter of 'E.P. Ode pour L'Election de son Sepulchre' in 1920); certain Provencal and Italian Renaissance poets and artists are 'clean, all without hell-obsession'; under false economy, the body of the people is

> no longer the body of air clothed in the body of fire; it no longer radiates, light no longer moves from the eye, there is a great deal of meat, shock absorbing—at any rate absorbent. . . . We appear to have lost the radiant world where one thought cuts through another with clean edge, a world of moving energies . . . magnetisms that take form, that are seen, or that border the visible, the matter of Dante's *paradiso*, the glass under water, the form that seems a form seen in a mirror, these realities perceptible to the sense, inter-acting, 'a lui si tiri', untouched by the two maladies, the Hebrew disease, the Hindoo disease, fanaticisms and excess that produce Savonarola, asceticisms that produce fakirs, St. Clement of Alexandria, with his prohibition against bathing by women. . . . For the modern scientist energy has no borders, it is a shapeless 'mass' of force; even his capacity to differentiate it to a degree never dreamed by the ancients has not led him to think of its shape or even its loci. The rose that his magnet makes in the iron filings, does not lead him to think of the force in botanic terms, or wish to visualize that force as floral and extant (*ex stare*).

In Canto XLIX Geryon's state wealth through debt is countered with a Chinese régime embodying people's needs—

'imperial power' checked by 'the fourth; the dimension of stillness./ And the power over wild beasts'—that is, both the Confucian centred, balanced man and a control over the Dionysian. But in Fascism, Pound mistook totalitarian control for this double quality, formed in Canto LI with the first appearance of the Ching Ming ideogram of 'right'/'name', or 'precise verbal definition', which serves him in both literary and artistic, and political, capacities. Canto LII cites centralized benefits in Nazism and Fascism, and backs it from the Chinese; and again the Jews who manipulate money are targeted.

A main strength of the *Cantos* is to have found a structuring technique for handling such materials within the Great Bass, creating a form which is not merely 'phenomena strung out in a neutral field of time, but rather as a succession of difficult, and often traumatic, reorientations of the human psyche'.[24] Canto CVII, for instance, is a fine example of such mosaic balance: pieces of information are suspended together within an over-all intention, both local and part of the epic process. The 'forma' is both firm and urgent in its presentation of inter-war policy changes. Common law is again the subject, praxis rather than divine rights or 'natural' laws which are in fact impositions *contra naturam* (Canto XLVI[25]). The early seventeenth-century lawyer Coke, who said 'Let us now peruse our ancient authors, for out of the old fields must come the new corne' and declared commerce to be part of law, is placed with Pound's beliefs that Malatesta, John Adams and Mussolini could be reconciled into a legalized dominance: 'The heritage of Jefferson, Quincy Adams, old John Adams, Jackson, Van Buren is HERE NOW ... at the beginning of fascist decennio.'[26] *Rock-Drill* and *Thrones* continually summarize such positions in deft maxims, obviously designed for use: 'The Government ceases to be independent/ when curency is at will of a company/ All property is at their mercy'; 'And the dogmatic have to lie now and again/ to maintain their conformity,/ the chuntze never/ And as for the original-sin racket ... the hex-hoax ...'; 'Monetary literacy, sans which a loss of freedom is consequent'. The concentrated splendour of these twenty-five cantos is too compact a poetic discourse to maul by brief analysis and reference. Suffice it to quote from Canto XCIV in summary of Pound's later poetic condition:

> To Kung, to avoid their encirclement,
> To the Odes to escape abstract yatter,
>   to Mencius, Dante, and Agassiz
>   for Gestalt seed,
> pity, yes, for the infected,
>   but maintain antisepsis,
> let the light pour . . .

> . . . So that walking here under the larches of Paradise
> The stream was exceeding clear
>   & almost level its margin

But within Pound's long series of 'altars to Zagreus', the fundamental cultural ideogram of value—grain, Demeter-Persephone, *nous* and *virtu*—is repeatedly violated by destroyers. As Robert Duncan points out, Pound's basis is not Christian but Gnostic—from Greece, the Eleusinian and Provence: 'the cult of Eleusis will explain not only the general phenomena but particular beauties in Arnaut Daniel or in Guido Cavalcanti.'[27] Pound fully believed that language, myths and art are '*functions* by means of which a particular form is given to reality and in which specific distinctions are effected', so that 'inside' and 'outside', I and the World, can be creatively articulated. The *Cantos'* process is by *quantum*, by ideograms carrying variable and defined values controlled by context and aggregative modification.

The *Cantos* remains one of the last major works of poetic privilege, since its poetic bases are a steady resource, and its cultural lapses, omissions and some of its aims undermining of its ostensible humanity. Pound failed to grasp that any form of sovereignty infers hierarchy and therefore loss through dominance and subordination, patronage and feudal decision-making. He had no revolutionary sense which would destroy class and caste. The dead rise in him to instigate a non-technological, non-revolutionary world. He cannot reach beyond totalization into its necessary critique:

> If totalization no longer has any meaning, it is not because the infiniteness of the field cannot be covered by a finite glance or a discourse, but because the nature of the field—that is, language

and a finite language—excludes totalization. This field is in
effect that of *play*, that is to say, a field of substitutions only
because it is finite. . . . there is something missing from it: a
centre which arrests and grounds the play of substitutions. . . .
One cannot determine the centre and exhaust totalization
because the sign which replaced the centre, which supplements
it, taking the centre's place in its absence—this sign is added,
occurs as a surplus. . . . there is always more.[29]

Pound's early twentieth-century quality is his worry about
origin and totality or coherence. Mallarmé's 'pli selon pli', and
Bataille's heterogeneity against homogeneity, show where
Derrida's 'play' can be creatively operative. Paradoxically, the
exhilarating strength of the *Pisan Cantos, Rock-Drill* and *Thrones*
is that they do open up the reading mind to a play of
abundance, a travel across borders, a relaxation of those
dogmas which tighten so many Modernists into intolerable
closures. Pound paid no regard to those nineteenth-century
American writers who investigated threats to the democratic
from the authoritarian and paranoid—Brockden Brown, Poe,
Hawthorne, Melville—and very little to the open-endedness
in Whitman. As Duncan puts it in an interview: 'We couldn't
have a more extreme instance of democratic composition out
of that man who kept hoping he'd rescue himself by having
totalitarian order.'[30] Bunting's obituary memoir presents
Pound as a man who 'looked more deeply into the processes of
poetry' than his allies and other contemporaries. The Great
Bass concept is the container of his discoveries, which remain
fresh:

It took critics a long time to forgive Ezra for puzzling them with
new, misleading, complex, endless poetry. . . . If you will read
the Cantos aloud and listen, without troubling your head about
their meaning, you will find, especially in the later Cantos, a
surge of music that is its own meaning. Every year more people
seem to hear it.

NOTES

Citations from Pound's essays and poems, unless otherwise stated, can be
found in: *Literary Essays of Ezra Pound*, ed. T. S. Eliot (London, 1954); *Selected
Prose 1909–1965*, ed. William Cookson (London, 1973); *The Cantos* (London,

1975); *Personae: Collected Shorter Poems of Ezra Pound* (London, 1952); *A Lume Spento and Other Early Poems* (London, 1965). Quotations from *Personae*, copyright © 1926 by Ezra Pound, and from *The Cantos of Ezra Pound*, copyright © 1956 by Ezra Pound, are reprinted by permission of Faber and Faber Ltd. and New Directions Publishing Corporation.

1. William Carlos Williams, *Selected Essays* (New York, 1954), p. 105.
2. *The Letters of Ezra Pound* (London, 1951), p. 418.
3. *Ezra Pound and Music*, ed. R. Murray Schafer (London, 1978), p. 467.
4. *The Translations of Ezra Pound*, enlarged edn. (London, 1970), p. 23.
5. Schafer, Appendix 1.
6. Charles Olson, *Human Universe and Other Essays* (New York, 1967), pp. 51–61.
7. Schafer, pp. 471–72.
8. (a) *Poetry*, March 1913, (b) Ezra Pound (ed.): Ernest Fenollosa, *The Chinese Written Character as a Medium for Poetry* (1918) (San Francisco, 1964).
9. *Letters*, p. 418.
10. Carroll F. Terrell, *A Companion to the Cantos of Ezra Pound* (Berkeley and London, 1981).
11. Ezra Pound (trans.): Sophocles, *Women of Trachis* (New York, 1957), p. 50.
12. *Letters*, p. 366.
13. Peter Makin, *Provence and Pound* (Berkeley and London, 1978).
14. Translation and commentary Ezra Pound, *Confucius* (New York, 1969), pp. 20, 131.
15. Ezra Pound, *ABC of Reading* (London, 1951), p. 46; *Make it New* (London, 1934), 'Date Line', p. 19.
16. René de Gourmont, *The Natural Philosophy of Love* (New York, 1922), pp. 13, 18, 186.
17. *Ezra Pound: Impact*, ed. Noel Stock (New York, 1960), p. 133.
18. Gourmont—Pound, 'Postscript', p. 217.
19. *Writers at Work: The Paris Review Interviews—Second Series* (London, 1963), p. 51.
20. Wendy Stallard Flory, *Ezra Pound and the Cantos* (New Haven and London, 1980), p. 209.
21. Makin, p. 3.
22. John Rockwell, *All American Music* (New York, 1983), p. 20.
23. *Impact*, p. 71.
24. Walter J. Ong, *The Presence of the Word* (New Haven and London, 1967), p. 176.
25. *Impact*, pp. 44 and 177.
26. Ezra Pound, *Jefferson and/or Mussolini* (New York, 1970), p. 12.
27. Robert Duncan, *The H.D. Book*, Part 2: Nights and Days, Ch. 3, *Io 6*, 1969.
28. Ernst Cassirer, *Philosophy of Symbolic Form*, Vol. 1 (New Haven and London, 1953), p. 91.
29. Jacques Derrida, *Writing and Difference* (London, 1978), p. 289.
30. *Unmuzzled Ox*, Vol. IV, No. 2, 1976.

6

'The Dark Magnificence of Things': The Poetry of Robinson Jeffers

by R. W. (HERBIE) BUTTERFIELD

Some fifty years ago, Robinson Jeffers, himself then in his middle forties, was as widely read, and as famous, as any other American poet. There had always been dissenters, those who found Jeffers either morally distasteful or aesthetically vulgar, and surely it was primarily to the bizarre violence and extravagant sexuality of his long narrative poems that he owed much of that readership and fame; but nonetheless it was solely on account of his reputation as a poet, and for no other activity, significance or antic, that on 4 April 1932 he joined the broad company of the momentarily renowned on the front cover of *Time* magazine. It had been, therefore, against a man conspicuous as a major contemporary poet that two years previously the young Yvor Winters had launched his fierce and damaging attack,[1] one which the remote Jeffers himself characteristically seemed not to notice, but also one which effectively prepared the way for the more general critical hostility that was to ensue. In part because his far-flung rhetoric, his romantic hyperbole and his loose-fitting, long lines were alien to the ascendant New Critics, and in part because his cyclical view of history, his political aloofness and, in the War years, his furious isolationism were unattractive to

93

liberal Democrats and Marxists alike, through the later 1930s
and the 1940s, Jeffers's once *Time*-honoured celebrity was first
translated into notoriety and then rendered into neglect; until,
in his last years, he became, in the phrase of his long standing
admirer and fellow-poet, Horace Gregory, a 'poet without
critics'.[2]

Forgotten or repudiated by most critics as he has been—
and by the general literary student readership virtually
ignored, perhaps a little less so during the hippy heyday,[3]
altogether more so in the microcomputerized, post-structuralist
present—Jeffers has at the same time never wanted for
individual adherents, poets both certain of his achievement
and angry at his neglect, whether scattered randomly like
Gregory, Richard Eberhart and James Dickey,[4] or concen-
trated in California in the persons of Charles Bukowski, Gary
Snyder, Jack Spicer, Diana Wakoski and, above all, his
disciple, editor and interpreter, William Everson, the erstwhile
Brother Antoninus.[5] I cite three poets, each quite unlike
Jeffers and quite unlike one another. Winfield Townley Scott,
himself a sadly underrated figure, found Jeffers in 1955,
'pushed aside, neglected', yet 'the greatest poet now living'.[6]
e.e. cummings, writing a month after Jeffers's death in 1962 to
Ezra Pound's daughter, Mary de Rachewiltz, who was
translating some of Jeffers's poetry into Italian, deemed 'his
neglect . . . immensely scandalous'.[7] And Czeslaw Milosz, the
Polish poet and 1980 Nobel Prize winner, after visiting
Jeffers's house and musing on his spirit, mourned that he 'has
been almost completely forgotten', because 'after all, whatever
his faults, he was truly a great poet.'[8]

His neglect is by no means surprising, for the self-assured
insouciance of his manner does not suit contemporary critical
preferences, and the self-styled Inhumanism of his matter can
appeal neither to people of benign, secular will nor to
quotidian materialists of left or right; whilst 'Jeffers country',
the actual world he recreated as his poetic world, can only be
imaginatively rather than immediately available to dwellers in
city, suburb, or agribusiness countryside. Yet if by no means
surprising, his neglect is still 'immensely scandalous',[9] for he
is 'truly a great poet', so that in forgetting him, though
doubtless we scarcely trouble his own austere ghost, we

diminish ourselves, and subtract from our own seriousness of spirit, our weight.

Back now to origins; for despite seldom speaking of his childhood and ancestry, Jeffers lifelong bore their visible impress. Of first-generation New England, Scottish and Ulster descent, and with a father who was a minister and professor of Old Testament literature, his heritage was deeply, vigorously Protestant; and though he was himself to discard Christianity, his mind and sensibility remained in important respects inextinguishably Protestant. He was born in 1887 in Pittsburgh, growing up there in a comfortable home, where his scholarly, reticent father was twenty-two years older than his gregarious mother, and where his privileged solitude was interrupted when he was 7 by the birth of a younger brother. In an ostensibly happy household Jeffers's inner world must also have been one more than usually crowded with forbidden desires, annihilating fantasies and excruciating guilt, if we are to make but the slightest connection between his childhood experience and the incestuous, implosive families that fire his narrative poems. After spending three years in Europe, the family moved in 1903 to Southern California, where Jeffers studied literature, medicine and forestry at a succession of Universities, before marrying the recently divorced Una Kuster in 1913. The following year the young couple made their way up the coast to Carmel, where amid hills and trees and by the ocean they knew they had come to their 'inevitable place'. Of his major American contemporaries, only Williams and Faulkner would be so firmly, productively attached to a particular place, this 'Jeffers country' that was both physical Carmel and symbolic farthest West, 'this shore, the very turn of the world, the long migration's/ End'. Their home, Tor House, and its adjacent Hawk's Tower were built by Jeffers himself, on 'foundations of sea-worn granite', hauled up from the beach, with hands that 'had the art to make stone love stone'. Around the house he planted and assiduously tended hundreds of trees. They travelled only occasionally, though twice to the British Isles, where Jeffers felt significantly more drawn to Scotland and to Ulster, lands of his forefathers, than to England's 'soft alien twilight/ Worn and weak with too much humanity'. Una died in 1950; his epitaph for her, a whisper of exquisitely tender

95

pantheism, concludes the narrative poem, 'Hungerfield'. He lived on until 1962 and the age of 75.

Jeffers was slow to arrive at his mature, distinctive manner. *Flagons and Apples* (1912), his first volume, was almost wholly derived from his youthful, pre-Raphaelite enthusiasms. And though, as its title suggests, *Californians* of 1916 was coming closer to the poet's proper mark, he was nevertheless still speaking in accents that were audibly Wordsworth's or Shelley's or Emerson's, rather than his own. It needed his father's death, the accidents of love and the spectacle, watched from afar, fascinated and aghast, of Europe's bloody carnival, for him to shake off extraneous literary influence and find his own unique voice.[10] Building his house had much to do with it too, the slow, patient, heavy, careful labour, within sound of the perpetual ocean:

> I did not dream the taste of wine could bind with granite,
> Nor honey and milk please you; but sweetly
> They mingle down the storm-worn cracks among the mosses,
> Interpenetrating the silent
> Wing-prints of ancient weathers, long at peace, and the
>   older
> Scars of primal fire, and the stone
> Endurance that is waiting millions of years to carry
> A corner of the house, this also destined.
>   ('To the Rock That Will Be a Cornerstone of the House')

There at last is the unmistakable sound of authentic Jeffers.

Once come upon, somewhere around his thirtieth year, the style with scant variation served him for a lifetime. 'Shearing' the rhyme from his poetry, as he expressed it in a poem from this time, and also 'breaking' the pentameter, Jeffers arrived by another route at the open ground that Pound and Williams had cleared for themselves a few years earlier. As his characteristic poetry emerged, it was often taken to be either a free verse broadly in the tradition of Whitman's *Leaves of Grass* or a prose-poetry deriving from the Authorized Version of the Bible. Certainly, Jeffers owed much to both these books. With Whitman he felt what has been called 'a profound fellowship',[12] despite their obvious great differences, and he made one of his very few literary pilgrimages in 1941 to Whitman's house in Camden. However, as far as form is concerned, what the poets share does not go much beyond the sheer, capacious length and adaptability of line, although this is enough to align Jeffers more closely with Whitman than with any other American antecedent.

In the case of the Bible, as the son of his father, Jeffers could not help but be saturated in the Holy Book, so that every now and again one may hear an echo of the verbal texture of the Song of Solomon or a rhetorical reminiscence of Ecclesiastes or the Book of Job. But as with *Leaves of Grass*, one staple element of Jeffers's verse is missing from the poetry of the translated Bible. And that is, for all Jeffers's absolute break with the world of rhyme and traditional metre, a *notion* of rhythmic regularity, of predictability, of prior aural design. For in principle, if only in principle, or in gesture, Jeffers's verse is governed by a rhythmic norm, which consists of a regular number of accents to the line or pair of lines, a stress prosody, for precedents to which he referred a correspondent to old English poetry, and to Coleridge's 'Christabel'.[13]

However, the primary influences on Jeffers's poetry are not literary but natural. Living within the sound of the ocean and within sight of the mountains, planting his slow-lived trees, handling, transporting, and positioning his granite boulders, Jeffers in his few remarks about poetry and poetics refers always to the qualities of the natural world—to 'tidal regularity' or 'tidal recurrence', to 'perpetual renewal', to 'physics, biology, beat of blood, the tidal environments of life'—and, for the subject matter, to the 'essential element' of permanence, 'permanent things, or things forever renewed, like the grass and human passions.'

What he was after was a natural condition, neither freedom nor strict rule, but the broadly timed recurrences and the variable regularity of nature. By analogy with Williams's 'variable foot', perhaps we may talk of Jeffers's variable line. A short poem, 'To the Stone-Cutters', written not long after he had made himself at home in his mature manner, may demonstrate the simple aural constituents of Jeffers's poetry: alliteration, constant but irregular, a stress pattern, regular but not fixed, and a 'tidal' alternation of longer and shorter lines.

Stone-cutters fighting time with marble, you foredefeated
Challengers of oblivion
Eat cynical earnings, knowing rock splits, records fall down,
The square-limbed Roman letters
Scale in the thaws, wear in the rain. The poet as well
Builds his monument mockingly;
For man will be blotted out, the blithe earth die, the brave
    sun
Die blind and blacken to the heart:
Yet stones have stood for a thousand years, and pained
    thoughts found
The honey of peace in old poems.

'To the Stone Cutters' appeared in *Tamar and Other Poems*, published in 1924 when he was 37. This book set the pattern for the great majority of Jeffers's volumes, consisting as they mostly do, of one or two long narrative or dramatic poems, supplemented by a score or so of short poems of broadly reflective kind. Beginning with 'Tamar', over a period of thirty years Jeffers wrote some fifteen narrative poems, all located in twentieth-century California, in 'Jeffers country', and half a dozen dramatic poems, based on Greek, Biblical, or Germanic legend; taken together they make up by far the larger part of the huge bulk of Jeffers's poetic output. Almost without exception, they are poems scarred, and scarred again and again, by violence, mutilation, murder, and suicide, by sexual sickness and aberration, usually within the family enclosure.

Though none of the modern narrative poems are without their impressive moments, though many shine with extended passages of luminous genius or ring with sonorous verbal magnificence, and though the best attain, like few other modern writings, something of the gravity and grandeur of ancient tragedy, it has at the same time to be admitted that all are more or less flawed, in ways that must disappoint or embarrass the Jeffers advocate. The faults may lie in bombastic overwriting or in slipshod underwriting, in stilted or inert dialogue, in structural incoherence, in ludicrous grotesquerie, in clumsy authorial intrusion, or, perhaps saddest of all, in an absence of that sense of the marvellous, the glorious, the numinous in the natural world, which is else-where for Jeffers life's redemptive quality, and without which his stories too readily collapse into bathetic horror and vileness. Especially was this quality lacking in the narrative poems of the 1930s and the War Years, and in that respect, though in that respect alone, the decline in his reputation during those years was deserved.

For all that during his middle life he returned time and again to his violent sagas, it seems to me obvious that Jeffers was not formed by gift and temperament to be a convincing interpreter of the intricacies, murderous or otherwise, of human interchange. Distant from other people, evidently horrified at the knowledge of what lies within the self, he lived his life in personal refuge, devoted to wife and children certainly, but at the most powerful level of his imagination in solitary communion with nature and God. He was a meditative or a rhapsodic or a prophetic poet, quite at his best in either the short poem or in sections of the longer poems that are in effect detachable, self-contained lyrics. What is unfortunate about the narrative poems is the extent to which the defects of the story-teller may distract attention from the excellences of the poet.

Nevertheless, the stuff of the long poems is finally of a piece with the whole, in so far as these poems picture for us, only too vividly, a fallen world, or a desperate world, inward-looking, self-obsessed and self-destructive, the human imbroglio from which, Jeffers was to tell us throughout his life, for health of mind and salvation of spirit it was necessary to turn away so as to look outwards upon the redeeming wonders of bird and tree and rock and star. Thus, whatever deeper, less rationally articulated motive there may have been behind his frequent focus upon incest, that particular sexual connection did precisely serve his purpose, as he explained, 'to symbolize human turned-inwardness, the perpetual struggle to get ahead of each other, love each other, scare each other, subdue or exalt each other, that absorbs 99 per cent of human energy'.[14] In shutting the mind to all that is not man-made, as, increasingly secular and socialized, we have done, the whole human race is, Jeffers felt, charged with 'a sort of racial incest'.

> It is all turned inward, all your desires incestuous, the
>   woman the serpent, the man the rose-red cavern,
> Both human, worship forever. . . .

So speaks Orestes, in 'The Tower Beyond Tragedy', as, taking to the high, wild country away from the human world, he 'cast humanity' and 'entered the earlier fountain'. And the woman, California, in 'Roan Stallion', sickened by her debauched, brutal husband, seeks in the beauty and power of the stallion she rides a God 'not in man's shape'. Implicitly or explicitly, the verse stories and dramas support the principal burden of all Jeffers's poetry: turn outwards and love 'the beauty of things, not men;/ The immense beauty of the world, not the human world'; and thus retrieve a knowledge of deity and an understanding of man's part in the divine whole:

> the stars, the winds and the people: one energy,
> One existence, one music, one organism, one life, one God:
> star-fire and rock-strength, the sea's cold flow
> And man's dark soul.

Thus, the Inhumanist in the poem of that name.

Unquestionably the best of the long poems are those in which the unhappy personal elements (the physical violence and sexual degradation) clearly subserve an exalting, spiritual purpose. The more they do, the more Jeffers is a great tragic poet; the less they do, he is the author of sensational, dispiriting shockers. Amongst the narrative poems, as those that should join the things of permanence, along with the 'grass and human passions', I would name here 'Roan Stallion', 'The Loving Shepherdess' (the gentlest of his stories, with about it a Franciscan quality), and 'Cawdor', chiefly because it contains in the description of the death of the eagle several pages of this century's most sustained sublime writing. Of their very nature the dramatic poems avoid the realist pitfalls of the narratives, and as a consequence are broadly more successful works whose imaginative and rhetorical power compensates for intermittent structural weaknesses. To be named here are three of the Greek adaptations, 'The Tower beyond Tragedy', 'At the Fall of an Age', and *Medea*; 'Dear Judas', Jeffers's idiosyncratic treatment of the Jesus story; and 'At the Birth of an Age', which, beginning as a dramatization of the closing part of the Volsung saga, concludes as a chilly, high-altitude meditation upon the rise and fall of cultures and ultimately of the human race. To this number must be added 'The Inhumanist', though it is neither a narrative nor a dramatic poem, but rather Jeffers's version of Whitman's 'Song of Myself', likewise in 52 sections, self-renewing at the close, as the old man, the Inhumanist, Jeffers's most exemplary creation, 'arose refreshed in the red dawn'. The Inhumanist's startling nihilism ('hear me, Lord God! Exterminate/ The race of man. For man only in the world, except a few kinds of insect, is essentially cruel') is systole to the diastole of his radiant adoration:

> There is one God, and the earth is his prophet.
> The beauty of things is the face of God: worship it;
> Give your hearts to it: labour to be like it.

'The beauty of things', that is where Jeffers begins, not with an aesthetic proposition but with a sensory commonplace: that the universe is beautiful, beautiful to behold as a spectacle, the eyes raised to the stars, beautiful to contemplate in its composition, the mind dwelling upon the cell and the atom. He does not ask us to ponder the nature of the beautiful but merely seeks to remind us, since we are continuously forgetful, that it is always there, beside, before and around us, to be discovered in human endeavour, in the 'bitter earnestness' of fishermen in great waters doing 'their business among the equally earnest/ Elements of nature'; in the 'beauty of inhuman things, sea, storm, and mountain'; and in the mind's slow dance to the natural rhythm that beats beneath the human world's fractured, frenzied cacophony:

> Sane and intact the seasons pursue their course,
> Autumn slopes to December, the rains will fall
> And the grass flourish, with flowers in it.

It is altogether appropriate, therefore, that the last words of his last volume invite us to expect and enjoy, while watching the activities of the natural world, 'not mercy, not mind, not goodness, but the beauty of God'.

God, the final word in Jeffers's work, just as it had been the final word of his first poem, published at the age of 16[15]: a lifelong Word. For Jeffers, God may be either immanent or transcendent, to be perceived within the world, or to be sought within the self. The immanent predominates; the universe is all-beautiful, the physical form of God, who is all, the all that is God. The eyes should merely have to see to believe, the lungs should merely have to breathe to inhale God's spirit. In 'The Answer' we are told, simply, that 'Integrity is wholeness, the greatest beauty is/ Organic wholeness, the wholeness of life and things, the divine beauty of the Universe.' In this virtual pantheism the American transcendentalist heritage is clearly visible: the links with Emerson, who was also introduced to the perfect whole by his sense of beauty; and with Whitman, who heard and beheld God in every object and saw something of him each hour of the twenty-four. Above all, God and his beauty, the beauty that is God, are experienced in natural and elemental power, whether in the stallion, the hawk and the eagle, or in the vast eons-long beating of the universal heart and in cosmic 'faceless violence, the root of all things'.

Jeffers could also own to another, more inward conception of God, one closer to that of his Protestant forebears, a transcendent or an exclusive God, to be awaited in the patient, mystic air of 'the soul's desert'. But however meditative and mystically inclined, he did not travel in spirit across the Pacific to the faiths of the Orient, like so many fellow-Californian poets, especially of the succeeding generation. He might express a considerable regard for Buddhism and Oriental religions, for their quietism and cyclical view of existence, and he might scorn the 'anthropoid God' of 'decaying Christianity'. But he was always at the furthest point of the West rather than at the beginning of the East. Differing from an Asian contemplative in his poem, 'Credo', he finds 'in my blood/ Bred West of Caucasus a harder mysticism'. The 'harder mysticism' is a philosophical materialism that attributes a prior reality to matter before mind, that sees the light shining first in 'the beauty of things, not men'. It is a poetic materialism that for closest analogy sends us back as far as 2,000 years to a figure to whom Jeffers several times pays tribute: the Roman poet Lucretius, author of the great expository poem, the epic of a joyous materialism, *De Rerum Natura*.

This sense of the marvellous 'divinity' of the universe and of the vibrancy of matter Jeffers felt to be drastically missing from the mind of modern, Western man. The basis for any sort of sanity, any sort of integrity, he felt, must be reverence for the cosmos, so that the best life that can be lived is one that leaves as much space as possible for silent wonder at natural processes and their invisibly slow evolution, for quiet amazement at the immense splendour and all the diminutive miracles. It should be a life lived in simple relation to nature, such as can be found most readily in the primitive agricultural or the pastoral stages of human development:

> What's the best life for a man? To ride in the wind. To
>   ride horses and herd cattle
> In solitary places above the ocean on the beautiful
>   mountain, and come home hungry in the evening
> And eat and sleep. . . .
> I will have shepherds for my philosophers,
> Tall dreary men lying on the hills all night
> Watching the stars, let their dogs watch the sheep. . . .
>   ('The Silent Shepherds')

But such are disappearing ways of life, or nostalgic myths and timeless idylls, as Jeffers knew only too well. The dominant theme in human history, certainly in Western history, has been quite other. It has been a history not of man's accommodation with nature, but of his separation from it, subjection of the earth, exploitation of its gifts, and self-appointment as lord of creation. In his lifelong treatment of our relationship with nature, Jeffers writes both within and against the Judeo-Christian heritage. He can be said to be within it in so far as he subscribes to an idiosyncratic, naturalistic version of the doctrine of original sin, the consequences of which his work continuously illustrates. He is against it, radically, in so far as he would regard that heritage, and even more so its secular succession of whatever political emphasis, as being from its very beginnings a direct expression of that original sin, in its initial presupposition of man's privileged or central place in the universe.

The sin, to put it in the most broadly traditional terms, is the sin of pride, man's arrogant promotion of himself above the level accorded him by God. And if God is identified with the Cosmos, then the original sin occurred at that mythic moment when man first felt himself singled out as distinct from the rest of creation and superior to it. In consequence, the race's few heroes include those whose scientific discoveries have had the effect of eroding man's conceit and returning him towards his rightful place in the scheme of things: Copernicus, for instance, 'who first pushed man/ Out of his insane self-importance and the world's navel, and taught him his place'. Because of this 'insane self-importance' and the breaking of the umbilical connection with nature, 'life's norm is lost' and 'monsters possess the world', toying with atomic power. Twenty years before the invention of nuclear weapons, in a poem entitled simply and comprehensively 'Science', Jeffers already envisaged the possibility of total destruction, as nature is reassembled into ever more terrifying new energies. For all his scientific genius, man

> being taken up
> Like a maniac with self-love and inward conflicts
> cannot manage his hybrids.
> Being used to deal with edgeless dreams,
> Now he's bred knives on nature turns them also
> inward: they have thirsty points though.
> His mind forebodes his own destruction. . . .

More than thirty years on, that vague, dark foreboding of destruction had lifted to reveal the clear prospect of 'war certain as sunrise', the conclusive disaster that overhangs our whole megalomaniac, introverted civilization. Such a vision afforded one relief:

> I have pitied the beautiful earth
> Ridden by such a monster as the human race. Now,
> if we die like the dinosaurs, the beautiful
> Planet will be happier.
>
> ('The Beautiful Captive')

For even while the bombs do not fall we are merely left, too clever, too prolific, to continue our heedless ravage of nature, ripping the parts from the whole. Decades before the word 'ecology' ventured far from the textbooks and before lip-service to conservationist sentiment became conventional piety, Jeffers was

> Mourning the broken balance, the hopeless prostration of
>   the earth
> Under men's hands and their minds,
> The beautiful places killed like rabbits to make a city,
> The spreading fungus, the slime-threads
> And spores; my own coast's obscene future . . .
>
>   ('The Broken Balance')

To repair that balance, to avoid, for a lifetime if fortunate, that 'obscene future', Jeffers went and held to Carmel, perched, like one of his hawks, on the land's furthest, Western edge. Indeed, it is impossible to imagine Jeffers living and writing anywhere except in the West of the American continent, perhaps anywhere except within sight and sound of the Pacific Ocean. For he is in every respect and in all assumptions a Westerner, an heir of the frontiersman of myth, a direct descendant of the westward-looking literary romantics. Behind him stand Emerson and Whitman, travellers in mind and gesture, and Thoreau, symbolic frontiersman in *Walden*, who like Jeffers absolutely required 'to be alone the greater part of the time'. And out of a further past looms Cooper's exemplary hero, Natty Bumppo, for whom also God disclosed himself in natural beauty, albeit in more Christian, less pantheist shape; and for whom also the greatest threat to that good life lay in the voracious, exploitative misuse of the natural world by a proliferating, densely packed population.

Thus, a redeemer, in the poem of that title, has to redeem a history of indiscriminate rapacity, mechanized utilitarianism, extirpation and genocide—the history of a people who

> have done what never was done before. Not as a
>   people takes a land to love it and be fed,
> A little, according to need and love, and again a little;
>   sparing the country tribes, mixing
> Their blood with theirs, their minds with all the rocks and
>   rivers, their flesh with the soil: no, without hunger
> Wasting the world and your own labour, without love
>   possessing, not even your hands to the dirt but plows
> Like blades of knives; heartless machines; houses of steel:
>   using and despising the patient earth. . . .

Oh, as a rich man eats a forest for profit and a field
    for vanity, so you came west and raped
The continent and brushed its people to death. Without need,
    the weak skirmishing hunters, and without mercy.

So, removing himself as far as possible from that continuous
process of history, Jeffers found himself a place where, with
'hands to the dirt', he planted his trees in the patient earth and
slowly built his house, not of steel, but of stone. It was a life's
work, a life's dedication; but in any time span longer than the
individual's, merely a moment's holding action:

> We have geared the machines and locked all together
>   into interdependence; we have built the great cities; now
> There is no escape. We have gathered vast populations
>   incapable of free survival, insulated
> From the strong earth, each person in himself helpless, on all
>   dependent. The circle is closed, and the net
> Is being hauled in. . . .
>
>   ('The Purse-Seine')

There was no further to go. Centuries, millennia even, of
westward yearning and outreaching were coming to an end.
The globe's circle was closed, and as he looked outwards, on
the edge of the ocean, away from humanity, he felt, within the
dimensions of human history, the end of the West piling up
and darkening the sky behind him.

This circular shape of westward movement around the
globe was repeated for Jeffers in the shapes he discerned of the
many cycles of culture. The cycles, smaller and larger, inter-
sected one another—Judaic, Greco-Roman, Nordic—and
were all contained within the vaster cycle of Western history.
During his lifetime, he believed, the Christian cycle had
turned, with its weight of at least fifteen centuries, heavily
downward. Rising swiftly to meet its fall, to cut its descending
path with terrifying, clashing possibilities, was the age of the
machine, of the robot, of the robotized, technologized human:

> Truly the time is marked by insane splendors and agonies.
>   But watch when the two curves cross: you children
> Not far away down the hawk's-nightmare future:
>   you will see monsters.
>
>   ('Diagram')

As with cultures, so with nations. As early as 1925, in 'The Tower beyond Tragedy', he has Cassandra in Ancient Greece foresee a cyclical future of ever swifter rises to ever wider power and ever greater catastrophe. She curses in succession Athens, Rome, Spain, France and England, yet there is still

> A mightier to be cursed and a higher for malediction
> When America has eaten Europe and taken tribute of Asia,
>   when the ends of the world grow aware of each other
> And are dogs in one kennel, they will tear
> The master of the hunt with the mouths of the pack: new
>   fallings, new rising, O winged one
> No end of the fallings and risings?

No, he saw little hope for the world, if by the world is meant the world of power politics and historical tendency. That story was just the one about original sin, the tale of hubris writ large, larger, and ever more destructive. As a result of such political pessimism, he has often been misinterpreted as nihilistic or life-denying or despairing. Such judgements are very far from the truth, for they ignore or are ignorant of that world of which the human is but a part, that greater world which Jeffers inhabited, knowing that 'to see the human figure in all things is man's disease/ To see the inhuman God is our health.' Upon the 'immense beauty' of that larger world Jeffers concentrated his rapt attention, celebrating its coincidence with God, who is 'rock, earth, and water, and the beasts and stars; and the night that contains them'. His is not a mental image or construct of eternity, but an intense, very material comprehension, nonetheless mystical for being material, of the actual universe, in perpetual motion, forming and re-forming, permanently impermanent, marvellous worlds upon worlds in miraculous grains of sand, 'desperate wee galaxies/ Scattering themselves and shining their substance away/ Like a passionate thought. It is very well ordered.' Within such an ordered perspective merely human history takes its proper, parenthetical place:

> Look at the seas there
> Flashing against this rock in the darkness—look at the
>   tide-stream stars—and the fall of nations—and dawn
> Wandering with wet white feet down the Carmel Valley to
>   meet the sea.

107

Or again:

> Men's 'powers and their follies have become fantastic,
> The unstable animal never has been changed so rapidly. The
>   motor and the plane and the great war have gone over him
> And Lenin has lived and Jehovah died: while the mother-eagle
> Hunts her same hills, crying the same beautiful and lonely cry
>   and is never tired; dreams the same dreams,
> And hears at night the rock-slides rattle and thunder in the
>   throats of these living mountains.'

('The Beaks of Eagles')

There have been cleverer poets than Jeffers in this century, and doubtless better and finer poets. We cannot be deaf and blind to his many failures of taste and mind and language. But there have been few, if any, poets possessed of such a simple power of being, drinking so close to the primal, originative source of all religious waters, brooding in his solemn, watchful contemplations upon 'the dark magnificence of things'.[16]

NOTES

1. Yvor Winters, 'Robinson Jeffers', *Poetry*, XXXV (February, 1930), pp. 279–86.
2. Horace Gregory, *The Dying Gladiators* (New York, 1961), pp. 3–20.
3. In July 1969 Friends of the Earth chose some words from a poem by Jeffers for the title of their bulletin, *Not Man Apart*. This is also the title of an outstanding book of photographs accompanying lines and poems of Jeffers, published in 1965 by the Sierra Club, San Francisco. It contains an exceptionally perceptive foreword by Loren Eiseley.
4. Richard Eberhart, 'A Tribute and an Appreciation', *Robinson Jeffers Newsletter*, XXVII (November, 1970), pp. 6–7. James Dickey, 'First and Last Things', *Poetry*, CIII (February, 1964), pp. 320–21.
5. See Spicer's poem, 'A redwood forest is not invisible at night' in *The Collected Books*; Wakoski's 'Cap of Darkness' in the volume of that name dedicated to Jeffers; Bukowski's 'he wrote in lonely blood' in *Mockingbird Wish Me Luck*; Snyder's remarks in Bob Steuding, *Gary Snyder* (New York, 1976), pp. 153–56; and, in addition to his book and several essays on Jeffers, Everson's 'The Poet is Dead' in *The Veritable Years*. Strangely as it seems to me, Kenneth Rexroth, whom I find to have affinities with Jeffers, was largely hostile to the elder poet.
6. Scott Donaldson, *Poet in America: Winfield Townley Scott* (Austin, 1972), pp. 283–84.

7. F. W. Dupee and George Stade (eds.), *Selected letters of E. E. Cummings* (London, 1969), p. 273.
8. Czeslaw Milosz, *Visions from San Francisco Bay* (Manchester, 1982), pp. 87–96.
9. There have nevertheless been a number of excellent book-length studies of Jeffers, notably by Robert J. Brophy, Frederic I. Carpenter, Arthur B. Coffin, William Everson, Laurence Clark Powell, Radcliffe Squires, and Kenneth White. Two especially interesting references to Jeffers within other contexts are to be found in Albert Gelpi's afterword to William Everson, *The Veritable Years*; and in Dudley Young's essay, 'Still Life Inside the Whale', *PN Review*, 18, Vol. 7, No. 4 (1980), p. 48.
10. Jeffers published no new volume during this period, but thanks to Everson's brilliant and painstaking literary detective work, two books now exist that represent Jeffers at this interim time of most radical change: *The Alpine Christ and Other Poems*, and *Brides of the South Wind: Poems, 1917–1922*.
11. Cf. Pound, Canto 81: 'To break the pentameter that was the first heave'; Williams, *I Wanted to Write a Poem*, p. 26: 'With Whitman, I decided rhyme belonged to another age.'
12. Frederic I. Carpenter, *Robinson Jeffers* (New York, 1962), p. 46.
13. Ann N. Ridgeway (ed.), *The Selected Letters of Robinson Jeffers, 1892–1962* (Baltimore, 1968), p. 173.
14. *Selected Letters*, p. 35.
15. 'The Measure', published in *The Aurora* (December, 1903) and reprinted in S. S. Alberts, *A Bibliography of the Work of Robinson Jeffers* (New York, 1933).
16. 'To the Stone-Cutters' and other excerpts from Jeffers's writings are reprinted by permission of Random House, Inc., copyright © 1938, 1948, 1963, 1968. Certain parts of this essay have been adapted from the author's considerably longer essay, 'Robinson Jeffers', published in *American Writers* Supplement II, Part 2, copyright © 1981 by Charles Scribner's Sons.

7

Marianne Moore: 'Transcendence, Conditional'

by MICHAEL EDWARDS

The first line-and-a-bit in Marianne Moore's *Complete Poems*:

> Dürer would have seen a reason for living
> in a town like this,

contains two unobtrusive, though vertiginous, double meanings. That Dürer should find a reason for living in a town like this while at the same time finding, in a town like this, a reason for living, uncovers in a single phrase the urgent within the relaxed, the momentous within the everyday. That he should 'see' the reason, travels from sight to insight—it is relevant that Dürer was a painter—from literal seeing to figurative.

The device continues through 'The Steeple-Jack'. The next words, 'with eight stranded whales/ to look at', move even more coolly between looking at whales and contemplating huge helplessness and mortality, while later passages allude to different kinds of seeing and reinforce them paronomastically with 'sea' or 'seem'. The opening of 'The Jerboa', within a hostile view of Roman and Egyptian culture, slips from a bronze cone that 'looks like a work of art made to give/ to a Pompey' to lords who 'looked on as theirs,/ impalas and onigers'. Even her first book-title, *Observations*, joined visual and intellectual observing; and one realizes that perceiving

110

with the mind, rather than being merely metaphorical—I may 'see what you mean' with my eyes closed—derives here from actual perception, and that a close relation of seeing to 'seeing' is being attempted.

A great deal of Marianne Moore's poetry is clearly concerned with the question, What can you see when you look? and it is a question for which she is not alone in desiring an answer. This is a basic issue in a period for which the largely Christian certitude of transcendence continues to become gradually more clouded. Strangely, what one is most aware of in her poems is the literally visible, which the descriptions of animals in particular deliberately and copiously promote. Surfaces do not give way to depth; appearances are not erased by hidden reality. Her poems seethe with ornament, yet the ornament is not there to ornament something; it is the something. Along with the eagerness to see, moreover, goes a care for the otherness of what she observes, a care that has been important for later poets and that has appealed to writers on her work. Denis Donoghue refers to her 'generous perception'[1]; she teaches one that there can be a generosity in perception as in human relations, that we can be generous of observation as of time. (Not, alas, that persistence and closeness in looking guarantee purity of motive.) The generosity even redeems aggression. In that first part of 'The Jerboa' there is 'Too Much', a decadent plethora, an excess of exquisiteness. Yet as object after object is handled by the eye:

> round bone boxes—the pivoting
> lid incised with a duck-wing
>
> or reverted duck-
> head;

or:

> Princes
> clad in queens' dresses,
> calla or petunia
> white, that trembled at the edge, and queens in a
> king's underskirt of fine-twilled thread like silk-
> worm gut,

111

scorn turns to delight, and a rhetoric of blame is transfigured into a rhetoric of praise.

Seeing opens to 'seeing', perceiving an objective world to 'perceiving' that it has a life of its own. And this 'ethical extension of fact', as Charles Tomlinson calls it, is wide and various, as 'the presence becomes a moral presence, or one that begets nuances of thought where a moral atmosphere asks for definition.'[2] Another way that surfaces speak is conveyed, again in 'The Steeple-Jack', not in a double but in a startling triple-take: 'it is a privilege to see so/ much confusion', where three, or maybe four, layered meanings progressively lengthen the phrase. One of the senses of 'confusion' here seems to be Latin, a mingling together, as objects clearly themselves are also related to others. The sea's purple is that of a peacock's neck. Boats advance as if in a groove. A summer-house is sugar-bowl shaped. Stars in the sky answer to a star on a steeple, at the point where it is a privilege to see so: the distinctness of the stars prevents them from merely merging, and the 'confusion' hinted at here is the major one, between heaven and earth. Varieties of simile link the world in Romantic analogies—she compares exuberantly, as Randall Jarrell says, 'everything to everything else'[3]—but in the manner of Marianne Moore. For there is a certain oddness in the connections she hits on. The flower salpiglossis, for example, described without ado as having 'spots and stripes', turns up later in a diffident little newt lingered over with a kind of luxury of precision—it has 'white pin-dots on black horizontal spaced-/ out bands'—whose colours, drained of detail, recur on a sign in plain 'black and white'. The diversity of things related is even accented by a nice yet bizarre insistence on numbers: eight whales, a twenty-five-pound lobster, four fluted columns, and so on.

Her poems also 'see', however, more mysteriously; presence becomes religious presence. The intervention of another painter in the book's second poem, 'The Hero', defines vision in a quietly euphoric metaphor, of an El Greco 'brimming with inner light'. Surfaces are depth, not because, as in later writers, there is no depth but because depth, well seen, rises to fill the surface: depth appears. All her animal poems, it seems, are sounded by 'O to Be a Dragon':

If I, like Solomon, . . .
could have my wish—

my wish . . . O to be a dragon,
a symbol of the power of Heaven—of silkworm
size or immense; at times invisible.
Felicitous phenomenon!

The dragon is legendary but there could be no better word
than 'phenomenon' to describe it, since it combines what is
prodigious with what is perceived. (The silkworm suggests a
delicacy of perceiving, as do the products of its own and our
spinning.) Even more than the jelly-fish of a few pages later, a
more material instance of something both 'visible' and
'invisible', the dragon, symbol of the small or immense, visible
or invisible, power of Heaven, quivers with intimation. It is
implied that all her lizards have this quality, and one notes
that, as well as salamanders 'on fire' yet 'unconsumed' ('Sea
Unicorns and Land Unicorns'), and basilisks 'whose look will
kill' ('The Plumet Basilisk'), an ordinary chameleon gets his
food by 'snap[ping] the spectrum up' ('To a Chameleon').
Concerned for wood-weasels and arctic oxes, she nevertheless
writes often of real creatures played-through by the fabulous.

If certain animals can be seen as phenomena, a number of
moments in her poetry see humans as similarly intensified.
Take the middle stanza of 'What Are Years?':

He
sees deep and is glad, who
accedes to mortality
and in his imprisonment rises
upon himself as
the sea in a chasm, struggling to be
free and unable to be,
in its surrendering
finds its continuing.

The poem's theme of a captivity that is freedom looks
traditional enough. Doesn't its power, however, lie in what the
comparison that it makes only hints at: the vastness of the sea
beyond the chasm, of the person beyond the prison? Acceding
to mortality secures, in Marianne Moore's world, a quite
incommensurate enlargement of life, an 'eternity'—the final

word—at once unattainable and already won. The depth is also accompanied by a rising movement, the centre of the poem's contradictory structure, that recalls a moment of calm in 'Marriage':

> the heart rising
> in its estate of peace
> as a boat rises
> with the rising of the water.

The comparison, whose source is given as Richard Baxter's *The Saint's Everlasting Rest*, buoyantly locates the agency this time as other, and under, and all around.

And what, in 'The Hero', of the decorous frock-coated Negro doing service at Mount Vernon, who tells a sightseer where Washington and his lady are buried, and is said to be 'standing like the shadow/ of the willow'? It is a truly strange simile, and while strange similes are easy, truly strange ones are rare, the doors to understanding. The Negro has a 'sense of human dignity' and 'reverence for mystery'; neither seeing the hobo nor being out 'seeing a sight'—Washington's very tomb—but seeing (or being) 'the rock/ crystal thing to see', what he 'sees' is mortality, a mystery more than human, as guardian of the grave. He is like the further willow withdrawn from appearance; the real willow on the grass but not of it, obscure yet revealed by the sun; the shadow that absorbs all of the willow, and all colour, into an adumbration, a dark, of possibility. . . . Like other trees, firs, in 'An Octopus', 'each like the shadow of the one beside it' (a line come upon in the seventh section of Ruskin's *Frondes Agrestes*), the Negro seems to stand beside himself, in a mysterious relation, larger than life.

It is here that reference is made to an El Greco brimming with light. Shadow and inner light are clearly not considered incompatible as images of seeing deep. Her poetry, like Eliot's, goes by both the opposing ways, noting 'how by darkness a star is perfected' ('By Disposition of Angels'), and in its few explorations of darkness being more suggestive than in its exploring of light. The end of 'Then the Ermine' (a poem most of which baffles me) indicates a 'Foiled explosiveness' that has a 'power of implosion', and is another 'perfecter' and also a

114

'concealer'. It then gathers those abstractions, across the mysterious threshold of yet another 'like', into 'violets by Dürer' (flowers that, instead of dazzling, implode, perfect, conceal), and concludes, after a long semi-colon, with the words 'even darker'.

There is some 'biblical' theorizing of the relation between the visible and the invisible. 'Blessed Is the Man', says the poem of that title, 'whose faith is different/ from possessiveness—of a kind not framed by "things which do appear".' Actually, it is a matter of some delicacy with Marianne Moore to know how much to attend to the context of any of her quotations; the quote in this case may exhaust its function by defining, as faith in what does not appear, a faith in various virtues, including courage. Her note does direct one, however, to *Hebrews* 11.3, which, as well as also providing the word 'framed', is concerned, like her poetry, with seeing: 'Through faith we understand that the worlds were framed by the word of God, so that things which are seen were not made of things which do appear.' In her poems, too, objects are sometimes seen on the near edge of an unseen hinterland. Well-known lines from 'He "Digesteth Harde Yron"':

> The power of the visible
> is the invisible.

may also have a scriptural basis, in *Romans* 1.20: 'For the invisible things of [God] from the creation of the world are clearly seen, being understood by the things that are made, even his eternal power and Godhead.' One notes, in this other fundamental text about the seen and the unseen, that the word 'power' would also have been lifted, to describe what the visible derives from the invisible; and one remembers that the dragon will be the symbol of the power specifically of heaven. The move in her poetry from seeing to 'seeing' may well relate to the fact that, according to St. Paul, invisible things (*aórhata*) are visible to the mind (*kathorhātai*).

The theorizing, nevertheless, is minimal; the indication is assumed to be enough. Whereas the charged moments in Eliot ('The moment in the arbour where the rain beat', etc.) are placed in a continuity of Christian speculation, in Marianne Moore they occur and are left, they are illumined by 'piercing glances' ('When I Buy Pictures') but not insisted on, and their imagery is not usually religious. She celebrates the variegations of the visible (God's world), that one is not ambitious to own, and the power and mystery of the invisible (God's world), with little show of having a design on us.

One also learns that to 'perceive' is to disturb. In registering visibilities so as to surprise invisibilities, her poetry operates a change on the world; it enacts a process of seeing, 'seeing', and modifying. 'Dürer' is the first word to be met in her poetry, and a major change is in terms of visual art. I am not thinking of her poems about artefacts, though there are many of these, and, although her ways of making poems have been interestingly compared with the ways of painters, especially Dürer, El Greco, the Cubists and the Chinese, it is not the relation of her poetry to painting that concerns me: rather, the relation, in her poetry, of the world to painting. The earliest figures in the *Complete Poems* alert one to this relation, when water in 'The Steeple-Jack' is 'etched/ with waves as formal as the scales/ on a fish'. The simile works inwardly within the world, fish being in the water, while 'etched' and 'formal' reach across for another, pictorial mode by which the world may be perceived. In fact it is usually the simile that draws in art: in the third stanza the colour-changes of the sea are compared ('as') to colour-changes in Dürer, and the poetry as a whole includes, among other instances, a lizard with tail-bands painted 'As by a Chinese brush' ('The Plumet Basilisk'), chiton-folds of a nautilus 'like the lines in the mane of/ a Parthenon horse' ('The Paper Nautilus'), and a conifer contrived 'in imitation of the glyptic work of jade and hard-stone cutters' ('The Monkey Puzzle'); along with a jerboa whose leaps are 'like the uneven notes/ of the Bedouin flute', and a mountain damned by the public 'like Henry James' ('An Octopus').

That the simile should largely preside over this change means that the scene is not interfered with, displaced, by art. There is, decidedly, delight in imaginative possibility beyond what is warranted by fact: commenting in a letter to Ezra Pound, of 9 January 1919,[4] on a passage in 'Old Tiger' about a leopard 'spotted/ underneath and on its toes', she acknowledges that leopards are not spotted underneath but adds, 'in old illuminations they are', and then, with gusto, 'and I like the idea that they are.' Yet she usually implies the artistic virtuality within the object to be itself a fact: looked at in this way, the folds *are* like a sculpted mane. When the frigate pelican is said, in the poem of that title, to realize 'Rasselas's friend's project' of wings uniting levity with strength, life is imitating art in the sense that it can genuinely be seen in its terms: the world of the imagination, however remote (that double genitive), closes with the world we call real. The scene, the creature, the object, is accomplished in being perceived as art, in convincing the mind's eye, the eye of possibility, of the artistry of the actual.

The process of change, and its theory, are clearest in terms of colour. 'In the Days of Prismatic Color' looks back to a time 'when Adam/ was alone' and colour was 'fine' (and so, etymologically, finished and bounded) with 'originality' (that is, with origin), not, as in art, refined and original; and when obliqueness, which may now suggest deviation and obliquity, was simply a variation of the perpendicular, 'plain to see'. Regretting that 'it is no/ longer that', the poem alludes to a kind of fall of colour—a fall from Eden being a recurring assumption in her writing—which is also a fall of the observable world, into complexity and indirection. Yet what is most evident about her own colours is that they are extremely choice: 'the crimson, the copper, and the Chinese vermilion of the poincianas', 'fifty shades of mauve and amethyst' ('People's Surroundings'), 'ivory white, snow white,/ oyster white and six others' ('Marriage'). If there is again a suggestion of 'too much'—an ordinary steeple-jack takes over as painter from Dürer at the other end of his poem to gild the star with a primary colour, and of Wallace Stevens's exultant grasp of spectacle with its similarly opulent colours she has commented that it 'might be alarming were it not for its persistent foil of dissatisfaction'[5]—her poetry moves nevertheless to reverse the lapse of colour, to draw felicity from the fall; to be, for a perceived world that is flawed, a way of seeing newly.

It is true that, time and again, her poems derive not from life but from art, not, for example, from animals but from pictures of animals. Many of her lines were also taken from other writers. One might conclude that the immediate reference in her poems is to art-works and writings; that life is removed behind its representations, as, in the six separate quotations that constitute the 'end of 'Novices', the sea as analogue of the Hebrew language is withdrawn behind phrases about the sea. Maybe her (American) poetry is a very superior form of tourism, which consists of staying at home, or a glossy catalogue of rather expensive items and, in some cases, sayings. And it is pleasing to think that her *Complete Poems* has preserved some quite select pieces from, among others, *The Illustrated London News*. Or is this her deliberate and provocative way of achieving what Stevens calls 'fiction'? For Stevens it is only through our fictions, and ultimately through a 'supreme', that is, a loftiest and a final, fiction, that we grasp the real, though he does not himself reach out through the fictions of others. Marianne Moore, while giving a closer account than Stevens of a perceivable world, insists even more than he on the fictionality of that account, by overtly mingling the world with representations of it.

Her perspective was unemphatically Christian, Stevens's was explicitly not; and one sees the need to think further with her about representation, though I am not sure that she would wish to follow me here. If one accepts the premise of a fallen world, subjected, in St. Paul's words, to 'corruption' and 'vanity' (*Romans* 8.20–1), is not meaning, or the deepest meaning, fictive in any case? No longer unproblematically present in the observed and to the observer, meaning is an absence, that has to be laboured for. When it is achieved, when the object forms into a legibility, meaning comes as a kind of aesthetic consonance; it is *there*, or seems to be, but it has an air of literature (or painting, or music). In attaining meaning, moreover, the real changes; meaning is the possibility of the real, for good or evil. For the discovery, or imposition, of meaning in a fallen world is related to the deepest change of that world, to its re-creation. And since art is arguably a metaphor that we have been given of that re-creation, to 'see', to perceive meaning, is to enter a fiction as of the world remade. Of course, there is all the difference in the world, and beyond, between seeing the real world in its meaning and projecting a fantasy, a delusion, a wilful dreamscape. The problem is to know the difference, in a fallen world; so she says of her Negro, about to be associated with an El Greco painting, that he speaks to the hobo 'as if in a play', and of her steeple-jack, that 'he might be part of a novel.' They and the world of which they are a focus achieve something like the status of an art-work; but they are presented in this way only within the hypothesis of an 'as if', or within a speculation about what might be, which is qualified by an immediate 'but', by a look at the everyday, and by a sign with an everyday message:

> but on the sidewalk a
> sign says C. J. Poole, Steeple Jack.

Even to talk of the real and of the fictive, as if the distinction were perspicuous, is in effect to ignore the Fall. And if acts of seeing involve representations—'Things seen', writes Stevens in *Adagia*, 'are things as seen'[6]—so do all phrasings and especially all poems; things said are things as said. So the second change that she works on the world is a change into writing. The change is quite conscious, and her poetry, it seems, both celebrates and mocks it. Within a dense context in 'The Pangolin', she describes man as 'writing-/ master to this world'. The poem has stated (her poems state often and without embarrassment) that 'To explain grace requires/ a curious hand'—a high-pitched idea, where 'curious' refers to a quality that she associates in her essay 'Idiosyncrasy and Technique'[7] with a sense of significance, itself an attribute of genius, and probably benefits from its etymological and archaic meanings to include 'careful' and 'skilled'. The hand, which as the later passage suggests is at least in part one's writing hand, is also related to the pangolin's hands and so connects our writing with our animality. The opposing strains, a concern with grace and the reduction of writing to a refine-ment of animal skill, continue when the writing-master 'griffons a dark/ "Like does not like like that is obnoxious" '. The 'darkness' of what is written is partly heroic, as is the fabulous suggestion of 'griffons'; 'griffons' is also mock-heroic. A verb which she seems to have invented, it reinforces the animal association through the dog and the griffon-vulture, and, since it derives from the French *griffonner*, it specifically demotes our

119

writing-hand to a 'claw' or *griffe* and our writing to 'scrawling'. The very phrase about the writing-master, while indicating mastery, only allows us the rôle of pedagogue; we don't master the world by writing, or even write the world, we merely teach it to write, and subservience is suggested in the preposition 'to' rather than 'of the world'.

Reality changes as Marianne Moore instructs it in writing itself out. I do not wish to exaggerate the burlesque, since the effect is often quite other, as in this line from 'Novices': 'the lucid movements of the royal yacht upon the learned scenery of Egypt'. The movements, the royal yacht and the scenery occur in a physical world, though 'scenery', reinforced by that carefully selected 'upon', is also partly mental, the mind's almost artistic mode of picturing a natural place; while 'lucid' and 'learned' move stages further into the mental, and so suspend that perceived world re-creatively between matter and conscious-ness, between the lucidity of light and the lucidity of the mind. Yet La Fontaine practised a writing not so different from this within a context evidently mock-heroic, and it is the burlesque aspect of Marianne Moore's writing that needs stressing.

Take, for instance, her over-writing. When Yvor Winters thought he had found among her weaknesses 'a tendency to a rhetoric more complex than her matter',[8] he made, surely, an enlightening mistake. The attitude that gives rise to such a comment, so often abstersive and by no means in itself mistaken, cannot deal with a use of language that delights in going too far, that phrases and re-phrases the world to the point where the matter *is* in part the rhetoric. Here is a swan under the willows in Oxford:

> Disbelief and conscious fastidiousness were
> ingredients in its
> > disinclination to move. Finally its hardihood was
> > > not proof against its
> > proclivity to more fully appraise such bits
> of food as the stream
>
> > bore counter to it.

('Critics and Connoisseurs')

The excess here, the wit, is in that inexhaustible investing of the bird-brain of the swan with cultivated, polysyllabic

abstractions. La Fontaine again comes to mind, who at one
point, in a cool parenthesis, challenged his readers to appreci-
ate his prolixity:

> *Les reines des étangs, grenouilles veux-je dire*
> *(Car que coûte-t-il d'appeler*
> *Les choses par noms honorables?)*

Marianne Moore's own translation is:

> These frogs or queens of the swamp, to speak with care
> (For what does it cost to use, when all is said,
> A name that is honorable?)[9]

Or take what one might loosely call zeugma. It may be that
the odd collocations in her poetry, to which I referred when
discussing her seeing of analogies, relate to the disorganization
and rearrangement of the visual in Cubist painting; yet they
are decidedly burlesque. In 'The Hero' one comes with neither
warning nor emphasis upon 'the semi-precious cat's eyes of
the owl', while birds in 'A Grave' contrive to 'swim through
the air at top speed, emitting cat-calls'. In 'The Steeple-Jack',
seagulls fly 'One by one in two's and three's', which is
perfectly feasible but seems wrong, and the volatiles do appear
to favour the sequence one, two, three; the 'fife-and-drum' of a
storm is recalled snappily in the next stanza by a 'trumpet-
vine', which is itself recalled in the salpiglossis, whose ety-
mological meaning, should one care to check, is 'trumpet-
tongue'; and a spiderwort turns up again when the jack lets
down a rope 'as a spider spins a thread'. The claw-hand of
Jacob links with the 'Chippendale/ claw' of the jerboa. It is a
singular way of yoking elements of the world one to another
almost willy-nilly in the new space of one's poem (only
Raymond Queneau, that I can think of, works in a com-
parable manner), a gravity delivered in quirks.

Similarly with her lists. Again in 'The Steeple-Jack', as soon
as she has announced that in a town like this 'you have/ the
tropics at first hand', there cascades an apparently interminable
catalogue of plants, which manages surreptitiously to include
any number of other objects, 'moon-vines', 'flags', 'ragged
sailors' . . ., and in particular an inventory of creatures: 'fox-
glove', 'giant snap-dragon', 'toad-plant', 'tigers', etc. One is

again reminded of Queneau. There is also the neat bathos at the new line, after such a jostling forward of different flowers, in:

> petunias, ferns; pink lilies, blue
> ones . . .

And when the list seems to be complete it starts up again:

> The climate

> is not right for the banyan, frangipani, or
> jack-fruit trees;

as if the writer were determined, having told us all that is there, to inform us of quite a few things that are not. (It was apparently Charles Tomlinson who persuaded her to reinstate the flower passage after its exclusion from the 1951 *Collected Poems*; I can't share his regret, however, that the more direct 'There are no banyans' has been replaced by the present transition,[10] where the suggestion of a new departure, 'The climate . . .', the expectant blank, and then the arrival of another list to be embarked on—a further bathos, in fact— seems consummately done.) One hardly needs reminding that her poetry abounds in jokes: following a passage on Handel in 'The Frigate Pelican', *'Festina lente'* looks like an interesting musical notation; and her lists, which are conspicuously acts of writing gathering up items of the real, clown the world into words. At the same time, 'heroically', they involve it in artistry, they employ the dumbest means of describing the world yet transfigure it with unflagging eloquence, since with Marianne Moore even lists are stylish and docile to numbers.

Which brings one to her prosody, and more particularly to her syllabics. Syllabic verse is an evident changing of the world, which it measures and numbers. The numbering even draws attention to itself more than in conventional verse: its order is not that of a known regularity already present within a tradition and referring to a wider system, but of an internally devised regularity peculiar to each poem; and its numerals are self-conscious in a way that the '14' and '10' of the sonnet, say, and the calculating of its line-groupings, are not. Even the devices by which, in our reading of a poem, she sometimes causes us to hasten over a line-ending, work also in that direction, since to end a line with a minor word or to break a word over an enjambment clearly points to the syllable-count as a constraint. Her technique, most evidently in her lengthy descriptions disposing detail after detail in a kind of prosodic joy, transposes the world, if not into a state of grace, at least into one of elegance and newness. It too, however, contributes to the burlesque: don't the numbers go, just slightly, over the top? Isn't the high seriousness of the writing the suggestion that our forms, our aesthetic transfigurations, are vulnerable and even rather comic, and that it would be correct if, while we delighted in them, we also saw the joke?

Marianne Moore certainly had her own way of writing Christian poetry—if indeed it is that. She goes about her business, and only occasionally drops an indication of the religious view that is sustaining her. The indications are not necessarily oblique or tentative; on the contrary, she can surprise by an air of making major claims about life with little supporting evidence. The reader stumbles rather suddenly on passages such as this:

> existence
>
> is flawed; transcendence, conditional;
> 'the journey from sin to redemption, perpetual.'
>
> ('To a Giraffe')

The same is true of her glancing at the world in its fallen condition. 'The Hero' does open with a 'creepy' vision of snakes' 'hypodermic teeth', a neglected yew, the 'twin yellow/ eyes' of an owl; and it does close with the Negro and with a hero who, by saying, 'It is not what I eat that is/ my natural meat', seems to be a pilgrim echoing Christ's words, 'I have meat to eat that ye know not of . . . My meat is to do the will of him that sent me' (*John* 4.32 and 34). Nevertheless, its central and far-reaching declaration, about 'hope not being hope/ until all ground for hope has/ vanished', emerges without any exploration of that vanishing and groundlessness.

Or is this a form of discretion? Objecting to what he considers her consolatory way of dealing with evil, Randall

Jarrell dubs her animal and plant poetry 'this last version of pastoral'[11]; in a letter to William Carlos Williams of 11 September 1920, Pound calls her attitude to what doesn't please her a 'spinsterly aversion'.[12] These are powerful voices, and they may be right. Yet the refusal to go down into sin and despair seems to imply, with courtesy and toughness, that one already knows what is wrong, even if one does not regularly attend a Presbyterian church and read *The Expositor's Bible* and studies of the Old Testament poets. 'The Steeple-Jack', by moving smoothly past stranded whales, a storm that 'disturbs stars in the sky', sin-driven senators and 'Danger' on its way to the final word, 'hope', seems to ironize by its own blandness about the blandness of the town which, for all its qualities and because it has 'cats' and 'not cobras', could do with being alerted.[13] The discretion does mean that her 'piercing glances into the life of things' fail to illumine many areas, and we would not look to her for a deeper understanding of the Fall, unless by implication. It also means, however, that she keeps her attention on what positively matters, leaving the rest to brief notations.

Besides, the moments in her poetry that strain for the invisible are accompanied by others that are content with the splendour or glory of the visible. 'The Pangolin' is central here. It asks why monks would have slaved to 'confuse' the many meanings of grace, binding the worlds in a word, uniting apparently disparate matters all the way from elegance to 'the cure for sins' in a confusion which, one may think, it is a privilege to see, if 'that which is at all were not forever'. Why marry the visible to the invisible if only the invisible is eternal? 'That which is' is not love or anything else elevated, but first the pangolin, whose perfection and otherness have already led to the sudden exclamation:

> Sun and moon and day and night and man and beast
>   each with a splendor
>   which man in all his vileness cannot
>   set aside; each with an excellence!

I take this to be another reworking of St. Paul, specifically of *1 Corinthians* 15.39–41:

> there is one kind of flesh of men, another flesh of beasts. . . .
> the glory of the celestial is one, and the glory of the terrestrial is

another. There is one glory of the sun, and another glory of the moon, and another glory of the stars.

The passage leads immediately into famous verses about natural bodies not being destroyed but being transformed into spiritual ones; her belief that what exists now will exist eternally is based on something more solid than sentimental hopefulness. So alongside the brimming of inner light it is the 'apparition of splendour', to quote one of her poem titles, that causes her to exclaim, as it does once more at the end of 'The Pangolin':

> 'Again the sun!
> anew each day; and new and new and new,
> that comes into and steadies my soul.'

For itself, her poetry does not claim a great deal; insofar as it is Christian writing, it sounds the world with all the devices of seeing at its disposal and works partial and self-critical changes on it. No doubt it is preferable for a Christian poet to leave matters to God, and to recognize that the essential has already been said. She was spared, after all, from being the maker of her own supreme fiction, by being a 'free . . . captive' of 'supreme belief' ('Spenser's Ireland'). She accepts the conditional nature of transcendence, expressing the idea by quoting someone else's statement, with reference to Homer, and at the end of a poem addressed not to truth but to a giraffe; and she seems to take 'the being we call human' as living in a kind of interim, where the continual and patterned reappearance of the sun is a focal event. It can be experienced as a newness in the natural world, which may be the earnest of a larger renewal.

NOTES

1. *The Ordinary Universe*, p. 50.
2. *Marianne Moore: A Collection of Critical Essays*, ed. Charles Tomlinson, p. 2.
3. *Poetry and the Age*, p. 164.
4. Reprinted in *Marianne Moore: A Collection of Critical Essays*.
5. *Predilections*, p. 34.

6. *Opus Posthumous*, p. 162.
7. In *A Marianne Moore Reader*.
8. *In Defense of Reason*, p. 71.
9. From 'The Sun and the Frogs', in *The Fables of La Fontaine*, translated by Marianne Moore.
10. See *Some Americans*, p. 42.
11. *Poetry and the Age*, p. 179.
12. *The Letters of Ezra Pound, 1907–1941*, p. 222.
13. See Bonnie Costello, *Marianne Moore: Imaginary Possessions*, pp. 195–96. The quotation from 'Oh To Be A Dragon' is from *The Complete Poems of Marianne Moore*, copyright © 1959 by Marianne Moore; from 'Blessed is the Man' from *The Complete Poems of Marianne Moore*, copyright © 1956 by Marianne Moore; and from 'To a Giraffe' from *The Complete Poems of Marianne Moore*, copyright © 1966 by Marianne Moore. They are reprinted by permission of Faber and Faber Ltd. and Viking Penguin Inc.

8

Hart Crane and the Riddle of the Sailor, in 'Cutty Sark'

by JEREMY REED

A recurrent and powerful presence in Crane's poetry is that of the drowned sailor, or the poet's alter-ego. We encounter it in many of the poems in his first volume, *White Buildings*, most noticeably in the 'Voyages' sequence, but also as a theme obliquely presented in 'Legend', 'Paraphrase', and 'Recitative'. And we encounter it again at the centre of *The Bridge*.

My concern in this essay is not to establish the epic failure or success of *The Bridge* in terms of its structural cohesiveness, but rather, with the sailor as chief object of attention, to enquire into Crane's employment of a dynamic of metaphor, and into his use of certain recurring symbols that may be identified as obsessively his own.

Writing to Otto Kahn, his financier-patron, of his progress on *The Bridge*, Crane had this to say of the 'Cutty Sark' section:

> The form of the poem may seem erratic, but it is meant to present the hallucinations incident to rum-drinking in a South Street dive, as well as the lurch of a boat in heavy seas, etc. So I allow myself something of the same freedom which E. E. Cummings often uses.
>
> 'Cutty Sark' is built on the plan of a fugue. Two 'voices'—that of the world of Time, and that of the world of Eternity—are interwoven in the action. The Atlantis theme (that of

127

Eternity) is the transmuted voice of the nickel-slot pianola, and this voice alternates with that of the derelict sailor and the description of the action. The airy regatta of phantom clipper ships seen from Brooklyn Bridge on the way home is quite effective, I think. It was a pleasure to use historical names for these lovely ghosts. Music still haunts their names long after the wind has left their sails.[1]

We know from his letters[2] that Crane composed 'Cutty Sark' in July 1926 on the Isle of Pines, during that short-lived, intense, febrile period of creativity in which *The Bridge* was born almost in entirety. This Caribbean interlude has much, I think, to do with the shape of the poem: 'a cartogram', as Crane was to refer to it in a letter to Edgell Rickword.[3] The years of frustration, profligacy and thwarted creative impulse, that saw Crane tied to advertising copy work in New York, were by patronage suddenly removed, and the resultant freedom allowed him to ruminate on his life in the city and on the fragments he had compounded towards his envisaged whole—*The Bridge*.

If Crane saw 'Cutty Sark' as a pivot of *The Bridge*, then it is also central to the poet's idiosyncratic preoccupations as a person. Not only does the poem incorporate echoes of Melville, and of the sunken city of Atlantis which finds an earlier correlative in the 'San Salvador' of 'Voyages II' from *White Buildings*, but the Brooklyn waterfronts become the symbol of Crane's physical obsession—the pulchritude of sailors.

Numerous suggestions have been put forward by Crane's critics as to the identity of the sailor in 'Cutty Sark', but it is my intention to enter the poem without preconceptions, and with the anticipation of the poet in South Street, about to enter the literal 'cooler hells' of his night itinerary. The complete acceptance of the meeting, which is not dependent on previous acquaintance, or initiated by conversation, suggests that the ulterior motive is a physical one. It is certainly brought about by the loosening of barriers that alcohol induces.

> I met a man in South Street, tall—
> a nervous shark tooth swung on his chain.

His eyes pressed through green grass
—green glasses, or bar lights made them
so—
    shine—
        GREEN—
            eyes—
stepped out—forgot to look at you
or left you several blocks away—

After the initial physicality of 'I met a man in South Street, tall—' (and the meeting is face to face, for the poet observes how 'a nervous shark tooth swung on his chain'), there occurs the depth-sounding of the other, who is seen in that alcoholic combination of opacity and heightened clarity. Thus it is that the sailor's green eyes, distorted as they are by bar lights and unable to steady their focus, are perceived by the poet as flickering through 'green grass', which also reminds us of seaweed and the image of the drowned man. These eyes 'stepped out—forgot to look at you/ or left you several blocks away—'. One notices here how Crane has successfully employed the typographical spacing of the lines to represent a drunken man's stolidity, weave, then abrupt sinking back into himself.

Let us enter South Street from another angle, bringing to bear on it Crane's obsession with Marlowe, whose name, or that of Drayton's, he would adopt in his drunken brawls.[4] Marlowe, who haunted the Deptford alleys in pursuit of his 'lewde loue', inevitably figures in Crane's projection of an imagined alter-ego. In a book published the year before Crane composed the major portion of *The Bridge*, J. Leslie Hotson had substantiated the manner of Marlowe's death, by drawing on contemporary accounts and that of the coroner's verdict. And one can see by reading Hotson's sources the affinities that Crane must have felt existed between himself and the dark Elizabethan,

> a Poet of scurrilitie, who by giving too large a swinge to his own wit, and suffering his lust to have the full raines, fell (not without just desert) to that outrage and extremitie, that hee denied God and his sonne Christ. . . .[6]

Crane, who like Marlowe prided himself on his masculinity and despised effeminacy, gravitated towards sailors and the waterfront bars that they frequented. Thus 'Cutty Sark' finds him on familiar territory, well qualified to counterbalance his dreams of a sunken Atlantis, with the drunken reminiscences of a sailor.

'Cutty Sark', the name of a clipper ship and, according to Caresse Crosby, of Crane's favourite brand of whisky, brings the poet into confrontation with his two obsessive symbols: the modern city and the sea. After the initial drunken encounter, we are introduced to the voice of eternity as it is relayed through a pianola. This belief in a mystic synthesis of time is a recurrent theme in Crane's poetry, so that it comes as no surprise that 'the transmuted voice of the nickel-slot pianola' should be that of the sailor's counterpart speaking from the submerged continent of Atlantis.

> in the nickel-in-the-slot piano jogged
> 'Stamboul Nights'—weaving somebody's nickel—
>   sang—

> *O Stamboul Rose—dreams weave the rose!*

> Murmurs of Leviathan he spoke,
> and rum was Plato in our heads . . .

The slant and, we guess, askew track of the needle across the record of a popular song, recalls the 'weaving' or drunken walk of the sailor, and at the same time evokes eternity through the language currency of a contemporary song. The refrain '*O Stamboul Rose—dreams weave the rose!*' recalls the imagery of 'Voyages II' from *White Buildings*, where 'sleep, death, desire,/ close round one instant in one floating flower.' The embodiment of that flower is the sailor, and its counterpart is a voice issuing from Atlantis. Intimations of Ahab's obsession with the White Whale in Melville's *Moby Dick*, and of Plato's account of the civilization of Atlantis in *Timaeus*, find crystallization in the hallucinatory imagery engendered by rum drinking.

In contradistinction to the drift of eternity, the sailor's preoccupation is with time. Time and its disciplined apportionment is paramount in a sailor's life, and even in his drunkenness the sailor is tensed to meet the sailing time of a former ship. The reminiscences that follow are the more effective for their fragmentariness, and in this they find their correlative in the twentieth-century idiom of speed that Crane more than any other poet of his generation was to succeed in conveying through the medium of poetry.[7]

> 'It's S.S. *Ala*—Antwerp—now remember kid
> to put me out at three she sails on time.
> I'm not much good at time any more keep
> weakeyed watches sometimes snooze—' his bony hands
> got to beating time . . . 'A whaler once—
> I ought to keep time and get over it—I'm a
> Democrat—I know what time it is—No
> I don't want to know what time it is—that
> damned white Arctic killed my time . . .'

In recalling the name of his ship, there is a fractional intimation of eternity in the syllables '*Ala*' before a specific sailing time is designated. One is tempted to think here of the relationship between Ishmael and Queequeg prior to embarking on the *Pequod*. But Crane quickly disperses specific time into the amnesia that is later associated with the 'running sands' of the sailor's mind. Senses that have maintained too long a night watch on the ocean, and now are dulled by rum, admit ' "I'm not much good at time any more keep/ weakeyed watches sometimes snooze—." ' The absence of punctuation recreates the disordered syntax of drunken speech; and in the interval between words, 'his bony hands/ got to beating time'—an image appropriate to the later evocation of 'the skeletons of cities' and one which also creates the rhythm of time as opposed to the voice of eternity.

When the sailor resumes talking (the pause, in terms of tidal motion, is sufficient to allow a drowned body to break the surface), his recollections again recall Melville's *Moby Dick*: ' "A whaler once—/ I ought to keep time and get over it—." ' The sense of having drowned, suggested by getting over time, would seem to imply that the sailor is aware of the timelessness of his drunken counterpart and in his maudlin state thinks that he too should have escaped time. But immediately, with the abrupt contradiction of a drunkard, he reasserts ' "I know what time it is" ', only to gravitate once again towards

131

oblivion—' "that/ damned white Arctic killed my time . . ." '[8]

Extinction of the temporal is answered by the voice of eternity, '*O Stamboul Rose—drums weave—*', before the sailor resumes his reminiscences. The image of the rose evokes 'Belle Isle' of 'Voyages VI' from *White Buildings*, where the drowned man is also 'Creation's blithe and petalled word'.

In the typographical lay-out of the poem, Crane isolates the transmuted voice arising from Atlantis, so that it is always a stratum separate from the sailor's monologue. It is the bass resonance heard after the sailor has ceased compounding the mosaic of his life's experiences into a series of incohesive images.

> 'I ran a donkey engine down there on the Canal
> in Panama—got tired of that—
> then Yucatan selling kitchenware—beads—
> have you seen Popocatepetl—birdless mouth
> with ashes sifting down—?
>   and then the coast again . . .'

What is particularly noticeable about the sailor's monologue is its monotonic account of experience. There is no qualitative differentiation between being a whaler, running ' "a donkey engine down there on the Canal" ', or ' "selling kitchenware" ' in Yucatan. The matrix of his mind is frozen, and his narrative is chipped out of the grey sunken matter of his brain. He also hints at the geographical boredom that we have come to associate with the twentieth-century sensibility. Because the frontiers of the physical world have been defined, only the sea seems to offer possibilities of the unknown, and thus continental travel can result only in the expectation of ' "and then the coast again . . ." '.

Once again the monologue is punctuated by the voice of eternity; and this time the transformation of a popular song into an evocation of the drowned city of Atlantis is made more explicit. It is as though after earlier hints and rumours, only now does the maelstrom subside sufficiently to afford a 'skeletal' glimpse of that submerged city of myth. This time the track of the needle across the record resembles the chop of water.

Hart Crane and the Riddle of the Sailor, in 'Cutty Sark'

Rose of Stamboul O coral Queen—
teased remnants of the skeletons of cities—
and galleries, galleries of watergutted lava
snarling stone—green—drums—drown—

Here the rose, religious symbol of mysticism that we have
remarked on in association with 'Voyages VI' as 'Creation's
blithe and petalled word', and that is later to be transformed
into the white anemone symbolizing Atlantis in *The Bridge*, is
seen as ossified. It is a submarine 'coral Queen', a fossilized
efflorescence of the sea-bed. Its significance is conveyed
through the implied reality of the myth: 'teased remnants of
the skeletons of cities—/ and galleries, galleries of watergutted
lava'. The wash of current over its reefs, and the possibility of
imminent violence (the bar is in South Street) leads to the
abrasive resonance of 'snarling stone' and the image of the
drowned man in '—green—drums—drown—'.

When the words of the record become inaudible, we are
returned with a vehement crackle to the sailor's protest. His
gravitation is towards his drowned alter-ego, that counterpart
which belongs to the Atlantean myth, and leaves him
impatient of his shore leave.[9]

> *Sing!*
> '—that spiracle!' he shot a finger out the door . . .
> 'O life's a geyser—beautiful—my lungs—
> No—I can't live on land—!'

A spiracle is the vent or breathing-hole of a whale, and here
too we have echoes of Melville's Ahab in the demonstrative
authority of 'he shot a finger out the door . . .', and in the
mountainous spray discharged by the whale's surfacing, ' "O
life's a geyser—beautiful—" ', before the contraction into
himself, ' "my lungs—/ No—I can't live on land—!" ' Here
the sailor is close to desperation, for the overpowering pull of
the sea enforces on him a consciousness of the spiritual aridity
of his sojourn on land. And it is at such a moment, with the
sailor's psychic defences temporarily down, that the poet
returns to his own presence in the bar, and proceeds with the
most exacting scrutiny to enquire into the other's mind.
Rather as a strip of sand, alternately covered and uncovered

133

by the advancing and retreating wave, so the poet discerns the 'frontiers' of the sailor's mind.

> I saw the frontiers gleaming of his mind;
> or are there frontiers—running sands sometimes
> running sands—somewhere—sands running . . .
> Or they may start some white machine that sings.
> Then you may laugh and dance the axletree—
> steel—silver—kick the traces—and know—

The sailor's apparent nihilism seems to echo the despairing sentiment of 'Voyages V' from *White Buildings*, with its vision of a 'godless cleft of sky/ Where nothing turns but dead sands flashing'. The quality of his thought, heightened by its longing for the sea, has about it the minted polish of a tidal beach. On land the rhythm of his mind anticipates the sea, his frontiers of perception broken down into 'running sands—somewhere—sands running . . .'. It is only in his tentative recognition of spiritual horizons that there appears to be a resolution of the ennui and despair the material world offers him. This resolution would seem to lie in the ambiguous 'white machine that sings', presumably an enigmatic reference to flight, specifically to the aircraft's conquest of space which forms the subject of the 'Cape Hatteras' section of *The Bridge*, more broadly to the twentieth century and to those dual powers of spirit and machine that Crane viewed as yet unreconciled.

In his essay, 'Modern Poetry', Crane had written:

> The emotional stimulus of machinery is on an entirely different psychic plane from that of poetry. Its only menace lies in its capacity for facile entertainment, so easily accessible as to arrest the development of any but the most negligible esthetic responses. The ultimate influence of machinery in this respect remains to be seen, but its firm entrenchment in our lives has already produced a series of challenging new responsibilities for the poet.

In 'Cutty Sark' the ultimate importance of the machine is left unstated; it constitutes little more than one of the sailor's many disillusionments, for although he may envisage it with excitement and 'laugh and dance the axletree', it is powerless to restore a spiritual purpose to his life. In an image that evokes the polar cold of 'that damned white Arctic', Crane seems to be suggesting the abandonment of man by his sleigh teams, so that he remains ruthlessly exposed to the glare in which he will die. I read the line 'steel—silver—kick the traces—and know—' as pertaining to dogs kicking loose from their traces and leaving man on the brink of the unknown.

It is with the reinstatement of the fugue, and the voice of eternity in which *'drums wreathe the rose'* and *'the star floats burning in a gulf of tears'* that the mystic symbol of Atlantis as a rose is transformed into a star—the constellated apex of the poet's and sailor's dual vision. But that vision is too transient to comprise more than an ideal, and the downward pull of gravity, the return to the physical, results in a descent in which the continent is left to

> *sleep another thousand—*
>
>   interminably
>   long since somebody's nickel—stopped—
>   playing—

With the cessation of the record, and the corresponding extinction of vision (it has in fact all happened within the time duration of the song), the poet finds himself returned to the cold night wind of the Brooklyn waterfront, and in keeping with his alcoholically disordered perception, the sailor is viewed objectively as a total stranger, as someone who could have left the bar ages ago, and is now weaving a detached and precarious route back home. The transition from subjective to objective is achieved with that masterful injection of accelerating pace that Crane could give to his poems. It is at such moments that his strongly individual voice enforces on us the recognition of his genius in encompassing the pulse of New York in the '20s.

> A wind worried those wicker-neat lapels, the
> swinging summer entrances to cooler hells . . .
> Outside a wharf truck nearly ran him down
> —he lunged up Bowery way while the dawn
> was putting the Statue of Liberty out—that
> torch of hers you know—
>
> I started walking home across the Bridge . . .

Crane's observation of the sailor's sartorial elegance—'A wind worried those wicker-neat lapels'—has the assurance of a man fastidious in his own dress, as we know Crane to have been, as well as highly observant of the attire of others. And by skilfully unloading the lines of an obvious full rhyme (lapels/hells), he tightens the tension of separation, and suggests the latent inferno concealed inside the sailor's drunkenness and his own precautions against possible violence. The displacement of the rhyme suggests the hostile angle that each presents to the other. Thus it is with a dispassionate tone that Crane is able to relate objectively how 'Outside a wharf truck nearly ran him down', for by this time the sailor is a depersonalized figure, one who 'lunged up Bowery way while the dawn/ was putting the Statue of Liberty out—that/ torch of hers you know—'.

The cold, unemotional manner in which events are related and minimalized—'that/ torch of hers you know'—would seem to indicate a cooling of personal relations. We know that Crane was often threatened with physical violence from drunken sailors, and this, or the depressant effects of alcohol, might account for the sudden estrangement of their parting, and the failure on the part of the poet to achieve any form of elation at the night city viewed on the skyline.

The sailor gone, we are returned to the centre-beam of Crane's vision, both in terms of his proposed epic, and in terms of the resonance that 'steel' afforded to the best poems in *White Buildings*.[11] The line is a simple one, but vibrant in the associations that it yields. 'I started walking home across the Bridge . . .' The note of personal defeat sounded in that line admits of that ambivalence between spiritual exaltation and physical disillusionment that so often creates the vital conflict of tension in Crane's work. The departure of the sailor directs us towards the poem's other key note—'the hallucinations incident to rum-drinking'.

In his evocation of the world of clipper ships, Crane is in effect extending the poem's epigraph from Melville—'O, the navies old and oaken,/ O, the *Temeraire* no more!'—into a distinctly personal vision. While this section comprises essentially a postscript to 'Cutty Sark', it does so not only as a brilliant act of self-indulgence, but also as a poem whose

stylistic innovations were to serve as a precedent for much of
the subsequent development in American poetry of the free
association of images, right down to the prose experiments of
William Burroughs. Crane recalls

> Blithe Yankee vanities, turreted sprites, winged
> > British repartees, skil-
> ful savage sea-girls
> that bloomed in the spring—Heave, weave
> those bright designs the trade winds drive . . .

In compiling his 'airy regatta of phantom clipper ships' Crane
is aware that the backwash of the poem must engender
sufficient tidal current to intersect with the tension established
between the poet and sailor in the South Street dive. Whereas
the initial friction was mental, its counterpart is physical, and
the muscular wash of the sea is captured in lines like

> Heave, weave
> those bright designs the trade winds drive . . .

Here the monosyllables seem set in opposition to a powerful
form of resistance, and the movement is that of a clipper ship
in heavy seas, as opposed to the prevailing motion of wind
arising from the voice of the fugue that recalls

> *Sweet opium and tea, Yo-ho!*
> *Pennies for porpoises that bank the keel!*
> *Fins whip the breeze around Japan!*

The reference to opium suggests not only the inspiration
behind Coleridge's 'The Ancient Mariner' and Poe's *The
Narrative of Arthur Gordon Pym*, and for that matter Baudelaire's
'Le Voyage', but also the frozen isolation that the drug
induces, thereby accentuating the poet's solitary vision of the
past. Thus it is in a time quite removed from that of the
incident in which the sailor 'lunged up Bowery way' that an
incisive wind finds its onomatopoeic correspondence in the
line *'Fins whip the breeze around Japan!'*
From the tense friction of a bar encounter in which space
opened up mentally, we are now deposited in a world where
space is physical, and where, confronted by his knowledge of
the limitations of the universe, the sailor can only recount his

inventory of disillusionment as a substitute for conquest of the new.

> Bright skysails ticketing the Line, wink round the
>   Horn   .
> to Frisco, Melbourne . . .
>   Pennants, parabolas—
> clipper dreams indelible and ranging,
> baronial white on lucky blue!

One senses the note of joy with which Crane opens up these sea roads, and how the sails appear to 'wink', a word conveying not only speed, but that peculiar quality of sea light that invariably coruscates on the horizon. One can extend the metaphor to include the semaphoring of lighthouses and thus see how Crane embodies an entire seascape in a word that is in itself fleeting and suggestive of transience. The alliterative resonance of 'Pennants, parabolas—' likewise suggests a running sail, and a choppy sea, and is another example of Crane's syllables resisting a forward motion, thus setting up the flow and counterflow of the ocean.

When Crane does come to evoke the fictitious names of clipper ships, and the feats of their nineteenth-century trade runs, he vitalizes their names with a wind from the past, so that in the conjunction of their names we not only see the outlines of their forms but also hear the very flapping of their pennants.

> Perennial-*Cutty*-trophied-*Sark*!

> *Thermopylae, Black Prince, Flying Cloud* through
>   Sunda
> —scarfed of foam, their bellies veered green espla-
>   nades,
> locked in wind-humors, ran their eastings down;

It would not be unreasonable to suggest that the typographical shape of the stanzas employed in the second section of the poem represent gradations of sea-level, with the clipper ships flying on the surface, and the symbol of the drowned man and the lost city of Atlantis finding a gradual descent to the seafloor, until they are finally represented as being an enigma that lies beyond the two question marks with which the poem terminates. The names *Thermopylae* (a city of hot springs), *Black Prince*, and *Flying Cloud*, both of which evoke sea moods, the one storm and the other wind, are held in partial suspension by their grouping, until flight is promoted 'scarfed of foam', and depth too in that 'their bellies veered green espla-/ nades', with the word 'bellies' suggesting girth and water volume, while 'green' takes us back to the image of the drowned sailor, and the sea colour of his eyes.

The fugue is maintained for the last time with a sudden insurgent rhythm as of wind freshening. And here the voice is that of the protean sailor, this time recalling his life on board a clipper ship:

> *at Java Head freshened the nip*
> *(sweet opium and tea!)*
> *and turned and left us on the lee . . .*

Thereafter the poem spirals into a vortex, and the evocation of names denotes loss; and thus the personal loneliness echoed in the line 'I started walking home across the Bridge . . .' finds its correspondence in the blank face of the sea uncombed by clipper ships, a sea that has closed in a vortex over the transient resuscitation of the drowned sailor and the sunken city of Atlantis.

> Buntlines tesseling (91 days, 20 hours and anchored!)
> *Rainbow, Leander*
> (last trip a tragedy)—where can you be
> *Nimbus*? and you rivals two—
>
>   a long tack keeping—
>   *Taeping?*
>   *Ariel?*

Crane's choice of names resonates with symbols peculiar to his poetry. '*Rainbow*', which recalls God's covenant to man, also suggests a veiled disclosure; it is through this prism that Atlantis or Belle Isle of 'Voyages VI' is to be perceived. And '*Leander*' who drowned in the Hellespont in quest of Hero, alludes not only to the image of the drowned man that runs throughout Crane's sea poetry, but also to Marlowe whose translation of Hero and Leander was completed by George Chapman. The reference to '*Leander*'—'last trip a tragedy'— reinforces my conjecture that the drowned sailor partly embodies the characteristics of Marlowe, while '*Nimbus*', the halo or sacred aura investing a God or Goddess, refers us back to '*Rainbow*' and the radiance of light that is a manifestation of deity. '*Taeping*', the Chinese word for the Pacific, with its connotations of 'opium and tea!' is united with the spirit of the Western world, '*Ariel*',[12] thus bringing the latter's creative inspiration to preside over the ocean of great calm.

In my reading of 'Cutty Sark' I have focused upon its merits as a lyric poem independent of its contribution to the unity or disunity of *The Bridge*. As such a poem I have found it to be brilliantly innovative, a poem in which Crane not only reworks obsessive symbols, but also accentuates the crucial tension between the poet and the modern city. 'The city's stubborn lives, desires' are nowhere more powerfully concentrated than in the pool of bar-light shared by the poet and sailor.

NOTES

1. Brom Weber (ed.), *The Letters of Hart Crane* (Berkeley and Los Angeles, 1965), pp. 307–8 (12 September 1927).
2. *Letters*, pp. 268–69 (29 July 1926).
3. *Letters*, p. 283 (7 January 1927).
4. 'In the intense energy and excitement of [his] lines, in the torrential imagination, so often cosmic in its reaches, one may find more than ample confirmation of Crane's belief that he was possessed by a Marlovian demon. The same qualities in his personality earned him the Elizabethan nickname of 'the roaring boy'. Philip Horton, *Hart Crane* (New York, 1937), p. 310.
5. J. Leslie Hotson, *The Death of Christopher Marlowe* (London, 1925), pp. 13–14.
6. Thomas Beard, *Theatre of God's Judgements* (London, 1597). Quoted in Hotson, p. 11.
7. 'Speed is at the bottom of it all—the hundredth of a second caught so precisely that the motion is continued from the picture indefinitely: the moment made eternal.' *Letters*, p. 132 (15 April 1923).
8. Crane had evoked such a landscape in his youthful poem 'North Labrador', as well as in the powerful 'antarctic blaze' of 'Paraphrase'.
9. 'He is a latter-day Columbus, driven always to pursue "the frontiers gleaming of his mind". He is mortality seeking eternity.' R. W. (Herbie) Butterfield, *The Broken Arc* (Edinburgh, 1969), p. 176.
10. *Letters*, p. 308 (12 September 1927).

11. Of particular pertinence here are 'Recitative' and 'For The Marriage of Faustus and Helen Part III'.
12. 'But I would rather do as I did yesterday—after a night of wine—wake up at dawn and dip into The Tempest, that crown of all the Western World.' *Letters*, p. 317 (22 February 1928).

The lines from 'Cutty Sark' from *The Complete Poems and Selected Letters and Prose of Hart Crane*, edited by Brom Weber, are reprinted by permission of Liveright Publishing Corporation, copyright © 1933, 1958, 1966 by Liveright Publishing Corporation.

9

Inaugural and Valedictory: The Early Poetry of George Oppen

by ANDREW CROZIER

Although *Of Being Numerous* (1968) and *Primitive* (1978) are arguably George Oppen's mature achievement, rightly attended to and admired as such by many of his readers, these late works are rooted in and a fulfilment of his early work, which they comment on and acknowledge. Yet reference to Oppen's 'early' work incurs immediate uncertainty, since his career can be seen to possess two separate points of departure, first with the poems written during the late '20s and early '30s assembled in *Discrete Series* (1934), and again in the poems of the late '50s and early '60s collected in *The Materials* (1962). To what extent these different beginnings, and the issues raised by the suspension of Oppen's poetic career, either derive from or affect the character of his writing are questions that ask to be explored. To assert peremptorily, with Hugh Kenner, that 'In brief, it took twenty-five years to write the next poem' (although Oppen quotes this remark with approval and apparent relief) is to pre-empt several important questions.[1] To what extent is an Objectivist poetics carried over from *Discrete Series* into *The Materials*? If Oppen did not simply start again where he left off, to what extent is the poetics of *The Materials* responsive to his experience, in the intervening years, of political activism, skilled factory work, infantry combat, family life in post-war America, and political exile in Mexico? Kenner's impatient formula shrinks the issues to fit the case that the contours of Oppen's poetic career can be traced through an as-if uninterrupted series of poems, distorts the relationship between his life and his work and, above all, circumvents consideration of Oppen's politics.

In this essay I propose an account of *Discrete Series* that leads me to conclude that its connection with Oppen's subsequent writing is autobiographical. One way of formulating the difference of *Discrete Series* and *The Materials*, among others, is to point out that whereas in the former there is a recurrent focus on a woman as companion and sexual partner, and on women in general, the latter is pervasively informed by the presence of a child or daughter. Around this figure cluster new issues of age, memory, cultural transmission and temporal process, which both extend and subordinate preoccupations in *Discrete Series* with machinery, work, idleness, and the diverse present-day life of the modern city, all disposed in such a way that time implodes, so to speak, within the simultaneities of the poetic moment. Oppen's renewed poetic scrutiny of the world, after a prolonged lay-off, produced a more fluent, less cerebral account of what there is, in which value identifies itself more confidently in the things named than it did in the naming of things. As a corollary of this but, I would maintain, preconditionally, *Discrete Series* and *The Materials* confront us with different rhetorics. This in itself might be taken as evidence of a fundamental discontinuity in Oppen's work. It is in terms of these rhetorics, totalities of the formal and discursive procedures of the writing, that any reading of Oppen, especially, must answer for itself, so much otherwise does his work seem incommensurate with writing with which we stand on more familiar terms. By and large existing discussions of *Discrete Series* have tended to describe its formal qualities as embodiments of some of the given features of modern poetic style, and given little attention to any specific discursive assumptions they might be bound up with. The Objectivist notion of a poem as a made thing, as a machine, has tended to confer on the reductive, almost (it might seem) arbitrary writing of *Discrete Series* a craftsmanlike authority and prestige that have gone largely unargued. The language strategies and decisions implicit in the writing, of which it is the outcome, have been readily taken for granted, neither analysed nor justified in relation to the interpretations they enable or forestall.

Discrete Series was an almost belated event within a briefly coherent literary milieu, the imprint of which it bore clearly but ambiguously. Oppen was associated with a grouping of young poets, convened initially in the pages of Ezra Pound's *Exile* (1927–28), where work by Carl Rakosi and Louis Zukofsky appeared, at a moment when Pound was anxious to consolidate and put on record the achievement of the previous fifteen years, and was looking for American disciples into the bargain. Rakosi and Zukofsky were put in touch with each other, and also with William Carlos Williams and other native survivors of Pound's generation. Pound wished this small force of younger poets to manifest itself as the new generation, and arranged for Zukofsky to edit the February 1931 issue of *Poetry* for this purpose.[2] *An 'Objectivists' Anthology* (1932), edited by Zukofsky and published by Oppen, established more explicitly, though with less publicity, the short-lived connection of the new generation and their predecessors. There are grounds for seeing Pound's *Active Anthology* (1933), which included Zukofsky and Oppen, though not Rakosi, as a late manifestation of Objectivism, although Pound's waning interest can be inferred from his comment that many of the young poets seem to have 'lost contact with language as language . . . in particular Mr Zukofsky's Objectivists seem prone to this error'.[3] Nevertheless, when *Discrete Series* came out the following year it carried a Preface by Pound saluting 'a serious craftsman, a sensibility which . . . has not been got out of any other man's books'.[4]

Oppen was by no means a prominent member of this milieu. He sponsored To Publishers, later The Objectivist Press, and saw to the production side of things. Apart from *An 'Objectivists' Anthology* the enterprise is best known for having published books by Williams and Pound. Oppen published very little of his own work: two poems in the February 1931 issue of *Poetry* that Zukofsky edited, and another four in January 1932; one poem in *An 'Objectivists' Anthology*; five in *Active Anthology*. Eight of the twelve were included in *Discrete*

Series. His junior status was seized upon in reviews of his book.
Not much good came to him either of Pound's Preface or an
enthusiastic review by Williams in the July 1934 issue of *Poetry*;
if anything, such connections defined Oppen too narrowly,
and comparisons were made at his expense by, for example,
Geoffrey Grigson and H. R. Hays. Grigson objected to 'simple
brevity' ('a push-bike for the simple-minded'), and found that
'when one attempts to permit these anti-poems to expand in
one's mind . . . one discovers them to be elastic, not organic—
fictions which can only be enlarged by pulling.' [5] For Hays,
Oppen's 'pretentiousness is not supported by any felicity of
observation', and whereas 'Williams is intent on capturing the
object as a whole; Oppen is apparently trying to derive
textures of objects.' [6]

It could hardly have turned out otherwise, perhaps. What
prestige had either Pound or Williams to confer at a time when
they still published with such hole-and-corner operations as
The Objectivist Press? As much as anything, they were
convenient sticks with which to beat poets who attended to
their outworn example. And *Discrete Series* cannot have seemed
an ingratiating or rewarding book. It is tightly organized, even
rigid, and gives very little away. It consists of thirty-one short
poems, the first of which, with its pastiche of a Jamesian
periodic sentence, is sufficiently anomalous in style to ask to be
regarded as standing outside an even more tightly-knit group
of thirty poems. The sense that this poem is in some way
prefatory is reinforced both by its promulgation of large-scale
thematic concerns in its concluding reference to 'the world,
weather swept, with which one shares the century' and by its
implicit repudiation of the values and conventions of Oppen's
wealthy middle-class background and also, I would argue,
their attendant boredom.[7] The narrow line trodden here
between boredom as knowledge of the world and boredom as a
particular knowledge of the world is typical of the close shave
Oppen's way with definitions and propositions administers.
Neither the book's programme nor the terms in which it is
proposed can put us at our ease. The book appears, if
anything, almost too deliberately calculated, with an uncon-
cealed but obscure polemic intention; it is decidedly self-
possessed, and comments on its properties as it proceeds, as

something both written and read, in a way that seems to attribute both graphic and three-dimensional qualities to its existence. It is so little like the majority of young poets' 'first books', neither haphazard miscellany nor an object of subsequent shame, that it might almost be taken for a valedictory rather than an inaugural statement. Indeed, it already bears traces of the diagnosis of social disaster that led Oppen quietly to abandon poetry (including the option of politically committed poetry) and take up the life of a full-time Communist Party worker in Brooklyn and subsequently in Utica.

The very title of *Discrete Series* is a sign of deliberate intent. Series are normally continuous, each term in succession deriving from its predecessors and determining those that follow. Oppen's later elucidation of his intended meaning represents it in terms that do not appear to have occurred to his readers at the time. Grigson thought that the writing itself was discrete, and gave credit at least for the fact that it had 'no pinned-on imagery'.[8] Williams, on the other hand, thought that the term was probably 'meant merely to designate a series separate from other series'.[9] Oppen's account of what he had in view, however, might well put us in mind of the position taken by Samuel Johnson in his 'Review of a Free Enquiry' (1757), namely that our partial knowledge of the creation, unbuttressed by theories of plenitude, is not inconsistent with feelings of awe in the face of a transcendent origin of being. Oppen describes a discrete series as 'a series of terms each of which is empirically derived, each of which is empirically true'. This empiricism was to be made to yield a method, in an 'attempt to construct meaning, to construct a method of thought from the imagist technique of poetry—from the imagist intensity of vision', based on 'a moment, an actual time, when you believe something to be true, and you construct a meaning from these moments of conviction.'[10] Elsewhere Oppen has remarked that the numbers 14, 28, 38, 42 comprise an exemplary discrete series: 'the names of the stations on the east side subway'.[11] Yet the intelligibility of such a series depends on a context of independent knowledge, some actual or theoretical reference. If after catching the Tube at Victoria I find myself at Earl's Court, I know that I am on the District Line, not the Circle, and that I am on the wrong train for Kensington High Street.

Oppen's comments, thirty and more years in retrospect, need to be approached with due caution. The appeal to conviction, for example, seems more fully in keeping with his concerns of the 1960s. The evidence of the few poems Oppen published prior to *Discrete Series* is helpful in this respect. It is clear both that he initially thought of some of the poems in *Discrete Series* under a different rubric, and that 'discrete series' was a generic term rather than a title designating a specific text. The two poems he published in the February 1931 issue of *Poetry* were jointly titled '1930'S', as was his poem in *An 'Objectivists' Anthology*. These three poems, arranged in a different order, became the first three poems of *Discrete Series*: the prefatory poem, and a pair numbered 1 and 2 to denote their correlation. This pair of poems refers to skyscraper lobbies and lunch-bars, and on the basis of this rendering of the texture of contemporary life, and the topical connotations of the discarded title, it might be concluded that for a time Oppen contemplated a series of poems in a contemporary documentary vein, but subsequently revised this intention to produce a more rigorous conception of the composition of a serial work. The term 'Discrete Series' first appeared as the collective title for Oppen's group of four poems in the January 1932 issue of *Poetry*, but of this group only one—the last—is to be found in *Discrete Series*. The first three poems refer to the confined orbit of the poet's room, the inadequacy to passionate life of the world of social refinement, and anticipations of the release of summer. They provide an antithetical version of city life, in which wished-for dialogue keeps giving way to fretful monologue. 'Cat-Boat', the concluding poem, is different; it objectifies the tense intersections of mast, sail, wind, water and sun as a single event, and now the beleaguered couple implied in the previous poems can glide unscathed over the infinite peril of the 'unrimmed holes' of the sea-bed. If in this series there is a sequence from alienation to fulfilment, its preliminaries contribute little to the outcome; their rôle within the discursive framework is at best thematic. The complex stasis of 'Cat-Boat' (for in fact the perils glide 'beneath us') is not subject to the recognition of directed feeling tone, but is the source of its own security. Even though the terms of this series are arguably discrete, in the sense that they are not derived successively from each other, there remains a definite sense of forward movement under schematic pressure (both in terms of seasonal progression and spiritual attainment), the initial stages of which, in relation to 'Cat-Boat', are finally redundant. The boat has no need to negotiate terms with its situation since it is so completely borne by and one with it.

Whereas the contradictions encountered in the first three poems are organized propositionally or interrogatively, their discourse articulated by means of an enacted central consciousness, in the final poem the contradiction between security and risk is sited without disrupting the sequence of indicative statements ('imagist statements') by anything more than a break in the line, the graphic/prosodic device indicating a shift in the weight the poem is carrying. The transition of feeling and evaluation between one reference and another has not been attributed to an imputed subject, and the poem's significance is thereby normative, in the absence of such personal witness, if the reader agrees. It is possible to imagine a series of such poems, imposing their conviction of the way things are or might be on their own evidence. But any such gain is accompanied by considerable risk, for the reader of *Discrete Series* is aware, as much as anything, of language operating under severe pressure, of a discourse loaded and compressed in order to test individual words. Far from being a dance of the intellect among words, Oppen's *logopoeia* implies considerable scepticism about available discourses and communal usage.

I allude to Pound's category deliberately, because Oppen's references to imagism, in particular his suggestion that it might provide a mode of thought, point beyond general notions of imagism as a technique of immediate presentation. In his Preface to *Discrete Series* Pound endeavoured to distinguish between Oppen's work and that of Williams, but this is misleading. Pound himself, if anyone, is the presiding influence in *Discrete Series*, even though Oppen's field of reference may remind us more of Williams than of Pound, and this influence is most discernible when we trace the basic strategies of Oppen's writing. At the same time, Pound's influence does not result in any very clear resemblance, for Oppen adopts Pound's method only to throw it into reverse.

In Pound's typically imagist poems we find a discourse constructed through the juxtaposition of elements, normally drawn from different conceptual orders of reality, the spiritual and the mundane. These elements are not so much opposed or contrasted as shown in terms of their possible equivalence, the completion of this discourse lying in some further, unstated term. The advantage of this method for Pound, which we might epitomize as the reciprocity of image and ideogram, is that elements so used, by virtue of their difference, can be scaled up or down, either by setting them parallel to other series of elements, or by subdivision into new series. The disadvantage of this method is the monolithic unity of concept it entails; its inclusivity breaks down under the weight of its own inertia—as we find in the *Cantos*—when it is developed beyond certain limits. This is experienced either as incoherence or as vulnerability to counter-discourses.

The poems in *Discrete Series* have a binary structure similar to that of the Poundian image, but whereas in Pound the elements correlated are different but equivalent, in Oppen they are similar (ontologically identical in some cases) but opposed. It is out of the collision between different versions of similar events, the discovery of mendacity or misrepresentation where discourses compete, that the meanings of *Discrete Series* arise. One of the book's least startling poems can exemplify Oppen's general procedure.

> The edge of the ocean,
> The shore: here
> Somebody's lawn,
> By the water.

On the face of it this is a charming vignette, suggestive perhaps of nature tamed to serve as an amenity to civilized living. But to read the poem thus is an act of selective attention, hardly adequate to the already stripped-down syntax. In the absence of explicit grammatical co-ordinators (there is no main verb, for example, and the consequent power vacuum destabilizes the adverb 'here') our reading is forced to rely more than usual on the interaction of semantic values, and indeed the poem immediately indicates that it is concerned with definitions. Surely in such extreme verbal economy there is no space for any surplus. If we give each word its due weight, we see that the poem turns on the opposition of 'shore' and 'lawn', 'ocean' and 'water', names for the same things in this instance, for we still understand a reference outside the terms of the poem to some actual situation, of which the poem's two opposed discourses are minimal predications. We are not even permitted the interval of relief that might be afforded by a here/there contrast: the 'here' of immediate location is shunted forward (a colon marks the point of impact) from a preliminary definition, if not to repossess 'somebody's lawn' at least to show how private property diminishes the natural world. 'Here' man's triumph over nature has been achieved at the public expense, if 'shore' and 'ocean' are the proper names for those things as they locate and define the conditions of human existence. But in the world this poem refers to the elemental conditions of our existence, on the edge of which we live, are seen to be hidden. They are obscured by such an innocent, domesticated little word as 'lawn', which under testing pressure reveals the weight of ethical censure. We can hardly feel, however, that the judgement here proceeds from concern for popular rights, from some sense of exclusion; the perceptions deployed in this poem are derived from somewhere beyond the social, beyond the edge of the inhabitable world and human history. If we want to look for this place, we should refer to the conclusion of Oppen's prefatory poem. If 'By the water' could stand for 'The edge of the ocean', the measure of the earth's waters would be taken on a scale that found them no bigger than a duck pond.

With this exemplary poem in mind, and seeing it in the light of Oppen's dismemberment of the original 'Discrete Series', it becomes possible to generalize the assumptions and procedures directing the writing of *Discrete Series*. In the first place, the poems are written in a way that does not permit them to be read progressively, as though leading the reader forward to some conclusion to be enacted at the moment of textual closure. (This can be understood to apply to the series as a whole.) The reader is required to bear in mind concurrently all the elements in a particular poem. But if the poems are non-narrative, no more are they the random and simultaneous notations of a moment; their detail is neither additive, accumulative, nor typical. Detail is organized to establish lines of association and dissociation, the parameters of discourses local to the poem. Moreover, language itself is treated as an empirical datum, in which reference is inextricably combined with its terminology; language cannot, on such assumptions, mediate neutrally between the reader and some other matrix of empirical knowledge. (Oppen's work contains no gestures towards authenticity of speech such as we find in Williams, for example.) Hence verbs cannot be relied upon to correlate relationships between details, so that throughout *Discrete Series* we find that transitive functions are regularly displaced on to adverbs and prepositions, and that participles and intransitive verbs are favoured.

In the light of the implications of Oppen's methods Hays's strictures on *Discrete Series* are seen to have at least some descriptive accuracy, for one important outcome of Oppen's procedure, we might say its very purpose, is a general levelling of usual figure/ground gradients. Oppen can take objects very much for granted, both as cultural and perceptual products. Motor cars and yachts, whatever their different values, are empirically very simple. Similarly, Oppen has little time for the braveries of figurative rhetoric. Both types of figure/ground relationship, the perceptual *gestalt* and the rhetorical trope, divert attention from the system or ground in which the figure is produced. In poetry that addresses the reader in terms of an array of figures it is always possible to see how the figures are produced within the general terms of the discourse, but it is not really feasible to provide them also with the empirical substantiation we find in *Discrete Series*. This is a mainly negative observation, as regards Oppen, and need not stop anyone from thinking of the poems in *Discrete Series* as discrete tropes if it is thought useful to do so. The substantive issue, in Oppen's practice, has to do with the way our knowledge of productive systems or grounds tends to be abstract and theoretical, subordinate to the configurations and entities they give rise to. 'Texture' is an approximate but less than adequate term by which to denote the outcome of Oppen's over-riding interest in retrieving the commonplace background of everyday life—pavements and street-lighting, systems of communication and transfer—in an attempt to bring within the range of discourse conditions normally taken for granted or imperceptible. (It is in terms of such a project, entailing the textual absence of determinate entities, that Zukofsky's remark that Oppen's work deals with the 'void' makes best sense.[12]) By taking basal conditions as the contexts for discursive juxtapositions in *Discrete Series*, Oppen is able in effect to figure one theoretical order of reality and its discourse against the ground of another.

Resistance of the solicitation of trope and *gestalt* leads to different kinds of engagement, but in each different case we can see that the outcome is compatible with the need to produce a textual effect of continuous groundwork. The fifth poem of *Discrete Series*, for example, starts with a series of attributive figures similar to those deployed by Williams at the beginning of 'Portrait of a Lady'.[13]

> Her ankles are watches
> (Her arm-pits are causeways for water). . . .

But these appropriative figures are checked and replaced by a more literal incursive discourse as the woman in question continues her morning routine ('She walks on a sphere// Walks on the carpet') so that her everyday, insignificant gestures reappropriate her being.

> Her movement accustomed, abstracted,
> Declares this morning a woman's
> 'My hair, scalp—'.

Here a continuous ground, between woman and morning, is established thematically and, to an extent, figuratively. The seventh poem, in contrast, specifies and comments on a setting for events that remain elusive.

> The lights, paving—
> This important device
> Of a race
>
> Remains till morning.
>
> > Burns
> Against the wall.
> He has chosen a place

With the usual considerations,
Without stating them.
Buildings.

Is this poem about the streets or the city authorities? What sort of race is referred to: the human race, or an athletic contest? Who is the referent of the abruptly intrusive pronoun? The poem provides no answers to such questions. What it does is dissociate the terms normally subsumed in such concepts as 'city' or 'environment' in order to divest such fictions of their contingency. However depopulated this urban night-scene appears, it is hardly mysterious; nor is it void of human purpose, however disavowed its social ideologies may be. The two discourses opposed in this poem interrupt one another, so that the reader is left in the dark about the precise character of each, but as they intersect their separate details combine in a different discourse, however fragmentary, which produces the base conditions of social forms and agencies. The transition from 'wall' to 'place', between location and decision, mediates the two discourses while indicating their discrepancy; the referent for 'he' can then be found, if anywhere, in 'a race'.

Throughout *Discrete Series* objects and configurations tend to be merged with temporal and spatial sequences, either by repetition or dispersal. In the eighteenth poem a bird—probably one of Williams's sparrows—is epistemologically complex within the terms of recurrent experience. In the twenty-sixth poem the Depression spectacle of a man selling postcards in the street is part and parcel of the urban scenery of traffic and cinema publicity. We might say that within the terms of Oppen's method the presentation of a determinate figure would be seen as a failure, since such an achievement would entail the subordination of one discourse to another by a too explicit inflection of the ground that the poems equally derive from and have as their formal aim. Oppen's suppression of significant figuration is perhaps most blatant, in terms of the available discourses of the '30s, when the poems raise the issue of photography. Here we can gauge both the extent to which Oppen distanced himself from any documentary intention, and the degree of his difference from Williams. The 'readers' of documentary photographs are presented, in familiar language,

153

with information that is remote from their experience. Their empirical relationship with such images is not corroborative but guaranteed by notions of authenticity, although the assumed values of authenticity are effectively subordinate to confrontation. The last people a documentary image is for are the people depicted in it. But where photographs are most clearly acknowledged as Oppen's sources in *Discrete Series*, they are treated as snapshots, their subject matter grounded in familiarity. In the seventeenth poem, for instance, which refers to what is presumably one of Brady's civil war photographs, we find 'The cannon of that day/ In our parks'. In several other poems the reader can infer that reference is made to a photographic image.

> This land:
> The hills, round under straw;
> A house
>
> With rigid trees
>
> And flaunts
> A family laundry,
> And the glass of windows

This reminds us, more than anything else, surely, of that 1930s photography of American landscape dominated by commercial signs, and we can see inscribed among the details of the poem a Walker Evans image of a window bearing the legend 'Family Laundry' somewhere in the middle of nowhere. If I am right to see this (and I could extend such speculations to deal with other instances, the tenth poem for example), it is because Oppen appeals to the inclusiveness of the photographic image, its inability to state preferences within its visual field. In this respect Oppen stands in marked contrast to Williams who, as Bram Dijkstra has shown, used Stieglitz's photographs to explore significant configurations of resistance between one object and another within the strict margins of the image.[14]

In his Preface to *An 'Objectivists' Anthology* Zukofsky designated 'condensation' as the technique by which the necessary craftsmanship of contemporary verse was hidden in the poem-object. 'Against obvious transitions, Pound, Williams, Rakosi,

Bunting, Miss Moore, oppose condensation. The transitions cut are implicit in the work, 3 or 4 things occur at a time making the difference between Aristotelian expansive unities and the concentrated locus which is the mind acting creatively upon the facts.'[15] Zukofsky's polemic opposition of particulars to generalization was not espoused by Oppen, but if we put Oppen within this general stylistic context, we might more precisely define his technique by saying that, while in his work the notion of the mind operating directly among facts remained problematic precisely because it showed the mediated nature of facts, he does indeed use condensation in order to effect transitions. We might go further and say that we recognize that a transition occurs while remaining in ignorance of the facts. The separate poems of *Discrete Series* are related by method as well as technique, but above all they are related by their collective reference to the presence of a continuum outside their series—the inferred continuum of the world accessible to empirical knowledge, however full of gaps that world might be. This reference occurs within the qualified and incomplete discourses the poems set in motion, and it is as an accompaniment of the friction generated by the inadequacy of specific discourses that a conviction of a totality beyond them arises. But there are neither large-scale axioms to provide a framework for an inclusive knowledge, nor the full discourse of a continuously knowing subject. We feel the presence of a consistent intelligence in the poems' method, of a certain sensibility in the range of empirical details responded to and acknowledged, but this intelligence and sensibility are not projected within the series as a point of view from which its various components are rendered intelligible as a whole. That is up to the reader. Above all, the reader is forced to resist any temptation to search for and identify with an authorial point of view, for the author can only occasionally be made out as another presence among the empirical data (a 'me' rather than an 'I') or heard as one voice amongst others.

When Oppen began to write again in 1958, shortly before his return to the U.S.A. from his Mexican exile, he did, in one sense, start again where he left off in 1934, for the poems in *The Materials* deal centrally with the relationship between the human, individual and social, and the non-human world. But

155

Oppen's procedures had to be radically different, inasmuch as starting from this point he effectively claimed authorship of the meanings of his earlier work along with the experience and memory of the intervening years. *The Materials* is extensively organized, in a way that *Discrete Series* is not, through co-ordinated thematic centres, and authenticates itself by referring back to a reflective consciousness, however scrupulous and hesitant its voice may be in stating and weighing the internal resistances of its meanings. But what was perhaps crucial in enabling this different beginning was Oppen's recognition of the divergence of the chronologies of the individual organism and the world it lives in, sharpened by the knowledge that under thermo-nuclear threat those chronologies might for once converge and close.

NOTES

1. George Oppen, interview with L. S. Dembo, *Contemporary Literature* X, 2 (1969) 174. See also *Ironwood* 5 (1975), 23.
2. For evidence of Pound's rôle in the 'Objectivists' issue of *Poetry* see Barry Ahearn (ed.), 'Ezra Pound & Louis Zukofsky: Letters 1928–1930', *Montemora* 8 (1981), 149–86.
3. Ezra Pound, *Active Anthology* (London 1933), p. 253.
4. Pound's Preface can now perhaps be more easily found in *Paideuma* 10, 1 (Spring 1981), 13 than in the original issue of *Discrete Series* (New York, 1934). (It was not included in the 1966 Cleveland reprint.)
5. Geoffrey Grigson, 'Baby Mustn't Touch', *New Verse* 9 (June 1934), 22.
6. H. R. Hays, 'Nothing But the Truth', *Hound and Horn* VII, 4 (July: September 1934), 738.
7. This and subsequent quotations from *Discrete Series* are taken from George Oppen, *Collected Poems* (New York, 1975), where they may readily be found on pp. 3–14. No further references will be given.
8. Grigson, loc. cit., 22.
9. William Carlos Williams, 'The New Poetical Economy', *Poetry* XLIV (July 1934), 221.
10. Oppen, interviewed by Dembo, loc. cit., 161.
11. George Oppen, letter to Rachel Blau, November 1965. Quoted in Rachel Blau DuPlessis, 'George Oppen: "What do we believe to live with?" ', *Ironwood* 5 (1975), 65.
12. Louis Zukofsky, letter to Ezra Pound, March 1930. Cited in Tom Sharp, 'George Oppen, *Discrete Series*, 1929–1934', in Burton Hatlen (ed.), *George Oppen: Man and Poet* (Orono, Maine, 1981), p. 271. Zukofsky's

term should be treated with some caution since it is somewhat premature in relation to the eventual shape given to Oppen's writing of 1929–34.

13. Williams's poem was first published in *The Dial* (LXIX, 2) in 1920, but might have been brought to Oppen's attention on its republication in *An 'Objectivists' Anthology*.
14. Bram Dijkstra, *The Hieroglyphics of a New Speech* (Princeton, 1970).
15. Louis Zukofsky, ' "Recencies" in Poetry', in Zukofsky (ed.), *An 'Objectivists' Anthology* (Le Beausset, Var and New York, 1932), p. 22.

Quotations from George Oppen, *Collected Poems*, copyright © 1975 by George Oppen, are reprinted by permission of New Directions Publishing Corporation.

10

The Poet as Archaeologist: Charles Olson's Letters of Origin

by GRAHAM CLARKE

> We must rediscover the structure of the perceived world
> through a process similar to that of an archaeologist. For the
> structure of the perceived world is buried under the sedimenta-
> tions of later knowledge—Merleau-Ponty[1]

> . . . The archaeological discoveries of the past century have
> supplied, directly from the ground, substantive and narrative
> physicality to previously discursive language and thought—
> Charles Olson[2]

1

American literature is full of beginnings and first moments—
of a (so called) adamic innocence seemingly capable of an
endless capacity to figure the possible creation of imagined
new worlds. Charles Olson's poetry (and poetic) digs deep
into this tradition to establish its energies and perspectives;
consistently impelled by its urge to break with Europe, its
object is a poetics of the real wholly reliant upon an American
condition and American space. But if Olson extends American
myth he does so through a radical reassessment of his
American roots. As 'archaeologist of morning' Olson elicits a

privileged pragmatism whose focus is a *world* perspective: a typology of being which at once enacts and transcends American promise. Thus his archaeology is forever extended backwards to a point of origin which, like *Moby-Dick*, is 'pushed back so far' that 'time is turned into space', a space which is itself the field of his projective act: a poetics whose 'metric' is 'mapping'.

Olson, then, is no Whitman who would 'strike up for a new world'. Just as, for Olson, Melville was the 'truer man' so Whitman remains (as he was for Pound) only a tentative ally—representative of a self-declared Americanism certainly, but one whose poetic achieves only a rhetoric of the self held within a compulsive geography of Western metaphor. Where Whitman moves across the continent always 'Facing West from California's shores', so Olson consciously follows Melville and follows him *east*, across space and time into prehistory. As both archaeologist and etymologist Olson's poetic seeks the recovery of a poetic (a 'being') which, for him, has been lost to us since 'at least 450 B.C.'. If in 'The Kingfishers' (an early poem) Olson suggests a beginning culled from his American inheritance, he does so, significantly, as he thinks 'of the E as the stone'—an epsilon carved into a sacred text. Such runic fragments declare his method and focus. The 'E' here is found evidence, a lost ideogram of precisely those verbal energies he would regain. He wants, thus, an *old* not a new America—a recovered language not an imagined alternative. Such a dimension underscores the extent to which he was critical of Williams whose effort, while valuable, 'missed' so much 'by not going behind Sam one Houston'. Olson's time-scale is wholly different and one which in *The Maximus Poems* he would bring to us through 'the first human eyes to look again' since '300,000,000 years ago'. The *Ground* of Olson's recovery is, then, at once millenial and alchemical: a typology of being underlying the attempt to both *re*-create and *re*possess a poetic adequate to the post-modern. He thus mines a 'contrary renaissance', a knowledge ('culture is knowledge'), a 'change of attention' intent on a mythic condition. Thus his declaration: 'I go back as far as I can'; endlessly back in order to release a poetics of the real. His archaeology is, by definition, an active etymology, a grammar

159

whose dynamic wants to be 'equal to the real, itself'.

Olson, then, inherits and rewrites an American poetics—opening his line into what he would see as a *muthologos*[3] of the word. He looks to his beginnings in order to 'make new' lost energies. Words become to him, like the E on the stone, letters of origin to which he would return and, out of the 'present condition of language', restore the experience of 'direct perception'.[4] *Moby-Dick* becomes one aspect of that search for origins and a central text in the displacement of the old 'discourse': the worn product of classical and renaissance civilization. Melville's 'fiery hunt' is a journey into history. As the whaleship becomes machine and Ahab will (power) and ego, so the chase becomes symptom and symbol of the inevitable relationship to nature which such egotism creates. Just as Olson wants to 'wash the ego out', so for him Melville isolated that self and, in tracing it to its origins, forced it to its conclusion. Ahab is, thus, seen as the product of a culture where reason and abstraction, logic and classification hold sway to such a degree that they are seen as leading to a brutal and mechanistic intentionalism: a misplaced power which, held in the destructive myth of individualism, cuts us away from the root, the relationship to nature, which Olson would release. To Olson Ahab's death suggests the 'end' of such individualism and the possibility of a return to an order of being, of creation, which Melville recovers in the Pacific. *Moby-Dick* thus discloses the 'New History' and does so by moving east, not west. As the *Pequod* moves across the Atlantic and into the Indian Ocean, so it signals a journey into past cultural basins. As it pushes through space and time, so it reverses Brooks Adams[5] and, as it were, *destructures* the fixed and fixing moulds of Ahab's eye. *Moby-Dick* thus becomes a text whose process is wholly archaeological: a provisional charting and uncovering of relative orders of knowing, seeing, naming, and of language. In *Call Me Ishmael* this is the direction Olson gives to Melville's epic, seeing it as a voyage of discovery back to a lost order which post-modern man (as American) has again entered. As the movement east displaces the rapacious individualism of the western frontier, so its space transcends history and recovers the Pacific as an 'American' Ocean which stands forth as the central integer of the consciousness to which it points: a flux which is itself 'America's primary'. In Ahab's death Olson reads the end of Ulysses and 'of the archetype of the west to follow'. It is a momentous symbolic event, for with it 'three thousand years went overboard'. Thus the great value for Olson is that *Moby-Dick* gives him 'a pull to the origin of things, the first day, the first man'. Melville's way parallels Olson's in that he 'went back, to discover us, to come forward'. The Pacific, as a 'Symphony',[6] a found unity, is both the text's and America's home: a position which allows Olson to insist that we, too, shall 'call' him Ishmael.

Thus Americans are the 'last first people' who, with the Pacific, 'Square the circle' and bring renaissance man to an end. Olson's history sides with Melville's. As one aspect of his archaeology it elicits an active re-reading of the past in all its terms for just as the whale blasted the *Pequod* so, in 1945, the 'bomb blasted history'[7] and confirmed for Olson the 'new history' he, like Melville, sensed in the Pacific—a return to mythological beginnings: myth as consciousness. Olson's history is that of recovery and, just as he left politics for poetry in the 1940s and rewrote *Ishmael* into what was to become his characteristic prose-style, so he becomes the seeker of that history, that origin, doing what he so praised Herodotus for: '*istorin*'—that is, 'to find out for yourself'.[8] The past thus becomes the site of his archaeology: an enormous map to be traced and dug. As archaeologist he seeks the evidence of a remade and recovered 'mappemunde'[9]: the measured world of *The Maximus Poems*. While, during the '50s and '60s, Olson exacted text after text to define his poetic, so, by *placing* Maximus in Gloucester, Massachusetts, he sought the verbal map of his being and inheritance—intent on the recovered energies of a poetic which would 'Take the natural for base' and, 'out of the slime', create an answer to the blasted word and world of what he saw as the product of a misplaced individualism.

2

The early essays and poems suggest the basis on which such a poetic might develop. 'Projective Verse', 'Human Universe' and 'The Kingfishers', for example, chart the way ahead, announcing their status as *Letters for Origin*. The focus here is consistently a re-statement of an American perspective enmeshed in what, for Olson, is part of a fundamental re-orientation of our relationship to the real. Olson thus insists upon his 'Americanism' but filters it through a discovered and developed field of reference. As American he seeks his 'primary', his past, in the way one of his mentors, Edward Dahlberg[10] did—placing myth over method and, like Lawrence, seeing in the continent an Indian past which itself signalled the dynamic that Olson felt the continent to have inherited. As *Call Me Ishmael* sides with Ishmael, so *Mayan Letters* disclose a complex (if intuitive) anthropological weighing of alternative cultures and histories in which Europe is displaced by a reawakened geography rooted in South West and Central America: an aesthetic which, as it did for Lawrence, spoke to a poetic, an aesthetic, long lost to language.

Olson's method reflects both that aesthetic and his search for its origin. In the poetry especially the alternative 'primary' often creates texts quite baffling to a reader intent on single-willed meanings. Indeed, the difficulties in Olson are precisely, so often, his refusal to adopt a seemingly 'ordered' poetic line or linear argument. Rather, as in Pound's *Cantos*, both prose and poems (as parts of an inclusive *poetic*) inhabit a mutual field of reference and activity: a spatial spreading which, in itself, creates an active map of discovered particles and energies. Words (nouns and verbs) become nodal points in a kinetic process whose 'meaning' asks for an active awareness of all possible directions at once: a maximum intensity and linguistic 'event'. Thus in *The Maximus Poems* the effect is not so much in what is completed as in what is realized: a finding and releasing of relative energies. The named particulars, as found fragments, discover their significance in the plotted measure of a larger 'being'. The poems become a 'geometry of occasions'. Never a 'border of ideas' they exist as a cutting edge of Olson's movement through his world—the tool by which he enters the real, the plotted evidence of his 'hunt among Stones'. Thus he names, digs, and scrapes—always intent on finding the evidence and holding the energy he wants: building the poems from restored denotative fragments; the intense phonemes of an awakened discourse. The prose speaks to this process and declares the poetic as part of an ever-widening field of activity and reference. Thus the 'bibliographies' become part of that act (for example, the *Bibliography on America for Ed Dorn, Proprioception*, and *Pleistocene Man*)—further maps and tracings of the alternative he wants.

And thus Olson's ever-widening effort. In the '60s, particularly, his focus is upon a 'map' far beyond America, just as the intensity and mythic dimension of *The Maximus Poems* moves it beyond the local. The sheer *range* of Olson's references and of figures central to his 'act' extol the mappemonde, the theogony he seeks: 'a total placement of man and things among all possibilities of creation'. Williams and Pound, like Lawrence and Rimbaud, are significant literary figures,[11] but the force of Olson's search, his alchemy, drives him to skid across subject barriers as he pulls allies into his ever-expanding poetic—Webb, Merk, Whorf, Frobenius, Jung, Sauer, Peirce, Merleau-Ponty, Sapir, Heisenberg, and Whitehead for example, all points on his widening base— further evidence of the active archaeology he seeks.[12] Thus he charts a world consciousness: an etymology of word and mind, a poetic compulsive and compendious enough to 'take the earth in under a single review.' Like Williams Olson wants 'by multiplication a reduction to one', an holistic map of his own making the force of which seeks to reground the basis of our relationship to the real. Taken as a single body the poetic offers an ecology of word and mind—a recovery of an order allowing 'A plausible "entry" for . . . man', or, as it were, a re-entry, a *gate* (to use one of Olson's metaphors) back into 'the real'. Thus his search for origins—a poetic whose alembic recalls the word to the continuing insistence of an American poetics (and mythology): what Emerson called 'an original relation to the universe'.[13]

3

Emerson, indeed, underlines the extent to which Olson's projectivism, and his 'theogeny', is so distinctively American. If 'Pound is verse' and Eliot 'the reverend reverse', so *Maximus* declares, in part, Olson's anti-poetic in answer to a European word order anterior to his sense of American meaning. What Olson called 'objectism'[14] is thus part of a continuing Americanist attempt to repossess a poetry of the real. Indeed, Olson's major debt, especially in the 'Projective Verse' essay is not to Pound, Williams or Zukofsky but to Fenollosa whose *The Chinese Written Character as a Medium for Poetry* plots a direct relationship to Emerson's *Nature* which, like Fenollosa (and Olson), gives absolute credence to the status and singularity of *poetic* language as a grammar of process, energy and contact—the origin which is forever the burden of an Americanist poetry.

Olson's archaeology is, then, at once etymological and ontological—a mining of central Americanist concerns wedded to a field of evidence the force of which creates a cosmology of meaning. Olson completes Emerson's ideal poetic figure but does so in the context of what he saw as post-modern man. And yet, in many ways, Olson remains quite essentially Emersonian. Indeed *Nature* remains central to the view of poetic language: a mapping of potential energies whose meaning is, ultimately, a divine presence. The poem seeks that (American) divinity. As 'man' is 'the instrument of definition and the instrument of discovery' so the poem becomes the text of that act: a *sighting* of the world (of 'nature') in all its assumed intensity—its 'being'. The 'eye-view' of Olson (as of *Maximus*) is, like Thoreau's, in search of a 'theology of facts'—a divine kinetic which incarnates a Whiteheadian event into its endless process. Thus Olson's recovery seeks an energy charge of origins—the act of recognition (of meaning) at a moment of original sighting and seeing. Definition and discovery suggest the double axis through which Olson works—as archaeologist and etymologist, as explorer and discoverer, as poet and map-maker. Noun and verb remain integral to the act: a world (and *word*) of objects alive with the energy (and radiance) basic to Olson's eye-view. This is the moment Olson finds so compulsive in *The Maximus Poems*, the first view of the American continent by Juan de la Cosa: an equivalent 'record' to John Smith's map of New England and Winthrop's *periplum*.[15] All remain, in a 'poetic' sense, original acts of knowing—images of simultaneous discovery and definition made by staters of 'quantity and/ precision'.

Hence Olson's reaction against the present state of language as corrupt and empty—lacking the energies of the 'real', the *force* of a natural world. As American he seeks his primary, an American lexicon cleaned of sediment. As he wrote to the German poet, Rainer Gerhardt, his primer is a reader of the real—a language (supposedly) free of social and historical contingents. Unlike the collapsing towers of *The Waste Land* or the willed silence of *Four Quartets* Olson's area of activity (as American) is an alternative to ennui and alienation. Thus his advice to Gerhardt:

> Come here [to America]
> where we will welcome you
> with nothing but what is, with
> no useful allusions, with no birds
> but those we stone, nothing to eat
> but ourselves, no end and no beginning, I assure you, yet
> not at all primitive, living as we do in a space we do not
>   need to contrive.[16]

Olson's perspectives are not those of Gerhardt's Europe but part of a regained consciousness through which Olson achieves his right of primogeniture. Indeed, part of Olson's millenial perspective is a world etymology—a return to a possible language capable of naming and enacting the 'original' meaning of a radiant America. As part of that process he fights history as one kind of disease. Just as in *Paterson* Williams seeks a root, a beginning, and, in the *Cantos* Pound wants a 'paradiso terrestre' freed from the 'greased slide' of a corrupted language, so Olson seeks a cleansed and active vocabulary. Pound, of course, went to the Chinese ideogram as part of his attempt to purify the 'language of the tribe', just as Williams wanted 'no ideas but in things' as part of his return to the 'radiant gist' of an animated world. Olson, in turn, goes to the Mayan hieroglyph, to Hittite and Sumerian cultures and, above all, to the Hopi Indians who (via the theory of the American linguist Benjamin Lee Whorf)[17] are seen as offering 'useful freshening of syntax'. Such language patterns offer him further evidence of the original letters he seeks, the 'original minting of words and syntax': an active recovery whose force is, for him, magical.

Always Olson is insistent on a purifying act: washing his

words as part of the return to a fresh and intensive denotative (but active) language. In 'Human Universe' his concern with the word is, again, similar to Emerson's. Thus we have lived in a 'generalizing time'—language has lost its 'true' function and leaked away the energy of the 'instant'. Olson would establish a poetic whose language stays close to the 'thing' within its energy field (a grammar equivalent to Heisenberg's view of energy and mass). To Olson this is the great strength of primitive language patterns—patterns which underlie the advantage of an 'American' alternative to the European and Classical traditions. From the Greeks (pre-eminently Aristotle and Plato) we have, for Olson, inherited a false discourse—a language of abstraction and description which, like Ahab, creates an order of the world dependent upon logic and classification. Against this Olson wants to regain his 'primary' and restore poetic language to its central status as enacting medium of a 'human universe'. He wants 'word writing not idea writing'. His insistence on a phenomenal world is part of his concern to recover a grammar of the real: a discourse whose kinetic 'does not seek to describe but to enact'. Instead of the old order of will, power and state he wants a poetic representative of an *humilitas*—an Ishmaelian right reason. This is both a *virtu* and a *claritas* (all Olson's terms)—a balanced language whose denotative function is simultaneous verb and noun. This is the basis of a poetry of 'direct perception'. The world is *seen* as a creation whose 'harmony' is 'post-logical' as 'is the order of any created thing'. The poem is, then, part of a wider cosmology—what Olson understood as 'creation as a structure'. A world of clean edges and, like Blake's, of hard lines: an 'energy box' of original energies.

This, once again, brings Olson close to Emerson's view of a healthy language. Consistently Americanist poetry has been concerned with a cleansing of the word, with a purifying vivification as part of an imagined 'freeing' process from the restraints, delusions and rhetoric of a corrupt European State. Puritanism is part of that inheritance, as is Transcendentalism. The political and social is purged in favour of a direct relationship between self and thing, word and object (as mass *and* energy), eye and land, and poem and God (the real). Here language is never artifice nor can it remain an object of man.

Olson's insistence on origins is, indeed, part of that cleansing, seeking the original moment of naming: the spoken act (ideally) anterior to the spoken word as written form, as history in which man will corrupt and defile it so that language lies. Olson's poetic, in contrast, is part of a poetic intent on 'letting the song lie/ in the thing itself'. When Emerson argues that 'The corruption of man is followed by the corruption of language', he emphasizes this basic concern for the purifying act and a sense of poetic language as a sanctified discourse. Thus for Emerson 'wise men pierce this rotten diction and fasten words again to visible things'. The poet here is 'the sayer, the namer', and 'the language maker'. As such 'every word was once a poem' and 'The Etymologist finds the deadest word to have been once a brilliant picture. Language is fossil poetry.' In its healthy clean state 'all language is vehicular and transitive.'[18]

Olson (like Emerson's ideal poet) would recover that brilliance, that *radiance* and freshness. Indeed part of the archaeology of *The Maximus Poems* is the naming and mapping of a Gloucester which yields, more and more, a sacred and divine world. Language is, thus, redemptive and restorative— a circuit of energy whose primary enacts the real. This is, once again, part of Olson's advantage as American and New Englander.[19] If the recovery is not achieved and the energy of origins wasted, then

> the present will lose what America is the inheritor of: a secularization which not only loses nothing of the divine but by seeing process in reality redeems all idealism fr[om]   theocracy or mobocracy. . . .[20]

And thus Olson's sense of the primitive—a language of process which seeks the source of its occasion. It is

> the replacement of the classical—representational by the *primitive—abstract.* . . . I mean of course not at all primitive in that stupid use of it as opposed to civilized. One means it now as 'primary', as how one finds anything, pick it up as one does now—fresh/first.[21]

Once again a language of origins and contact: one that will 'hew' to experience 'as it is'. The 'primitive' is a lead into a ('secularized') divine: at once Whiteheadian process and

Heideggerian being. If we follow Olson's reading of Melville this is where *Moby-Dick* leads us—into a speculative cosmology intent on an ungraspable 'other', an original moment before 'the unhappy consciousness of history'. Olson's poetic language is, in the end, a sacred diction—a discourse 'equal to the real itself' but seeking the 'wondrous' depths' and 'unspeakable foundations' of the cosmos. Such is the 'mythological present' Melville discloses and Olson defines: not the inversions and vacuities of *The Confidence-Man* but a restored world based on trust in the word as a regained commodity—what Olson calls in *The Maximus Poems* 'an actual earth of value'. Language must thus 'Lie in a world on an Earth like this one we/ few American poets have/ carved out of Nature and God.' Not the lies of a false grammar but the achieved passivity of a 'divine inert': the centre of a sacred continuum. Olson's *Anima Mundi*.

4

This is the active process of *The Maximus Poems*, Olson's epic poem which, building upon *Paterson* and the *Cantos*,[22] inscribes his poetic into a realized locale in order to make it yield its wonder: the creation of a text whose centre reaches the 'divine inert' of a cosmology which is itself the muthologos of the American poem. Maximus, the poem's persona, seeks the divine through the restoration of an eye-view: an original sighting of American as clear and fresh as Smith's. In part by *placing* the poem in Gloucester, Massachusetts, Olson sets up a locale of interpretations: between sea and land, fishermen and landsmen, discoverers and settlers, heroes and villains, process and fixity which opens out into an inclusive image of an American and world condition—the state, as it were, we all inhabit. Through the local Olson seeks his alternative 'universal' in that 'it was the earth all the time I was after.' The poem enters Gloucester as both geography and history, with Maximus seeking a restoration of the human house: a polis based on an original condition. As the poem develops so the three volumes establish (and achieve) an ever-deepening inscription of the locale as a totality, a *cosmology* upon which Olson is intent. Thus the search for an original eye and word takes place within a perspective where 'the world/ is an eternal event and this epoch solely/ the decline of fishes.'

Indeed, the covers of the three volumes speak to this development. The first, a literal map of Gloucester (as land and sea); the second a map of Gondwanaland; and the third a *periplum* of the Massachusetts coast drawn by John Winthrop. All speak to a history of the earth and eye—the map as history and geography, the trace of our eye's view over and through 'nature'. *Maximus* develops an ever inclusive and expansive verbal map—moving from its Poundian foundations into an order of myth and mappemonde where Gloucester stands forth as a revealed and recovered cosmology: 'creation as a structure'. To map the area is thus to bring it into being via a poetic where 'image is knowing, and/ knowing, confucius says, brings one/ to the goal.'

The goal is what Olson finds in a fellow (nineteenth-century) Gloucester artist, Fitz Hugh Lane, whose luminist paintings of the area offer Olson an image of 'the mathematic of the Creation surrounding us'. What Lane does with the painted image, so Olson would do with the word—redeeming it as a point of contact and revelation with that mathematic. Thus Maximus inhabits a land of loss and cheapness. The inhabitants of Gloucester are 'estranged from that which is most familiar'. They cannot see to see. Maximus, through his letters, will restore that sight as he will restore the word: grounding both in place, in contact with the compulsive and sacred geography of an original America. Language, thus, has been cheapened, flattened out and emptied of meaning. It surrounds the people, defines and prescribes their limits as a bankrupt and corrosive structure. 'Words' have been 'adver-tised out' with newsprint, 'Tell-A-Vision' and 'mu-sick' as part of the 'greased ways/ of the city now'. America has become a 'pejorocracy', its 'nascent capitalism' and 'mer-cantilism' redolent of a commerce whose commodity is 'trash,/ industrial fish/ are called which Gloucester/ now catches'. Man is an 'ugliness and bore' surrounded by 'filth and lumber'. Maximus fights this condition, finding in explorers, fishermen, and carpenters figures of like *humilitas* and *virtu*: balanced eyes which admit that 'The light of the body is the eye, let it be clear.' They thus offer exemplary acts of the kind

Olson wants where 'The Real/ is always worth the act of/ lifting it, treading it/ to be clear, to make it/ clear. . . .'

Consistently Olson seeks a return to a clarity and purity as he wants a Gloucester untouched, untrammelled except by the *eye* for 'the newness/ the first men knew was almost/ from the start dirtied/ by second comers.' It is thus that he is archaeologist of the area, seeking a return to 'Lane's eye-view of Gloucester' which is also a 'Phoenician eye-view': a sighting 'equal to the real', at once divine and active. Thus *The Maximus Poems* open up to a dimension essentially mythological—inscribing earth sky, and sea into a complex of felt and seen energies. Thus 'backwards I compare/ Gloucester/ to yield'—back to a language of the pure and intense, the double axis of definition and discovery in which the divine inert (and the archaeological past) is held. In the third volume of the poem this mythology is announced, finally, in relation to an ideal world: 'the sky,/ of Gloucester/ perfect bowl/ of land and sea'. So Maximus moves to 'the brilliance/ earth': a poetic language of the kind Emerson announced. The earth 'shines' in a radiance where all is energy and all is divine: the 'Golden life, golden light on western harbor'. Gloucester becomes a city, a *land* of recovered light equal to Winthrop's ideal. The poet, so to speak, arrives home and reaches his archaeological object:

> On my back the
> Harbor and over it the long arm'd shield of Eastern
> point. Wherever I turn or look in whatever direction,
> and near me, on any quarter, all possible combinations of
> Creation. . . .

This is Olson's divine condition: a recovered 'creation' and language of the real, of energy and light. Olson thus extends Emerson's (American) grammar into an archaeological dimension. He wants, like Melville, the original *letters* of his condition, just as poet (and Gloucester postman) he is always the letter carrier. The effort, in the end, it seems to me, is enormous: a realized world which recalls American poetry to its primary. If 'projectivism' is a myth, it is so in the mainstream of central American ideals. Its force, nonetheless, extends that myth into a world dimension: a sacred energy made alive and spoken from its inscribed place on the page.

The Poet as Archaeologist: Charles Olson's Letters of Origin

Thus Olson's letters of origin are centrally American. If the ideal image is a compulsive passivity, it is equally active, ultimately transcendent and impossible. But always, for Olson, the *act* (the effort) was the thing. He offers lines of direction rather than completed meanings—doors into the ideal condition he would enter: the artistry and 'syllabary' [23] of 'How to dance sitting down' or 'to lift an arm flawlessly'. In *Maximus*, as in all Olson's writing, 'so there is, signs of this awakening'.

NOTES

1. *The Primacy of Perception*, ed. J. M. Edie (Northwestern, 1964), p. 5.
2. *Additional Prose*, ed. George F. Butterick (Bolinas, 1974), p. 50.
3. For a discussion of the meaning of this term for Olson see George Butterick's *A Guide to the Maximus Poems of Charles Olson* (Berkeley, 1980), pp. 146 and 147. Any essay on the work of Olson must be provisional. In recent years a number of full-length studies have been published, e.g. P. Christensen, *Call Him Ishmael* (Austin and London, 1979); Sherman Paul, *Olson's Push* (Baton Rouge and London, 1978); and Robert Von Hallberg's *Charles Olson: The Scholar's Art* (Harvard, 1979). See also Don Byrd's *Charles Olson's Maximus* (Urbana and London, 1980). Of the essays *Boundary II*, a special Olson issue, still contains a number of important pieces (Fall 73/Winter 74, State University of New York).
4. See 'Human Universe'. The *Selected Writings*, ed. Robert Creeley (New Directions, 1966), is still a good introductory text.
5. That is the theory propounded by Adams in *The New Empire* where the movement of civilizations 'west' parallels the rise and fall of commercial areas based on land and sea routes. The *Pequod* reaches the Pacific via the Indian Ocean. In *Mayan Letters* (London, 1968), p. 89, Olson recommends *The New Empire* 'for the scope of its trade-and-money story . . .'.
6. The title, of course, of Chapter 132 of *Moby-Dick* which is itself a 'coming together' in a harmonious interlude. For a fuller discussion of Olson's relationship to Melville see Ann Charters, *Olson/Melville: A Study of Affinity* (Berkeley, 1968).
7. This, according to Fielding Dawson, is what Olson said in 1951 during one of his lectures at Black Mountain College. See Dawson's *The Black Mountain Book* (New York, 1970), p. 94. For the background to Black Mountain see Martin Duberman, *Black Mountain: An Experiment in Community* (London, 1974).

8. For a discussion of the value of Herodotus and his *Method* to Olson (i.e. '*istorin*', 'finding out for oneself') see *The Special View of History* (Berkeley, 1970), pp. 19–21. See also Olson's review 'It Was. But It Ain't' in *Human Universe and Other Essays* (New York, 1967), pp. 141–43, where the method of Herodotus is contrasted to that of Thucydides.

9. In *The Maximus Poems* (Volume 2) Olson says that 'I am making a mappemunde. It is to include my being.'

10. See, for example, Dahlberg's *Do These Bones Live* (1941).

11. 'Pound and Lawrence more and more stand up as the huge two of the 1st half of the 20th century . . .' *Letters for Origin* (New York, 1970), p. 63.

12. See *A Guide To The Maximus Poems of Charles Olson* and, for example, *A Bibliography on America for Ed Dorn* in *Additional Prose* (California, 1974).

13. See Emerson's 'Introduction' to *Nature*.

14. Olson uses this in the 'Projective Verse' essay to distinguish 'objectism' from the 'objectivism' of, for example, Williams and Zukofsky. Williams quoted at length from the essay in his *Autobiography*.

15. See, for example, 'On First Looking out Through Juan de la Cosa's Eyes' (*Maximus* Volume One) and 'Captain John Smith' in *Human Universe and Other Essays* (New York, 1967) pp. 131–34.

16. See 'To Gerhardt, There Amongst Europe's Things'.

17. The central essay by Whorf for Olson is 'An American Indian Model of the Universe'. See *Language, Thought and Reality* (Cambridge, Mass., 1956) and *The Special View of History*, pp. 23–4.

18. See Emerson's *Nature* and *The Poet*.

19. In *Letters for Origin* (p. 127) Olson speaks of himself and other American poets (Robert Creeley, for example) as 'New Englanders' who are part of a 'landgeist which has now, again, reasserted itself . . .'.

20. See *Additional Prose* (*Proprioception*), p. 26.

21. 'Letter to Elaine Feinstein' in *The New American Poetry*, ed. Donald M. Allen (New York, 1960), p. 398. The 'letter' is important for Olson's sense of 'archaeology'.

22. In *The Mayan Letters* Olson refers to Williams and Pound as 'halves'. See pages 26–31.

23. See Olson's 'A Syllabary for a Dancer' in *Maps*, No. 4, 1971.

Quotations from Charles Olson, *Selected Writings*, copyright © 1951, 1953, 1959, 1960, 1965, 1966 by Charles Olson, are reprinted by permission of Jonathan Cape, Publishers, and New Directions Publishing Corporation.

11

J. V. Cunningham's Roman Voices

by JACK HILL

In 1970 a 722-page anthology of twentieth-century American poetry was published. It was well-received, Robert Lowell going so far as to aver that it was 'Not only the best of its period, I think, but is even perhaps safe from the competition of rivals'—a view which, not surprisingly, is now the front-cover blurb for my eighth impression. What first caught my attention though, as intended, was its title (a line from Wallace Stevens), *The Voice That Is Great Within Us*, which is by any standards an uncompromising value-judgement, the phrasing of which sounds a trifle oddly in the European ear. The anthology is, as far as I can judge, a useful one, but the title does, I think, deftly twin two of the tendencies of American poetry at its worst, and the two which the best American poets have striven (not always successfully) to avoid: the fraudulently biblical, and the daemon solipsistic.

The former, afflicting Whitman at his worst and others nearly all the time, depends heavily on the cadences of the King James Bible, with Swinburne hovering in the wings, dispenses with logical connectives in favour of the aggregative 'and', and is, depending on personal bent, theological pre-dilection, and the accident of history, alternately millenarian, messianic, or apocalyptic in tone (the 'And-I-Saw-The-Mushroom-Cloud-In-the-Supermarket-And-Duluth-Was-A-Blinding-White-Flower' ploy). The latter offers a series of personal statements juxtaposed with historical analogues, dispenses with logical connectives in favour of the blunt phrase or clause, and leaves the reader to infer an extreme psychological tension in the poet, his family, his city, his times, youth, wives (especially these) and friends (boozy evenings shared but now dead, the bourbon and the car-crash). ('My mother cold-eyed, plucks chickens in the yard. I once saw Grandpa cry. George, Princeton '22, napoleons round the ward.') Great inner torment struggles to be revealed, and the wrath of the son of man (or Peleus) is externalized not in a battle with a cross or Trojan, but in confession to the psychiatric page.

One might come close to a stylistic characterization of the two voices by adapting the famous antithesis, formulated by Erich Auerbach,[1] of hypotactic *versus* paratactic: the psychotic writer offers degenerate hypotaxes, where the argumentative logics are submerged into jagged contrasts, while the apocalyptic chants his rite; the classical historian's analysis becomes the New Englander's analyst, the Frisco rhapsode incants a Pacific astrology, and the Boston Strangler stares suspiciously at Manson across the creative writing class.

Many American poets are still fighting out an intellectual battle between two of the great cities of antiquity, Jerusalem and Athens, between 'Worship Jehovah' and 'Know thyself', egged on by, in opposite corners, the rabbi and the shrink, and the 2,000 years of companionable war between Saint Peter and Saint Paul, the Hebrew and the Hellene, now have their battle-lines somewhere in the mid-West (Iowa, perhaps?).

The voice that seldom sounds is the voice of the third great city of Mediterranean antiquity, Rome (oddly, one thinks, in view of the grip which the Roman republic held on the imaginations of the early American politicians, but less oddly when one reflects that the greatest Roman poets were imperial protégés, with the exceptions of Catullus, whom propriety, and Lucretius, whom piety, excluded from the puritan mind).

The Roman voice, uttering its close-woven language, tends towards the lapidary, the epigrammatic. It distrusts the paradisal, for had not Rome acquired great power and wealth while still leaving the Roman subject to violence, fear, lust and hangovers? Its love-poetry is sharp, knowing, passionate, but realistic; its lovers are clearly defined both in their beauty and in their imperfections, for the Romans believed neither in the perfectibility of the individual nor in the ecstatic contemplation of the individual's guilt. Each person was original, but not an original sinner. All were fools, some wicked; and to ask a beautiful body to provide a simulacrum of infinity or a solution to the problems of history and personality was a silly way of preventing the body from providing what it could provide, namely a thoroughly pleasant evening, often rendered more sharply enjoyable by the inevitable preliminary difficulties. To express this the Roman began not in paradox, that Christian mode, but in epigram, the short poem in short lines, and Cunningham, almost alone among American writers of this century, is an epigrammatist, having written more than a hundred of them. (Even his sequence on driving westward *To What Strangers, What Welcomes* is a set of short poems in short lines, and such a topos does not usually stir the American writer to brevity either of whole or unit.)

Among his epigrams there are first the good simple jokes, as in No. 68:

> *Arms and the man I sing*, and sing for joy,
> Who was last year all elbows and a boy.

The neat, brisk metre takes Cunningham here closer to Ogden Nash than to Martial, but the double mockery of the Roman hero and the adolescent is effective enough. In No. 42, however, we are on different ground:

> Soft found a way to damn me undefended:
> I was forgiven who had not offended.

A sharp formulation of a peculiarly obnoxious form of moral hypocrisy acquires an added complexity from the world-weary cadence of the feminine rhyme. The characteristically Latin separation of the relative clause from the nominative pronoun gives a legal formality and inevitability, the sense that the poet is summing up once what has often happened before, and will as often recur. And the scansion of the second line moves us forcibly out of a potential pastiche of English Augustanism into Roman muscle, consisting as it does of dactyl and trochee (the end of a hexameter), followed by pyrrhic, spondee and trochee again:

175

/ ˘ ˘ / ˘ | ˘ ˘ / / / ˘
I was forgiven | who had not offended.

In No. 49 we are back to iambs, but to Cunningham's favourite octosyllabic iambs, favoured also by seventeenth-century epigrammatists:

> Lip was a man who used his head.
> He used it when he went to bed
> With his friend's wife, and with his friend,
> With either sex at either end.

Stripped of the connotations which are liberatedly hyped into the vocabulary normally chosen to glamourize such coitions, these plain words combine with the comic relentlessness of the metre to expose the activity (the fashion, one might add) as absurd, mechanistic and vulgar. The tone is not repelled and fascinated, but aloof, amused, and contemptuous: in a word, aristocratic.

The best of Cunningham's epigrams succeed because of this neat bluntness, this inscriptional quality involved in the meaning of the Greek word *epigramma*, a short verse written on tombstones or votive offerings. The form combines with astute social and self-knowledge to present a final judgement, a usually humorous summing-up of those inescapable limitations of human life which always underlie the human being's sexual or moral posturings:

> Jove courted Danäe with golden love,
> But you're not Danäe, and I'm not Jove. (No. 4)

or

> This humanist whom no beliefs constrained
> Grew so broad-minded he was scatter-brained. (No. 43)

or

> You ask me how Contempt who claims to sleep
> With every woman that has ever been
> Can still maintain that women are skin deep?
> They never let him any deeper in. (No. 62)

Since this style is destructive of hyperbole, of the glorious mendacity which is the very essence of other more opulent modes, it does not easily allow the broad evocative sweep, the

176

bravura gesture. The lyric can encompass it, for song, however far removed from incantation, still moves us away from general social knowledge towards individual inspiration. The epigram does not, and when Cunningham injudiciously tries to mix the two forms, the result is unhappy:

> This garish and red cover made me start.
> I who amused myself with quietness
> Am here discovered. In this flowery dress
> I read the wild wallpaper of my heart. (No. 14)

Our discovery is more, and less, than the poet intended. Even worse, since more is at stake, is:

> I had gone broke, and got set to come back,
> And lost, on a hot day and a fast track,
> On a long shot at long odds, a black mare
> By Hatred out of Envy by Despair. (No. 55)

The conceit is laboured, the rhythm, all-too-obviously setting up the last line, banal, and the sentiment both hyperbolic and commonplace. The personifications give a general wash of indulgent gloom rather than information, and in the facile chiaroscuro of pseudo-Romantic agony the epigrammatist's knowledgeable hauteur and humour are quite lost. Not only does the form demolish its content, as in the preceding poem, but one pose destroys another—Gibbon cannot be Poe, especially in four lines. (The only man who successfully fuses the two is Byron, and then only in very long poems.)

This is not to say that the epigram cannot be tender, or sad; its first function was elegiac, and when Cunningham writes his own epitaph, he correctly blends an almost seventeenth-century octosyllabic wit with a half-proud resignation:

> When I shall be without regret
> And shall mortality forget,
> When I shall die who lived for this,
> I shall not miss the things I miss.
> And you who notice where I lie
> Ask not my name. It is not I.

The 'this' in line 3 may refer either to poetry or to the general condition of being alive or to the skill which has gone into the writing of this very poem, but the non-specificity is a source of strength, not weakness. Cunningham is writing an American *exegi monumentum*, where he asserts that what Ovid called the 'better part' of him is not limited by the body, the grave, or the epitaph, but survives in what may be known of his life, and what he has written. Horace asserted that he would not wholly die (*'non omnis moriar'*), Ovid that the better part of him would live, and Ronsard demanded that his name survive almost as a natural phenomenon:

> *Et voyant mon pays, a peine pourra croire*
> *Que d'un si petit champ Ronsard se vante ne.*

But Cunningham's crisp finale asserts the value of a life and a metier, a value which has nothing to do with name or with survival, though it obviously hopes for the latter. And the conventions of the Greek epitaph (the passing stranger, the chosen anonymity), scrupulously observed, root the poem in a deep historical awareness of the poetic tradition (the metier) to which the individual is indeed important, but strictly speaking incidental, just as a link is a constituent but not a definition of a chain. It is a fully classical poem.

In many of his (slightly) longer poems, Cunningham begins from epigram. For example, in 'For My Contemporaries' he opens with a brilliant one,

> How time reverses
> The proud in heart!
> I now make verses
> Who aimed at art.

successfully binding self-mockery and general satire. But the wry and sharp-edged stance cannot, if it is to succeed, be mistaken for that very unaristocratic posture, disappointed pique. And in the next stanzas the poet, although expressing an understandable distaste for the vulgar rhodomontade of some of his contemporaries, falls into vulgarity himself:

> But I sleep well.
> Ambitious boys
> Whose big lines swell
> With spiritual noise,

Despise me not,
And be not queasy
To praise somewhat:
Verse is not easy.

The lines about the ambitious boys are meant to sound *as*
empty as the boys' own poems, but they just sound bad-
tempered, and the queasy/easy rhyme is itself queasy,
especially as Cunningham here is asking for praise, which is
not a gentlemanly thing to do. And the slickness of the last
stanza expresses not a precisely-poised balance of knowledge
and wit, but ungentlemanly self-satisfaction:

But rage who will.
Time that procured me
Good sense and skill
Of madness cured me.

In another poem, 'The Predestined Space', however,
Cunningham brings off a technical tour-de-force, using an
only slightly longer stanza to express the identical operations
of human behaviour, theology and the craft of the poet.

Simplicity assuages
With grace the damaged heart,
So would I in these pages
If will were art.

But the best engineer
Of metre, rhyme, and thought
Can only tool each gear
To what he sought

If chance with craft combines
In the predestined space
To lend his damaged lines
Redeeming grace.

The basic premise of the poem is that fallen man may
occasionally express a perfection which he cannot perform—or,
in other more secular words, that language may realize
potentials outside the scope of action, the works of imagination
thereby surpassing those of reality. Such occasional perfected
expression may not be achieved by 'will' but by craft and

179

chance which combine to add aesthetic grace to the bare form, just as the grace of God redeems the damaged heart from sterile predestination. The repetition of the adjective 'damaged', applied to both 'heart' and 'lines', associates them inextricably together, just as repetition of the adjective 'green' in Marvell's 'The Garden' inter-identifies 'thought' and 'shade', though Cunningham risks a much bigger gap between the doubled epithet than Marvell. This repetition beautifully sets up and reinforces the final splendid *double-entendre* of 'grace' (aesthetic and theological) and the silky perfection of rhythm and rhyme in the last stanza gives an optimistic certainty which refutes the tentative opening with the conditional 'If'. The argument (fundamentally syllogistic) harks back both to mediaeval Christianity and to the English poets of the seventeenth century, but Cunningham goes further than either for he is not reworking a simple syllogism ('Had we but world. . . . But. . . . Therefore. . . . Thus') or refuting a proposition (as Aquinas refutes, for example, in the *Summa contra Gentiles* the proposition that happiness consists in the practice of art[2]): his poem is asserting that identical logical (and hence inescapable) processes inhere in the creation of a poem and in the operancy of grace. And the clear, formal stanza is the only form which can enact this. Just as a Shakespearean hyperbole may express an over-reaching vision which neither the actor's human physique nor the details of plot can embody, or as a Petrarchan oxymoron may express the simultaneous co-existence of emotional antitheses which resists reasonable formulation, so may the neat verse, with the 'exclusions' of its rhymes, express the inevitable certainty of rational process—granted A, therefore B, if C. It is a Latin way, more Christian and Catholic than Augustan and Horatian, but Latin nonetheless.

Again using a blend of theological and literary vocabulary, though less successfully, Cunningham[3] admits to scepticism of

> the new
> Regenerate elect
> Who take the social view
> And zealously reject

J. V. Cunningham's Roman Voices

> The classic indignation
> The sullen clarity
> Of passions in their station
> Moved by propriety.

But his classic-Christian disbelief in the natural virtue of humankind saves him from facile whatever-is-is-rightery; the clarity is sullen, and the indignation may be classic but is still indignant. Faced with eternal verities, and Cunningham believes in them, innovation is rash:

> The hot flesh and passionless mind
> In fancy's house must still abide
> Each share the work, its share defined
> By caution under custom's guide.[4]

And literary education provides, he points out gently but firmly,[5] neither a *modus vivendi* nor a scrutiny of self, but a trade:

> For you have learned not what to say
> But how the saying must be said.

Cunningham in many quotations and references, more deeply in his selection of forms (and, one should add, in his translations from Latin), acknowledges his roots. (One of his most unfashionable lines—'Radical change, the root of human woe'—must be that rarity in a modern poet, an opinion which would attract nods of approbation from Horace, Saint Jerome and Burke.)

He rarely quotes from non-Latin writers, and it is odd that in one of his early poems[6] he should mention Beardsley and Dowson, characterizing them in these lines

> Their verse, sepulchral, breathes
> A careless scent of flowers in late July,
> Too brief for pleasure, though its pleasure lie
> In skilled inconscience of its brevity.

The words offer a kindly critical appraisal of the feel of '90s' poetry, but they also refer both in matter and manner to a whole long tradition of lyric verse, itself defined less by form than by one of its dominant topoi—*carpe diem*. Awareness of the evanescence of pleasure may destroy pleasure, but may also sharpen it, as the sharpness of form of the best *carpe diem*

181

writers deepens the reader's pleasure both emotionally (this delight is the more to be loved since it is short) and aesthetically (so much said in so little). The apparent contradiction of the phrase, 'skilled inconscience', contains, beneath the criticism of Dowson, both the effortless ease of the skilled technician and the poise, the *sprezzatura*, of the knowledgeable and fashionable man of the world. And since this poem is being addressed by one poet to another about their predecessors, we may legitimately infer that these qualities are important to him. (It might also be pointed out that as the poem was written in the early '30s, its apparently anachronistic references and opinions are in fact polemic.)

But the phrase itself, 'skilled inconscience', takes us further into another aspect of Cunningham's classicism. The late J. B. Leishman[7] pointed out that one of the important strands of a certain type of classical verse, and one which unites writers as chronologically distant as Horace and Marvell, is a kind of witty play. But this witty 'play' is not merely frivolous, but a manifestation (one might also say a re-enactment) of that condition of mind when the creative intellect, emancipated from the doings of the mundane world (what Shakespeare called 'all these'), is able to form those imaginative insights which are given by such meditative freedom into a delightful artifice. It is the result of *otium* rather than of *negotium*, and may only be expressed by wit in the Renaissance sense (the surprising but irresistible formulation of a novel imaginative insight in a melodious but sequential form). It is, through humour, removed from the narrowly personal, and a precondition of its success is a quick awareness of the true, as opposed to the apparent (daily or conventional), importance of things. (Among other scholars Huizinga,[8] Rahner[9] and Levin[10] have written on this theme at length.) The witty delight is achieved not *despite* but *through* the acceptance of rule, just as delight (and the only possible efficiency) in a game of rugby or bridge is expressed through a sequence of accepted limitations. Such 'play' does not mean that the poet is bound to be a comedian, though he must have many of the comedian's qualities, and it does not mean that he cannot write of unhappiness and failure; it does mean that jokes shall be economically phrased and timed, and it also means that the unhappinesses shall not ramble, but be checked by the same proprieties of expression as the jokes. In other words, both the form and the style transmit grief as a facet of sanity, not as a periphrasis of *in*sanity. The psychiatric ward may be the setting for an egocentric memoir, which we may agree for the purposes of convention to call a poem, but the quatrain, octosyllable and sonnet are better settings for a definition of life. Only the brake makes the efficient car, just as only the rules of play enable personal feeling to be expressive of general truth. And only a sane man may simultaneously receive into his consciousness both immediate personal feeling and an objective awareness of its relative importance in history and scale. Cunningham always adopts that most classical and difficult of postures, and the one without which very little truly great verse can be written: that of the sane adult writing for an audience of equals. The general truths, the *sententiae*, are newly present, and must emerge neither from obediently followed commonplace nor from an illogical novelty, for the sane and educated reader can spot both; and the reader's good eyesight, just as much as the difficulty of the stanza, is one of the constituent difficulties of the classical poet, which he has to accept, with (one hopes) both pleasure and success.

As Petronius points out,[11] the poet must

> take care that his sententiae do not seem to detach themselves from the body of his discourse, but that they shine like colours which have been woven into garments.

Cunningham's entire poetic output seems to obey, or at its worst unsuccessfully to try to obey, Petronius's rule. Stanzas and whole poems are organized so that the final statement or sententia, whether it be literary heir to the Romans or to the English metaphysical wits, emerges as naturally as the colours shine from a garment. His last lines often seem like quotations, though they seldom are, partly because of the precision of phrasing, and partly because, as one reads the poem as a whole, they seem to be arrived at by a process of indisintricable logic. Here are a few examples:

Your mute voice on the crystal embers flinging.

Nor live curiously
Cheating providence.

Naked you lie in an unknown grave.

Love's wilful potion
Veils the ensuing,
And brief commotion.

And David equally with Venus
Has no penis.

Was it unforgivable,
My darling, that you loved me?[12]

Through the arguments, the rhymes, and the play, exercised for neither therapy nor reward

Insight flows into my pen
I know nor fear nor haste.
Time is my own again.
I waste it for the waste.[13]

a cannily ancient voice is heard. It needs and accepts drink, sex, travel and art, but never mistakes them for absolutes, or avers that the pleasures and pains they bring are themselves absolute. It does not believe that in the acts of enjoying and speaking about these pleasures any grand gestures should be struck, or, using a less virile participle than struck, pirouetted. It distrusts statistics as much as ecstasies:

Error is boundless
Nor hope nor doubt,
Though both be groundless
Will average out.[14]

It mocks itself. It depends not on sensuousness for its effect, but on a knowledge of sensuousness's bounds. It is logical, partly Christian. It is sometimes stoic, more often epicurean. It is humorously resigned to the limitations of man's small pleasures, but also knows that the limitations of pleasure do not stop it from being pleasurable:

J. V. Cunningham's Roman Voices

Reader goodbye. While my associates
Redeem the world in moral vanity
Or live in the casuistry of an affair
I shall go home: bourbon and beer at five,
Some money, some prestige, some love, some sex,
My input and my output satisfactory.[15]

Despite the references to bourbon, cars and Montana, this voice comes from Rome—or if not from Rome as it was, from Rome as it was understood by Horace and Ovid, by Saint Thomas Aquinas, and by the wits of the seventeenth century.

I do not consider Cunningham a great poet, though I am sure he has written poems such as the world will not willingly let die. It might seem strange to set him in a tradition which includes Horace, Ronsard, Shakespeare and Marvell. But we should make our judgements in comparison with what Matthew Arnold called 'the glorious company of the best', and I believe that Cunningham himself would require, indeed demand, such comparisons. And it is only by a continual reference to the classics, whether of antiquity or of our own vernacular tradition, that poets and critics may avoid becoming provincial in their judgements. If wit, poise, sadness, clarity and shape are the virtues of Roman verses and voices at their best, and I believe they are, then at *his* best Cunningham is a classic.

NOTES

1. *Mimesis* (Princeton, 1968), pp. 71 *et seq.*
2. Cunningham discusses Marvell, the syllogism, and mediaeval logic in his 'Logic and Lyric', reprinted in *Tradition and Poetic Structure* (Denver, 1960).
3. 'The Symposium'.
4. 'Fancy'.
5. 'To a Friend on her Examination for the Doctorate in English'.
6. 'Obsequies for a Poetess'.
.7. In *On Translating Horace* (Oxford, 1956).
8. In *Homo Ludens* (London, 1949).
9. In *Man at Play* (London, 1963).
10. In *The Myth of the Golden Age in the Renaissance* (London, 1968).

11. '*Praeterea curandum est ne sententiae emineant extra corpus orationis expressae, sed intexto vestibus colore niteant*', *Satiricon* CXVIII, quoted and translated by Leishman, op. cit.
12. The last lines of, respectively, 'The Phoenix', 'A Moral Poem', 'The Helmsman, an Ode', 'Ars Amoris', 'I, too, have been to the Huntingdon', and *To What Strangers, What Welcomes*, No. 14.
13. 'Coffee'.
14. 'Meditation on Statistical Method'.
15. Epigram 100. All the poems by Cunningham cited in this essay are to be found in J. V. Cunningham, *Collected Poems and Epigrams* (London, 1971). They are reprinted with the permission of the Ohio University Press.

12

For Lizzie and Harriet: Robert Lowell's Domestic Apocalypse

by GABRIEL PEARSON

1

The circumstances of *For Lizzie and Harriet* are the common stuff of broken marriage, its emotions the familiar blind hurt, confusion, remorse. Though all its poems have appeared before, as the prefatory note makes clear, 'in another order, in other versions', they here achieve an integral completeness and definition. By turns celebratory and harrowing, its unique feature is that its protagonists are both eminent writers. In this it differs from that other sequence which plots the desolation of divorce, Snodgrass's *Heart's Needle*, which remains an important precedent. In Lowell's sequence both partners are obsessed with writing as, in his lament for Berryman in *Day by Day*, Lowell has said he and Berryman 'had prayed to be . . . and were'. The sequence then is 'for' Lizzie as it can be only potentially 'for' Harriet. It presumes a writerly compact, not necessarily reciprocated. This makes for further moral equivocalness; a purely writerly opportunism masquerades, arguably, as reparation and contrition. With these protagonists the issue of writing itself is bound to figure as significant and perplexing.

Indeed, the issue of writing further complicates the already reflexive nature of the sequence. Dissected out of the massive torso of *Notebook*, the poems re-ordered in this volume alter function, becoming themselves agents in the story they compose. It is also as literary people that husband and wife communicate, quarrel and suffer. The agony of their separation engages their individual literary culture which shows itself pitiably unfitted to contain or mitigate it. It merely adds the articulacy of insult to marital injury to enlist Dr. Johnson ('some small passage in our cups at dinner/ rouses the Dr. Johnson in a wife——') or to pit Byron against Kant ('Emmanuel Kant remained unmarried and sane,/ no one could Byronize his walk to class'). Alas, here 'the wo that is in marriage' is all too eruditely told.

Quotation itself is capable of becoming the locus of turbulent emotion. One moment of crisis indeed provokes a quotation famous for its linguistic poverty, when the only words that Lizzie's anger, despair and exhaustion can find are those of Bartleby's obstinate whisper of refusal:

> I toss a white raincoat
> over your sky-black, blood-trim quilted storm-coat,
> you saying, *I would prefer not*, like Bartleby. . . .
>   ('No Hearing' 4; Late Summer, 11)

Elizabeth Hardwick has given some subtle paragraphs to teasing apart the layers of this shadowy saying by Melville's scrivener; it is evidently a long-standing fascination.[1] Bartleby's 'preferences' manifestly exclude the elaborate and the explicit, which may well cause one to ponder Lowell's detailed welter of colour and clothing. Is this manic hysteria? Heightened perception engendered by shock? Mental pain displaced into observation? Or just the inappropriate and perhaps aggressive display of idiosyncratic virtuosity? The effect of Lizzie's intertext is to rebuke the poet's own descriptive excess. But is this what Lizzie did say or might have said or what Lowell's writerly complicity thrilled to hear it as? Compliment, rebuke, self-dismissal, because it is after all Lowell's poem that has her saying it, Lizzie's quotation remains inescapably locked in the prison of self-reference, which no literary art, only that life which literature fails and Bartleby's refusal refuses to engross, can hope to unlock. 'Ah, Bartleby! Ah, humanity!'

'For Lizzie and Harriet': Robert Lowell's Domestic Apocalypse

Throughout the sequence the writerly interests on both sides are shown as insidiously, generously or self-protectively alert. Matrimonial intercourse entails writerly complications, elements perhaps even of competition. It says something for Lowell's tact, not usually considered his most prominent feature, that none of this comes over as ridiculous while permitting the play of some humour. If the girl in his Mexican escapade was blessedly 'no artist', Lowell cannot refrain from appending a wistful-humorous 'perhaps':

> No artist perhaps, you can see the backs of phrases,
> a girl too simple to-lose herself in words—
> I fall back in the end on honest speech. . . .
>
> (Mexico, 9)

Whatever honesty might have been managed at the time, it is likely to look a shabbier commodity in the light of Lizzie's inspection. She is expert in both the backs and fronts of phrases, inclined, one would suppose, to suspect artfulness if not artistry in these alternative ladies and likely to take a jaundiced view of their simplicity. Lowell's lines curl a little in the breeze of Lizzie's silent appraisal, composing his own naïveté and his sophisticated sense of what that amounted to then and does now. His 'perhaps' should be read as his own defensive mutter fluttering in the tailwind of Lizzie's brisk scepticism.

These accounts of infidelity are also of course addressed over her shoulder to a more general reader, inevitably sounding the note of bravado, the brazen pitch for condonement. But implicit throughout, it seems to me, is an appeal to Lizzie as fellow writer; its subtext is that since as writer herself she has loved the writer in him, even such a personally wounding narrative must challenge her regard. In any case, it is not unprecedented for erring husbands to expect their wives to take an interest in accounts of their adulteries. It might be the last degree of insult but may also be a curious testimony to the inveteracy of marriage. It is the 'poor Child' of the Mexican escapade that gets shortest shrift, offered in oblation to two hungry literary lions 'famished for human chances'.[2]

In a number of poems ('Dear Sorrow' 1 and 2; 'Seals'; 'Obit') the writerly compact is honoured or saluted, not least

189

in 'Elizabeth' ('Summer' 3). Here, for the only time and with dramatic effect, Lowell uses Lizzie's full Christian name as title. The last lines present her in something like the plenitude of her own deferred longing for creative autonomy:

> We're fifty
> and free! Young, tottering on the dizzying brink
> of discretion once, you wanted nothing
> but to be old, do nothing, type and think.

A truly imaginative inversion turns 'discretion' itself into an ocean—Lowell's permanent site of creative turbulence—by way of a murmurous echo from *King Lear* (Edgar's Dover cliff speech has 'dizzy' and 'extreme verge'). This queer identity of 'discretion' and 'ocean' is already anticipated in the preceding lines:

> Squalls of the seagull's exaggerated outcry
> dim out in the fog . . .

which encompasses both the matrimonial quarrel and its exhausted cessation. One looks in vain however for the genitive plural in 'seagull's'.

This marine imagery connects reconditely with 'drinking . . . soaking in the sweat of . . . hard-earned supremacy . . .'. The poem is concerned in the first instance with their life as an ageing, quarrelling, married couple of 50, caught in precarious equipoise between ripeness and rot. The preoccupations with words however ('All day our words/ were rusty fish-hooks') and the tissue of Shakespearean associations, link the words of the poem with Lizzie's wish 'to type and write'. Words are imaged in their double power to wound and to assuage (the nuncial '*pace*' adding an almost ritual emphasis):

> *Pace, pace.* All day our words
> were rusty fish-hooks—wormwood . . . Dear Heart's-Ease,
> we rest from all discussion. . . .

'Wormwood' replicates, duplicates and reorganizes the acoustic profile of 'words'. At the same time, it sets up 'Hearts-Ease' as its verbal as well as herbal antidote, which in turn looks quizzically towards the later 'pills for high blood'. Heart's-ease is the Pansy, which we know from *Hamlet* is 'for thoughts'—not any old thoughts, but specifically thoughts of

190

love, touchingly appropriate in this context. This in turn
would appear to flirt towards 'think', the last word of the poem
which in turn embraces 'brink' in the concordat of rhyme.
'Type' too, more remotely, picks up the 'ripe' in 'ripeness', in
the first line: 'An unaccustomed ripeness in the wood . . .'.
There is, unusually, even a couplet rhyming doubly and
emphatically on 'smoking' and 'soaking'. The incidence of
rhyme here has its own resonance in the flow of ostentatiously
blank sonnets. The whole poem exhibits Lowell's compressed,
polyphonic idiom at its richest and most flexible, deploying its
own exaltations of craft to celebrate Lizzie's freedom—or at
least the wish for it—'to type and think'.

'Obit', the final, valedictory poem of this volume, as it was
of *Notebook* before it, dispenses apparently with the writer's
compact in favour of more broadly human themes: failed
marriage and vain love. . . . I find it a moving poem, despite
its conscious design to be so, because it manages to give formal
expression to its edginess and embarrassment, transmuting
them to praise, sad intimacy and the high bravery of lament.
In the last couplet, for example, the *you* trembles almost
beseechingly between line's end and line's beginning, not
willingly released from the couplet's lips into 'eternity':

> After loving you so much, can I forget
> you for eternity, and have no other choice?

Lizzie as writer has already been peeled (and pealed) away
with those other good trusty things that might have retained
him in the old life:

> old cars, old money, old undebased pre-Lyndon
> silver, no copper rubbing through . . . old wives;
> I could live such a too long time with mine.

'Old wives' creeps in to the end of the list, not without some
circumspect preparation, but it is in these terms that the
poem now seems to handle Lizzie: sterling certainly but not
quite granted the accolade of fellow-artist. Yet this is more
subtly awarded as she is made connoisseur of the purple
patch, the *locus amoenus*, which carries the verse into conscious
self-celebration even as husband and wife fall apart into
otherness:

> I am for and with myself in my otherness,
> in the eternal return of earth's fairer children,
> the lily, the rose, the sun on brick at dusk,
> the loved, the lover. . . .

The Sartrean phraseology (albeit derived through Marcuse)[3] puts one in mind of some such marriage of intellect as that of Sartre and de Beauvoir; the invitation to delight in the heightened cadence, of that of another literary pair, Elizabeth Barrett and Robert Browning (another Lizzie and Robert!). These are, I had better admit, my own associations; nonetheless the poet seems to be reaching for a transcendence partially realized in the implied spiritual communion it supposes for its proper appreciation. It is to be a charm designed to outlast the 'unconquered flux, insensate oneness, painful 'It was . . .' which afflicts common terrestrial lovers. The pure literariness of the hope is not the least part of its pathos.

2

The volume is also 'for' Harriet, 'offering a child [its] leathery love'. Three of its first set of five poems ('Summer') bear her name as a title; the first adds her birth date. All this advertises her centrality in the bane and bliss that is to follow. The second poem already sounds the apocalyptic note:

> A repeating fly, blue-black, thumb-thick—so gross,
> it seems apocalyptic in our house—
> whams back and forth . . .
>
> ('Harriet' 2; Summer)

seeming a horrible caricature of the manic productivity of the blank sonnets themselves. 'Blueblack, thumbthick . . . gross' catches also the child's surreal perception of the writer-father as grotesquely out of scale, random, obsessive, dangerous to himself and others, a mechanical menace as in the comparison with

> a plane
> dusting apple orchards or Arabs on the screen
> one of the mighty . . . one of the helpless. . . .

We move across the elipsis from parental omnipotence to childish insecurity. Harriet features here as any child is likely

to for her parent as a memory-mirror of his own childish
incompetence, as an example of which his own relationship
with his child may now figure. Poor fly, poor Harriet, poor
poet, poor poem, all seem equally busy, bemused and lost in
their dishevelled existences, all equally part of some random
and inscrutable activity on a screen.

The *it* in 'I kill it' becomes, among other things, the poem
itself which reports the deed and which is itself sterilely
deathless—'wrinkling to fulfilment'. Yet blessedly the poem is
lightened by some amused self-recognition:

> It
> bumbles and bumps its brow on this and that,
> making a short, unhealthy life the shorter. . . .

Lowell depicts himself here as so often in his double rôle of
monster and victim, malign yet inept fury. As the fly becomes
part of the muddle of Harriet's own possessions, the poet
allows implicitly that he may be no more than one of her
objects, a toy, one of her

> ephemera: keys, drift, sea-urchin shells
> you packrat off with joy. . . .

There is a touching hope that what is malfunction in the
parent may be converted by the child into the harmlessness of
play. However, fear for the child's vulnerability is the
predominant concern:

> The fly
> whams back and forth across the nursery bed
> manned by a madhouse of stuffed animals,
> not one a fighter. . . .

The nursery bed is manned ineffectually, its mimic guardians
infected with the madness that threatens them, the child's
capacity to contain psychic damage in doubt. She is herself
as helpless as the fly before the abrupt act of violence—'I kill
it', just like that, offhand, instant, adding it 'to the horrifying
mortmain/ of ephemera'. By happy chance, the *Oxford
English Dictionary* illustrates the figurative sense of 'mortmain'
by a quotation from Lowell's own kinsman, James Russell
Lowell:

> Sir George Beaumont, dying in 1827 . . . contrived to hold his
> affection in mortmain by the legacy of an annuity of £100.
>
> *Among My Books*, Series 21, 228

The Harriet poems are partly an effort 'to hold affection in
mortmain', to grasp with the dead hand of verse the living
relationship the father has relinquished. All this is amply
acknowledged; Lowell may have the firepower of an Israeli
fighter-plane, but this Arab is his own flesh and blood.
'Mortmain' admirably suggests the dominant negative feelings
of the whole volume: mortification, penitential self-accusation,
helplessness, loss. The 'for' of 'For . . . Harriet' essays an act of
reparation by maintaining in imagination the family's integrity
by the exercise of the same arts which in practice seem to
threaten it. There is some effort to incorporate Harriet herself
within the charmed circle of art, as artist in embryo, remem-
bered as hammering 'the formidable chords of *The Nocturne*,
your second composition' ('These Winds'; Summer 6) and
'writing a saga with a churl named Eric' ('Growth'; Late
Summer 6), but the consciousness of psychic injury is the
prevalent concern:

> Do I romanticise if I think that I
> can be as selfish a father as Karl Marx,
> Milton, Dickens, Trotsky, Freud, James Mill,
> or George II, a bad son and worse father—
> the great lions needed a free cage to roar in . . .?
>
> ('Dear Sorrow' 4; New York 7)

The list returns accusingly upon itself, as George II heaves
round the line's end to bring in a double indictment. The
lion's roar, carrying across to the next sonnet, 'Harriet's
Dream', combines with the 'burnt-umber' of Lizzie's dress,
glowing 'as if it had absorbed the sun' to blend into the
nightmare of the burning bungalow. Clearly her father's
'name' threatens Harriet with the loss of her own; he
consumes her, entirely engulfs her in his Lowell substance and
leaves no space for 'Harriet' to flourish in:

> We met a couple, not people,
> squares asking Father if he was his name—
> none ever said that I was Harriet. . . .
>
> ('Harriet's Dream'; New York 8)

194

One can hardly fail to interpret the 'couple' as a disguised version of Lizzie and Lowell, reduced to nonentity as she feels reduced: 'not people,/ squares'. What follows seems to arise out of the turning in of aggression against herself in punishment of her own aggression:

> They were laying beach-fires with scarlet sticks and hatchets,
> our little bungalow was burning—it
> had burned, I was in it, I couldn't laugh. . . .

Again 'they' would appear to be the parents. Harriet, in ducking through this death, eludes and represses psychic trauma that she fears she cannot endure. The parataxis seems to enact the rapid, gulping movements by which she moves through her death, holding her breath so that she will not have to feel it. You could say that the poet has committed a final transgression here, appropriating the very dream for his literary purposes that acts out the appropriation of her identity that seems to be its content. Yet Lowell has been true, one senses, to the movement of the dream, at least in the form narrated by Harriet. He realizes with nervous precision the sharp montage, the jumps, the dissolves of dreamwork. One has to say, however, that these closely resemble the general, cinematographic techniques of the blank sonnets. Still, one would like to think this was a hard poem to write and not patently to tamper with. If anything its technique seems to have worked towards an authentic, though not necessarily literal account. Thus he preserves essential ambiguities, as in the last line:

> While sleeping
> I scrubbed away my scars and blisters, unable
> to answer if I had ever hurt.

The verb conserves a genuine ambiguity between the transitive and intransitive senses: 'had I ever hurt someone' or 'had I been hurt'? (I would suppose that, ultimately, granted the process of introjection, these would be identical.)

Again, the last word of the penultimate line separates out into a kind of cry: don't make me undergo all this (quarrels, divorce, your mutual cruelty); I am unable (to stand it, to be thought to be able to understand it, to allow it, you demons). Finally, we notice the metrically abbreviated last line, amputated upon the word 'hurt', again unable—or defiantly refusing—to complete the measure. If something like this reading is correct, then one may wonder at the preternatural accuracy of what one may term Lowell's psychic ear. His verse is not only an organ of speech but also of a special kind of hearing, peculiarly sensitized to inner rhythms, catches of the breath, gasps, stammers and gushes. Here he does seem to give Harriet a voice, releasing her into her own first person. One even senses that slight glazing of the parental eye as the child at last snares the momentous and distracted father in the net of her narrative. It is too early to tell her how boring other people's dreams are apt to be. Still, Lowell has found a paradoxical way to release Harriet from the authority of his reading of her. Indeed, he licenses and liberates her answer, her narration back, letting her force him to put his art at her service.

The problem of how to release children to the authority of their own fate is in any case a broadly human one which Lowell meditates with considerable eloquence in the next poem:

> but to know you were happy would mean to lead
> your life for you, hold hard and live you out. . . .
>> ('Term End'; New York 9)

One solution taken here is to grant Harriet some healing effect upon his darkest malaise. 'The Human Condition' is a very dark poem indeed, its savage depression prepared to accept nuclear annihilation as a suitable punishment for our mutual cruelty, in marriage for example, which is seen as a nightmare of engulfment from which

> I wake to your cookout and Charles Ives
> lulling my terror, lifting my fell of hair,
> as David calmed the dark nucleus of Saul.
>> ('The Human Condition', Circles 5)

Here Harriet is a source of healing and release, a kind of innocent, therapeutic artist. Finding her way to the 'dark nucleus' of her father, she dissolves the constriction which knots together his psychic violence and the nuclear violence threatening all futures. Finally, it should be noted in Lowell's favour his willingness not only to countenance Harriet's collaboration, but her supersession of his own gift:

> '. . . You've got to call your *Notebook, Book of the Century*,
> but it will take you a century to write,
> then I will have to revise it, when you are dead. . . .'
>
> ('Growth': Late Summer 6)

Which is of course the common task of all children, cast in the curious terms of this book.

3

Though the whole book is 'For Lizzie and Harriet' their names are bracketed together with reference to only one poem ('Outlivers'; Late Summer 12). It is true that Harriet asks the questions and Lowell himself is a largely silent presence. Most of the talk is Lizzie's, presented as talking for victory in her 'Dr. Johnson' vein, widely discursive in a perfectly Lowell-like manner, evidencing no doubt much cultural and domestic symbiosis. In the event, the poem brackets father and daughter in childish collusion:

> '. . . I hope, of course, that you will both outlive me,
> but you and Harriet are perhaps like countries
> not yet ripe for self-determination.'

It is hard not to read this as an unjust performance, still animated by the marriage grudge, casting Lizzie in an especially ungracious, hectoring rôle. Such judgements raise the issue of the reader's own response to what Lowell has called with simple candour, describing *Notebook*, 'the story of my life'.[4] Critical reading and moral judgement are likely to be messily embroiled with each other when certain poems—and arguably the whole volume—do double duty as words and actions within a highly charged personal situation. I believe that 'Outlivers' is crudely manipulated by *parti pris*, and though I would like to believe that critical analysis would demonstrate that bad morality and bad writing coincide I cannot be sure. Perhaps all one can say is that this is a lumpy bag of a poem that assimilates its materials without obvious grace or felicity. What I think we should not do is to treat this story as plain fiction or fail to register that people still living move, suffer and speak within the body of these poems. Though *Dolphin* has been denounced for the more flagrant breaches of trust in its handling of intimate, confidential material—letters and conversations—*For Lizzie and Harriet* no less parades private events and intimate susceptibilities.

Arguably that is what makes this story relevant to our times. The destruction of private space is one of the more prevalent violences that beset us. Our intimate lives are narrated by so many intrusive influences that there is a perverse heroism in seizing the levers of the plot oneself, even if it results in a cruel, shameless and abject chronicle. It involves transgression at many levels, a Faustian pact which in the logic of the bargain entails 'not avoiding injury to others,/ not avoiding injury to myself'.[5] The blank sonnet enterprise, from the first version of *Notebook* onward, seems to have amounted to a massive act of transgression. In collapsing the private and public into each other, it simultaneously debauched the publishing process; 'I have handled my published book as if it were manuscript',[6] Lowell has stated of his three versions of *Notebook*, and the subsequent recapitulations in *For Lizzie and Harriet* and *History* have emphasized the magnitude of the desecration.

In this régime, the identity of the individual poem becomes unstable, volatile, when so much revision is publicly exhibited. It gets reduced to the ragged trace left by its successive versions. I exaggerate of course. Yet it is difficult not to feel a connection, in the depths of Lowell's creative adventure, between these forms of transgression and what is recounted in the poems of destructive passions, incongruous loves, quarrels and adulteries. This is to ignore those form-enhancing dimensions still very much alive in the blank sonnet volumes, which are allied to much that is sane, decent and compassionate. But the transgressive energies are predominant and remain the fuel of much creative vitality.

The Greeks regarded such transgressions as pollution, arising from forbidden mixtures, a failure of categorical hygiene. Thus, interior things should not be exposed, mixed states—the living body in the dead form of matter—were radically unclean. Yet polluted things could also partake of the sacred.[7] If there is a kind of holy terror involved in the presence of Lowell's self-narration, then perhaps it lies in some secular version of these primordial discriminations. Perhaps they lend themselves to prophecy. Perhaps at least a decade ahead, one of our most traditionally formal poets dreamed through and acted out many of the appalling freedoms and capabilities of the electronic era now at our throats. The technical situation already exists whereby we can all handle our published work as if it were manuscript. The question remains whether there would then be any public space in which they could be produced as objective forms.

4

Much remains in the volume which is simply grievous and hurtful; the four 'No Hearing' poems, for example, are all peculiarly harrowing, not least for their remarkable verbal control amid a vortex of violent emotions on the edge of breakdown. The two sequences that deal with Lowell's infidelities in Mexico and Harvard ought to be equally painful but on inspection prove to contain a surprising amount of genial and controlled humour and dramatic vitality. They are among the most brilliantly executed sections of the book, gaining much from their context and proving that the isolation of Lowell's personal story from the rich welter of *Notebook* make for impressive gains in clarity and impact. Lowell said of *History*, that he had 'cut the waste marble from the figure',[8] but this applies more appropriately to *For Lizzie and Harriet*. While it has no new poems to set against *History*'s eighty, it still emerges from the cutting-room as a fully autonomous and integral work.

The Mexican and Harvard sequences share broad similarities, though their emotional register is very different. Both, despite their prevailing sanity, are heightened and surreal. Both deal with sexual experience overtly, though not crudely. They are related antithetically in terms of heat and cold, south and north, a region void of personal associations (the igneous region of Lowry's *Under the Volcano*) and a landscape teeming with them. Both, finally, blend a good dose of sore conscience with a sense of helplessness and, in the case of the Harvard sequence, of comic incongruity:

Chaucer's old January made hay with May.
In this ever more enlightened bedroom,
I wake under the early rising sun,
sex indelible flowers on the air—. . .
you rival the renewal of the day,
clearing the puddles with your green sack of books.

('Morning'; Harvard 3)

Here at first blush there is more desolation than exaltation.
The poem I suppose is an aubade, though traditionally it is
the male love who sorrowfully decamps. This one remains
abed, catching his half-soporific responses as they bubble to
the surface of his mind. At first, there is a grimy self-distaste:

I cannot sleep, my veins are mineral,
dirt-full as the arteries of a cracked white cup;
one wearies of looking expectantly for the worse—. . . .

One probably should not lean too heavily on the Chaucer
reference. Nothing, it is true, could be more disenchanted
than the situation in Chaucer's story, and Lowell is content at
first to share its sour humour, not unmixed with self-derision
and post-coital disillusionment. The making 'hay with May' is
not a feeble line but a strong line about a man breaking a
feeble jest against himself. Sex, having failed to muffle the
verbal engine, can still provoke some puritan qualms: though
sex 'flowers', it does so 'indelible'; aspiring to be an 'indelible'
experience, it is more like a bad stain. There is, too, a muted,
not self-excluding jibe at fashionable sexual enlightenment 'in
the ever more enlightened bedroom'. Perhaps a certain glow of
geniality in the *double entendre* allows a surprising shift of tone
from the black bleakness of its beginning to the spring-like
spurt of feeling at the end.

This has something to do with the shift from what is largely
self-excoriation to direct address, which involves a search for a
more appropriate if still inadequate set of responses. The lines
I have omitted pose a question:

shouldn't I ask to hold to you forever,
body of a dolphin, breast of cloud?

The question dissolves even as it raises itself. It is a failed
metamorphosis, where images rise too sketchy and bland for

200

emotion to take hold. But they do give the impetus to lift into a purer form of feeling. The penultimate line, 'You rival the renewal of the day', is very pure indeed in diction in Donald Davie's sense: tight, formal, almost toneless, delicately antithetical, with 'rival' and 'renewal' playing off each other acoustically while repelling each other in terms of grammatical function. It is becomingly and cleanly clinched by the rhyme with 'May'. All in all, a line that Dryden might have written while adapting Chaucer but not one Chaucer would have written himself.

The last line opens itself out metrically and in its defiant refusal of rhyme seems to enact an avoidance of closure, an openness to wonder and sympathy. Rhythmically, the line swings on a long parabola on its way to becoming, without quite resolving into, an alexandrine. It too just clears any such limiting identity. The 'green sack' takes up the spring-like associations of May; Lowell's marvellous, rapid eye for significant detail coming into play again is itself the sign of a released vitality. 'Clearing' rejoices in its double sense as both the girl's child-like buoyancy and the clearing of line and vision. This is after all a poem which settles for what it can get, which appears to be more than this grizzled puritan had any right to expect.

The final poem of the Harvard sequence ('Sleep' 3) mingles in its Christmas scene a winter world of urban squalor and an interior of wildly domestic and moral confusions, while retaining an adroit, humorous poise. Here Lowell's imagination ensconces itself with some security on the sharp edges of incongruity. There are elements of irresponsibility and manic gusto but mainly a kind of relief as the girl acts out his own dilemmas in a spirit of comic innocence. The situation is disreputable enough to be normally unforgivable:

> Your child, she's nine keeps shrewdly, inopportunely
> reappearing—you standing up on your bed
> in your Emily Dickinson nightgown, purely marveling
> whether to be sensible or drown.

This has a certain hilarious charm, not least because of the mention of Emily Dickinson in such a context, but the dangerous edge it walks relates the nine-year-old to Harriet

201

and that 'pathos of a child's fractions' considered in the very first poem. Moreover, it woos comparison with the family Christmas in New York which is to follow contrasting the two Christmas trees. The Harvard tree is 'untinselled, asymmetrical, shoves up askew, blessing a small sprawl/ of unsealed brown paper Christmas packages'. 'Blessing' is more warmly affirmative than ironic, while 'asymmetrically' and 'askewly' comment underisively on Lowell's own oddball involvement in the scene.

Lizzie's tree is necessarily a grander affair:

> Twenty or more big cloth roses, pale rose and scarlet,
> coil in the branches—a winning combination. . . .

('Christmas Tree'; New York 4)

A palpable hostility hisses in 'coiled', and paranoia later finds its perch in the detail of the 'twenty small birds . . . [who] nip the needles'.[9] Even the cats are requisitioned to point the contrast:

> A tiger cat sentinelled on the record player
> spies on a second stretching from a carton-
> dollhouse to bat a brass ball on a string.

This gently reduces paranoia and aggression to play; amid a tangle of wrecky improvisations, the cats enjoy their sportive autonomy, sweetly captured in the far from sure-footed sway across the line gap of 'carton-/ dollhouse'. The general impression is of wobbly comic poise; even the concluding terms in 'whether to be sensible or drown' are lightened by the unimpeded flow of their syntax, posing the girl-friend's 'pure marveling' against the 'shrewdly reappearing' of the nine-year-old. In New York, 'minnowy/ green things, no known species, made of woven straw . . .' turn into 'small dangling wicker hampers to tease the cat'. But is all this fiddle of detail then a kind of optical irritation, a journalism of the nerves? Certainly the eye appears as much transfixed by this flickering variety as the cat with its brass ball. But more is involved than the welter of detail reproved by Lizzie's Bartlebyan murmur in 'No Hearing' 4. It is in the life of all this detail that human hopes and happiness declare themselves or die, and it is through and among these objects that Lowell's family apocalypse is finally unfolded.

'For Lizzie and Harriet': Robert Lowell's Domestic Apocalypse

NOTES

1. See Elizabeth Hardwick, 'Bartleby in Manhattan', *Bartleby in Manhattan and Other Essays* (London, 1983), pp. 217–31.
2. Robert Lowell, 'Afterthought', *Notebook* (London, 1970), p. 262. 'Accident threw up chances, and the plot swallowed them—famished for human chances.'
3. *Notebook*, p. 263.
4. *Notebook*, p. 262.
5. Robert Lowell, 'Dolphin', *Dolphin* (London, 1973), p. 78.
6. *Notebook*, p. 264.
7. I have—no doubt crudely—absorbed these notions from (i) Jean-Pierre Vernant, 'The Pure and the Impure', *Myth and Society in Ancient Greece* (Brighton, 1980), pp. 110–29, (ii) James M. Redfield, 'Purification', *Nature and Culture in the Iliad* (Chicago, 1975), pp. 160–223.
8. Robert Lowell, 'Note', *History* (London, 1973).
9. The English reader should be aware that you have to have decorated an American Christmas tree to take the force of this detail.

Excerpts from *For Lizzie and Harriet* by Robert Lowell, copyright © 1967, 1968, 1969, 1970, 1973 by Robert Lowell, are reprinted by permission of Faber and Faber Ltd. and Farrar, Straus and Giroux, Inc.

13

Robert Duncan: 'To Complete his Mind'

by CLIVE MEACHEN

'In the West some intense fire burned red in the evening',
writes Robert Duncan in *The H.D. Book*, adding later that

> I have seen such desolate and wrathful landscapes at night
> where man's devastating work has raised great mountains of
> slag and left great pits in the earth, burning wastes and
> befouled rivers that appear an earthly Hell.[1]

Projections of apocalypse are central to the imagination of
many American poets; many of Charles Olson's earliest poems
seem for instance to be directly initiated by the hell of the
Second World War. Fielding Dawson tells us that

> *Call Me Ishmael*, which he began, as it happened, the day FDR
> died, and ended the morning of Hiroshima, formed an exit from
> politics and the influence of Pound, and created the entrance
> into his personal poetic experience.[2]

He also records this:

Spring, 1950

> Charley stood on a street in bright daylight, Washington,
> D.C. Something was in the air, he looked up.
> There was a Soviet bomber in the sky. He stared at it in a
> gathering anxiety and fascination. It held the Bomb.
> He woke, frightened.

He told us that morning, on the porch, spellbound, looking out over the lake, astonished eyes drilling into space. What did it mean?[3]

The anxiety we see registered here is nevertheless coupled with a fascination; Duncan and Olson don't just stand braced against such horror but, rather, seek to find in their identification with it a key to our transcendence of it. As Duncan notes, 'the visitation is, like those actual landscapes, a just rendering of some desire of man's fulfilled.' Or, as he will write in another passage of *The H.D. Book*,

> Were it not for men's thoughts and dreams, we realise, there would have been no war. The realization, once it is there, never ceases to trouble H. D. The terror and evil of war give power and beauty to the poem ... from the fearful scene a proud music takes over, and the poet's voice takes on strength and resonance. The poem evoking, summoning forth from where it was hidden, this meaning of war, wrath and the fulfillment of prophecy—is apocalyptic.[4]

The drive towards destructiveness is also a yearning for self-transcendence; relativity, so close to the Principle of Life, has also given birth to the Bomb, that assertion of the Principle of Death.

> Yet, with this vision of what was at last, of lasting things, there remained the work of the last days. . . . I had my work to do. . . . I was terrified . . . cowering and praying in the dream that these strokes pass over my head.
> Then came the breakthrough of astral forms, a streaming down into this landscape, where Bosch's vision and my own San Francisco were already mingled, of another world, a coming together of universes. . . . It was the sign in the dream whereby I knew what must be done. I had known from the beginning and told those about me that we were in the Last Days—in the Glory, then. Now the change came.
> 'The astral worlds have fallen down,' I told those about me. 'We must redirect the spring' or 'we must *draw* the springs in the first direction' or 'the right direction'. . . .
> . . . Here, the Doctor and I must restore the Milky Way, the spring of stars that is our mothering universe.[5]

Here the twin streams of the Last Days cross and commingle; the Terror of the End and the Glory of a new

205

Beginning are found cohabiting in the single image of the springs of life. As Henri Corbin says:

> The union of the two terms of each pair constitutes a *coincidentia oppositorum*, a simultaneity not of contradictories but of complementary opposites.[6]

Or, as Duncan has put it:

> Poems then are immediate presentations of the intention of the whole ... a unity, and in any two of its elements or parts appearing as a duality or a mating, each part in every other having, if we could see it, its condition—its opposite or contender and its satisfaction or twin. Yet in the composite of all members we see no duality but the variety of the one.[7]

Apocalypse presents both collapse and renewal; these contenders are also twins, linked by a mutuality which transcends their opposition.

> Thus, I say, 'Let the light rays mix', and against the Gnostics, who would free the sparks of spirit from what is the matter, and against the positivists and semanticists who would free the matter from its inspirational chaos, I am glad that there is night and day, Heaven and Hell, love and wrath, sanity and ecstasie, together in a little place.[8]

Sometimes it is useful to focus the mind on an image; indeed, in the spectrum of imaginary phenomena, it could be that it is the image that generates the ideas, not the ideas that generate the image. So it is that I have come to think of Robert Duncan in the image of the cross-eyed king in the *Maximus Poems* of Charles Olson; 'twisted sinews' constantly underlie his work, a 'crossing and recrossing'[9] of associations as he tries to give breath to his sense of wholeness without excluding any element of what he is.

> To speak my mind,
> unfold the secret of the heart,
> breathe word of it,
> take soundings in the passage out—
>
>   even as my hand
> writes, thumb and fingers
> hold the pen in attention.

Robert Duncan: 'To Complete his Mind'

My whole life
needs to be here
to come alive in this
consideration.[10]

Constantly taking new soundings in the passage out, his poetry yet returns to a singleness of consideration. Referring to his background as a romantic and a theosophist, Duncan has said that

> our whole tradition was to identify with heretics throughout the world, and as a matter of fact, my parents . . . believed that they were identical with the Demolays, the Knights Templars. . . . So they had this long business—we have been exterminated over and over again by the dogmatists (actually exterminated) but we were perennial, so I find the perennial doctrine instead of established central doctrine. You find a cosmos that's perennial and that's destroyed—the law constantly *destroys* the law, which is not a dogma but a thing devouring itself and undoing itself, and you will find that in my poetry I undo my propositions.[11]

Such an attitude has certainly created in Duncan's poetry both a sense of continuity and a wide-ranging permission rare even in twentieth-century poets. A follower of Pound, he yet has room for Pound's despised Milton; a singer mingling in his song the high-toned strains of a rhetorical tradition, he yet has room for the childish, the naïve, the sentimental.

> The Symposium of Plato was restricted to a community of Athenians, gathered in the common creation of an *arete*, an aristocracy of spirit, inspired by the homoEros, taking its stand against lower or foreign orders, not only of men but of nature itself. The intense yearning, the desire for something else, of which we too have only a dark and doubtful presentiment, remains, but our *arete*, our ideal of vital being, rises not in our identification in a hierarchy of higher forms but in our identification with the universe. To compose such a symposium of the whole, such a totality, all the excluded orders must be included. The female, the proletariat, the foreign; the animal and the vegetative; the unconscious and the unknown; the criminal and failure—all that has been outcast and vagabond must return to be admitted in the creation of what we consider we are.[12]

One of the orders most recently excluded from our account of poetic creation is precisely that area of the dark, of the unknown Duncan points to in the passage quoted above. Duncan's poetry bears continuous witness to 'the releasing pattern of an inspiration', a fact that Robert Creeley has emphasized in a review of one of Duncan's books:

> Most primary is the assertion that what one *can* say, in any circumstance of poetry, is informed by a 'voice' not ours to intend or to decide.[13]

Duncan has also pointed to the importance of the 'sub-meaning level, because it's that one that's making the shifts'[14] in the creation of a poem. Such an insistence has been tempered and extended by Duncan's study and re-enactments of, for instance, Freud's theory of parataxis and Gertrude Stein's treatment of language, but no cultural grid can explain away such an imperative, as a prose poem in *Letters* beautifully illustrates:

> When I was about twelve—I suppose about the age of Narcissus—I fell in love with a mountain stream. There, most intently for a summer, staring into its limpid cold rush, I knew the fullest pain of longing. To be of it, entirely, to be out of my being and enter the Other clear impossible element. The imagination, old shape-shifter, stretcht itself painfully to comprehend the beloved form.
>
> Then all windings and pools, all rushings on, constant inconstancy, all streams out of springs we do not know where, all rush of senses and intellect thru time of being—lifts me up; as if out of the pulse of my bloody flesh, the gasp of breath upon breath (like a fish out of water) there were another continuum, an even-purling stream, crystal and deep, down there, but a flow of waters.
>
> I write this only to explain some of the old ache of longing that revives when I apprehend again the currents of language—rushing upon their way, or in pools, vacant energies below meaning, hidden to our purposes. Often, reading or writing, the fullest pain returns, and I see or hear or almost know a pure element of clearness, an utter movement, an absolute rush along its own way, that makes of even the words under my pen a foreign element that I may crave—as for kingdom or salvation or freedom—but never know.[15]

This is Duncan's primary sense of language, a language we first heard in 'infant song and reverie' that 'we acquire

without/ any rule for love of it/ "imitating our nurses" '. He
will often recall us to this sense, seeing language, like Dante, as
a thing drunk in with our mother's milk, redolent with
rhythmic and essentially physical vibrations:

> from the beginning,   color
> and light, my nurse;   sounding waves
> and air, my nurse;   animal presences,
> my nurse;   Night,   my nurse.
>
>   out of hunger,   instinctual
>   craving,   thirst for 'knowing',
>
>   toward oracular tits.
>
> This,
>
> being primary,
>   natural and common,
> being 'milk',
>
> is animal—
>
>   lungs sucking-in the air, having
>   heart in it, rhythmic, and
>   moving in measure,
>   self-creative in concert
>
> —and therein,
>
> noble.[16]

This is, says Olson, 'language as, root, graphic', where all is
'sound . . . as object in space', an actual 'mass, to be pushed
around, to be heard as things are eaten'; he insists that this is a
process 'of the organism not the "mind" or "taste" or
"aesthetics" '.[17] 'Secondary', says Duncan, 'is the grammar
of/ constructions and uses, syntactic/ manipulations, floor-
plans',[18] but we must not assume that Duncan's poetry simply
eschews the secondary acts of manipulation in favour of the
wild promptings of the inspirational. Out of love for the places
where we first heard such possible music, we imitate the craft
of those who initiated it. Duncan is a master craftsman,

steeped eclectically in the lores of a multitude of craftsmen, and that is certainly one way in which we can see him primarily as a *maker* of verse. But there is another sense of maker operative in Duncan's world, a sense which finally unites the twin worlds of inspiration and craft. 'Perhaps', he has written,

> the sexual irregularity underlay and led to the poetic; neither as homosexual nor as poet could one take over readily the accepted paradigms and conventions of the Protestant ethic. The structure of my life like the structure of my work was to emerge in a series of trials, a problematic identity.[19]

Not being able to find an identity in the social fabric outside of him, Duncan had to make up his own world:

> By my eighteenth year, I recognized in poetry my sole and ruling vocation. Only in this art . . . could my inner nature unfold. I had no idea what that nature was, it was to be created in my work. But I could find no ready voice. I was, after all, to be a poet of many derivations.[20]

Trying on identities for size, lost to himself, he is also looking for the hidden thing he knows he is projecting; in this case, the immediate location for the hidden is his homosexuality, a natural thing he must nevertheless invent an alternative world for, that its boundaries might be known and its true nature revealed. Yet the autobiographical reference should not dull us to the fact that this movement takes on in Duncan a far wider applicability:

> Were it not for this recurrence of the idea, Man, we would not imagine that the great Imaginer seeks His own self and knows not what It is but only that It's hidden in what fails, what falls from Him, what fouls the light in knowing with heat and drives the Holy Spirit Itself into Form and stories into Story to be undone. It is only to say that He will not know who He is until *we* know; He'll know nothing of seeing until *we* see. O, He is all we know of war, for we are no more than he *contends* we are. But He has also just that hope of freedom from what He is He has in us we feel as a yearning to pass beyond His conditions. He'll have no peace, for He has no peace in Him, until *we* make peace; no Love until we *make* Love, that now is no more than the regret or lure of a broken promise in us or a persistent wish.[21]

Such an interdependence of God and Man here expresses itself in a language almost torn apart by the pressure to maintain its sense of interrelatedness, yet it is crucial to an understanding of Duncan's 'perennial doctrine'. Charles Olson, Duncan's Doctor of the springs referred to earlier, puts it this way:

> God's purpose,
> to complete his mind, to bring
> creation
>
> into being, all error,
> of neglect, of laziness,
>
> of unequalling
> desire, of sleeping
>
> when the night
> is there to be used
>
> to undo the failure
> of yesterday, and wet
>
> tomorrow to match
> the uses
>
> of the sun: the race
> is incapable
>
> of its own possibility
> when any single one drops
>
> one power
> of his or her
>
> being, God
> is slighted.[22]

And yet, as Duncan says, how can we ever see what is hidden except 'in what fails, what falls from Him, what fouls the light in knowing with heat'? These powers that drop from us, what are they but tokens of the very attempt 'to complete his mind'?

*   *   *

Duncan's poetry has grown in confidence over the years, but it would be a mistake to treat this growth as a linear progression. Earlier modes which some critics would have us drop from the body of his authentic voices continually return. Looking back in 1966, he explained:

> What has happened in the almost two decades since *Heavenly City, Earthly City* was written, is that I have come not to resolve or eliminate any of the old conflicting elements of my work but to imagine them now as contrasts of a field of composition in which I develop an ever-shifting possibility of the poet I am—at once a made up thing and at the same time a depth in which my being is—the poems not ends in themselves but forms arising from the final intention of the whole in which they have their form and in turn giving rise anew to that intention.[23]

Such close interdependence of part and whole produces a startling result in the reading of the poems. Primarily it is our sense of time which is at stake here. Each new poetic event recalls us back to earlier poetic events; these, in turn, seem to apprehend their future realizations. It is as if we experience that sudden liberation from spatial and temporal conditionings that Ezra Pound referred to. Duncan talks of 'a series having no beginning and no end as its condition of form':

> The sequence we hear belongs to a field in which we know there is no consequence. In the true form of the poem all its parts co-operate, co-exist. What we hear at last has long preceded what remains of what first we heard. It is our own Memory-field as we listen in which the truth of that form is created, in which, as we comprehend the form, all its parts are present in one fabric. We wove strand after strand, line after line; but for those who at last see the cloth there is no first strand or second strand; the design does not begin in a certain place but where the admirer's eye chooses to begin in seeing.[24]

This seems to me to be a stranger power than it usually has been taken to be; Duncan, in trying to give us a sense of that whole the poem both addresses and brings into being, here talks of it in a decidedly mystical fashion:

> But in this moment of writing, in this reading, it is not into a later flow of energies this current enters. What we took to be a stream of consciousness, we take now to be a light streaming in a new crystal the mind ever addresses.[25]

Robert Duncan: 'To Complete his Mind'

It was Charles Olson who first recognized the existence of this power latent in what he termed composition by field:

> And I wanted to convince Duncan, or any one, of what he has proved to me by any number of his poems—that he has had the experience that a poem is ordered not so much *in* time (Poe's Poetic Principle) or *by* time (metric, measure) as of a characteristic *of* time which is most profound: that time is synchronistic and that a poem is the one example of a man-made continuum 'which contains qualities or basic conditions manifesting themselves simultaneously in various places in a way not to be explained by causal parallelisms'.[26]

Jung has called synchronicity an acausal principle and much could be said here about its effects and its powers. However, it seems to me that we are only just now beginning to understand something of the true importance of these matters; I offer the following therefore not as proof but as evidence. There is a way in which a book may be used in the manner of the *I Ching*; it may be opened randomly at any page, the randomness, itself a token attempt to disrupt the pre-arranged purposes and expectations of the reader. The disruption is of *conscious* senses of purpose, that the truer intent may reveal itself, and the book is thus approached with a heightened recognition that it is *right* to approach it. As Duncan says, 'the design does not begin in a certain place but where the *admirer's* eye chooses to begin in seeing.'[27]

So opening the book, I read this:

> Often in the obscure being dwells a hidden God;
> And like a nascent eye covered by its lids
> A pure spirit grows beneath the skin of stones.[28]

The passage revealed to me a thought that was imminent yet which nevertheless required the stimulus of the unpremeditated to be brought out. Yet this thought seemed more to possess me than I possessed it; seeking to find a fuller focus for the energy it evoked I dipped back again into the book. This is what I then found:

> Adam grows inside the Pod that swells upon Dame Nature's vine like a sleeping eye, a spirit hidden beneath closed lids of sleep that sends from the embryonic brain stems of sight into the depths of vision where eyes form in the skin between the Irreal and the Actual Real.[29]

Until we concede the existence of 'the skin of stones' we do not feel fully the pressure of 'a spirit hidden beneath closed lids of sleep'; such a revelation includes the necessity of admitting to the presence that which would disrupt it. There is surely no more arcane a sense of poetry than as a power; today, bludgeoned by the superstitions of a vast technological empire, poetry has come close to losing that sense. Duncan would return us to it; not to a poetry offering drably illustrated modest propositions, but to a poetry charged with the often dangerous energies of the primary imagination.

We are on the brink here of evoking a Promethean fire; it is a risk Duncan is well aware of and here, in this passage from *Bending the Bow*, directly confronts:

> He should have a straitend his ways and not taken so easily what the daemonic suggestion gave so easily, gave away to him, but, head in the honey, he would be taken in by whatever sweetness moved him or deep sounding thing or flaming that came on him in reading the green of a tree, the promise taken in a star, or the wisdom texts of Plutarch, Boehme. . . .[30]

It seems that this passage wants to pour the waters of its calming wisdom on to the heated consciousness of the poet immersed in the field of daemonic suggestion. Yet haven't we seen Duncan in an earlier passage with his 'head in the honey', longing to 'be of it, entirely, to be out of my being and enter the Other clear impossible element'? Hadn't this lifted him up, 'as if out of the pulse of my bloody flesh, the gasp of breath upon breath (like a fish out of water) there were another continuum, an even-purling stream'?[31] Such immersion cannot be denied— it is fundamental to the risk implicit in his poetic act. And yet, pushing against restraint, the fact of restraint returns; pushing beyond breath, we yet have to breathe:

> This,
>
> being primary,
>   natural and common,
> being 'milk',
>
> is animal—

> lungs sucking-in the air, having
> heart in it, rhythmic, and
> moving in measure,
> self-creative in concert.[32]

The salmon, immersed in the rushing obstruction of the waters, gathers his fire to leap up and beyond all obstruction; dashed back down again, he takes what breath his pounding heart permits. Ascent and descent leave us with the primacy of pulse:

> life shakes like a drum and would discover resonance of what it loves in its own beat, the old man wetting and heating the head of the drum until it answered the tone he sought that sought him.[33]

Neither the wisdom of water nor the risk of fire define the act of tuning the music of such a pulse. Both are necessary to that act's successful conclusion but neither are sufficient causes alone; rather, they must be blended in the alchemical balancing of the act of tuning–and who but the man who tunes can say when that balance is achieved?

Yet balance is itself an unsatisfactory word to use in a situation as open-ended as this one; it implies a finality this image of process cannot support. As Duncan says,

> Charles Olson, how strangely I have altered and used and would keep the wisdom, the man, the self I choose, after your warnings against *wisdom as such*, as if it were 'solely the issue of the time of the moment of its creation, not any ultimate except what the author in his heat and that instant in its solidity yield'.[34]

It is not that the wisdom is not there; the heat of the immersion demands a quenching peacefulness of pouring water if the poet is not to be entirely undone. The water the salmon fights with his heat is yet the water he must return to in order to breathe. But without the struggle, without the immersion in fire, there is no testing or extension of self, no way of finding that primal pulse that conditions us. Duncan believes that this pulse we seek is also seeking us; while such a conviction sounds ultimate, what evidence do we have for it but the evidence of any one specific occasion, 'not any ultimate except what the author in his heat and that instant in its solidity yield'?

*　　　*　　　*

As we stretch to uncover finalities we see that the only finalities we can know belong solely to this time, this place. Nevertheless, haunted by the present horror of apocalypse, we remember the pressure of such imaginings throughout all the times of man:

> The apocalyptic picture of the world that is also the heart under attack is a complex image of correspondence between what is felt as inflicted and what is felt on projection, of wishes for vengeance that we are also fears of punishment seen fulfilled in actual events.[35]

Seen this way, the imagination of apocalypse is as ultimate in the London of H.D. as it is years later in the San Francisco of Robert Duncan.

> Behind the war is an old war against Tiamat. On a psychological level, an analytical level, the war is sensed in pressures of inner wrath—of the 'Jehovah' within—upon living organs. Such a condition demands of the imagination a new heart and a new reality in which there is the germ of survival.[36]

The germ of survival might well lie hidden in Duncan's restoration and retranslation of the springs of poetry. As we turn almost full circle, we yet have his voice to lead us out:

> The old man tunes his drum between the bowl of fire and the bowl of water, listening to the music that is about to come.[37]

NOTES

1. Robert Duncan, *The H.D. Book*, Chapter 11, in *Io 10*, p. 212.
2. Fielding Dawson, *The Black Mountain Book* (New York, 1970), p. 85.
3. Dawson, *The Black Mountain Book*, pp. 84–5.
4. Duncan, *The H.D. Book*, Part 2, Chapter 3, *Io 6*, p. 130.
5. Duncan, *The H.D. Book*, p. 214.
6. Henri Corbin, *Creative Imagination in the Sufism of Ibn Arabi* (Princeton, 1969), p. 215. I use this quotation not only for its aptness but also to direct the reader to a complex work which sheds a great deal of light on many of the matters discussed in this essay.
7. Duncan, introduction to *The Years As Catches* (Berkeley, 1966), p. x.
8. Duncan, 'Ideas of the Meaning of Form', in *The Poetics of the New American Poetry* (New York, 1973), pp. 195–96.

9. Duncan, 'Passages 2', in *Bending the Bow* (New York, 1968), p. 11. Copyright © 1966, 1967, 1968 by Robert Duncan. Reprinted by permission of New Directions Publishing Corporation.
10. Duncan, *Dante* (New York, 1974), n. pag.
11. Duncan, et al., *Robert Duncan, an Interview* (Toronto, 1971), n. pag.
12. Duncan, *The H.D. Book*, 'Rites of Participation', in *A Caterpillar Anthology* (New York, 1971), p. 24.
13. Robert Creeley, 'To disclose that vision particular to dreams', *A Quick Graph* (San Francisco, 1970), p. 198.
14. See note 11.
15. Duncan, 'Source', *Derivations* (London, 1968), p. 130.
16. See note 10.
17. *Charles Olson and Robert Creeley: The Complete Correspondence*, ed. George Butterick, Vol. 5 (Santa Barbara, 1983), p. 109.
18. See note 10.
19. Duncan, *The Years as Catches*, pp. i & ii.
20. *The Years as Catches*, p. i.
21. Duncan, 'Narrative Bridges for "Adam's Way" ', *Bending the Bow*, p. 107.
22. Charles Olson, 'April 24 1959', *OLSON, The Journal of the Charles Olson Archives* (Number 9, Spring 1978), University of Connecticut Library.
23. *The Years as Catches*, p. x.
24. Duncan, 'Preface to a reading of Passages 1–22', *Maps*, Vol. 6, ed. John Taggart (Lawhead Press, Pennsylvania, 1974).
25. See note 10.
26. Charles Olson, 'Against Wisdom As Such', *Human Universe* (New York, 1967), p. 70.
27. See note 10.
28. 'Golden Lines', *Bending the Bow*, p. 92.
29. *Bending the Bow*, p. 104.
30. Duncan, 'Reflections', *Bending the Bow*, p. 38.
31. Duncan, 'Source', *Derivations*, p. 130.
32. See note 10.
33. See note 30.
34. See note 30.
35. Duncan, *The H.D. Book*, Part 2, Chapter 4, *Caterpillar* (No. 7, April 1969), p. 50.
36. See note 35.
37. Duncan, 'Reflections', *Bending the Bow*, p. 39.

14

The Poetry of Edward Dorn

by DONALD WESLING

Edward Dorn is now in his fifties, with nearly thirty years of publishing to his credit, with work including a *Collected Poems 1956–1974* (1975), a novel and other prose, translations—and *Slinger* (1975), one of the masterworks in the tradition of the American long poem. Dorn has protected his integrity by means of an early decision to publish with small houses, and by choosing to confront a political subject matter which addresses the contradictions of a historical moment. When the possibility of taking a new look at American realities seems removed by his country's entrepreneurial systems, he invents a language of the moral imagination that is capable of blowing such entrapment to rags. If English and American writers are to recover the means of facing the urgent public concerns of the era without giving up the rectitude of a personal witness (or elegance of style), Dorn's achievement will need to be known.[1]

Theory

Risking a vulnerable sentence, Dorn writes in his Preface to the *Collected Poems 1956–1974* that for him the work is ratiocinative, not bardic: 'From near the beginning I have known my work to be theoretical in nature and poetic by virtue of its inherent tone.' At least since Wordsworth we have

218

known this to be a possibility in poetry, and this self-definition might be true of nearly all good poets after 1800. It affiliates Dorn, in this regard only, with more recent figures such as Wallace Stevens, with his Black Mountain College mentor Charles Olson of course, and with the open-field poetry which represents in its sequences of syllables and perceptions the act of the mind. Both in theory and in tone, particularly in the managing of transitions, the drive of thought in an extended meditation like 'The Land Below', the declarative qualities are Wordsworthian. Such statements must of course lead on to a minimal cataloguing of what the values are which Dorn's statements express, and which are the special signature of his intelligence; for as a writer whose work is theoretical in nature, he would like us to respond to the cogency, precision of detail, and political credibility of his account of America.

The theory involves an account of human history from the earliest hunter-gatherers to the present 'North Atlantic Turbine' of commodity-production, international trade, and warfare between conscienceless collectives called nation-states: an account which is fully historical (if permissibly patchy), but also, in Black Mountain language, *areal*—locating in place as well as place-in-time certain types of material and intellectual production. One other determinant in this attempt to see the way things work is the kind of class-placing which is also, even in our Democratic Melting-pot, a form of voice-placing which can be of interest to a poet. The end-and-cover maps on some of Dorn's books are symptoms of the need to make the geographical relations particular, while images of a detonator, grenades, revolvers on at least three covers suggest one central concern: the marvellous American competence, in its benign use so humane and liberating, is also an energy that can be deflected into violence that is swift, even scientific, aesthetic. In a poetry that proposes to itself such a degree of inclusiveness, the themes which absorb other American writers—the nature of poetry, landscape and perception, heightened states of con-sciousness, primitivism, fraternity and sexuality—are by no means de-emphasized; they are merely, here, secondary.

At its largest stretch the theoretical concerns are political and economic, not in value-neutral, established definitions but in Charles Olson's Poundian-sounding ones from the *Bibliography on America for Ed Dorn* (1964):

> politics & economics . . . are like love (can only be individual experience). . . . I don't myself know how you master them except by practicing them. . . . Economics as politics as money is a gone bird. It's much more now power as state as fission.[2]

The hiddenness of contemporary power, which makes all of us victims in some measure and which has brought into much recent American history and writing the theme of the unseen assailant, becomes matter for comedy in the characters' quest for 'an inscrutable Texan named Hughes' in *Slinger*: 'Howard? I asked/ the very same/ . . . . He/ has not been seen since 1833.' Yet it would be wrong to conclude, from any review of such themes, that 'theoretical in nature' means the defecated-to-a-transparency free-verse style of a starved diction and predictable syntax. Nor does it mean Dorn's insistences are necessarily dogmatic in tone. We find him in an interview of 1972, in the midst of writing *Slinger*, hoping that his early sixties 'responsibility to say how you feel . . . has entirely gone' from a writing which now values more highly the aesthetic textures of American English.[3]

The adequate theory realizes its own limits. For Dorn as for other Black Mountain writers theory, like the poem, is not enough: not commensurate with politics, the world, or experience itself in its 'presyntactic metalinguistic urgency'. (That phrase from Book II of *Slinger*, a joking contradiction, demonstrates how Dorn can shoot academic phrases with the best.) Hence a certain sadness, and an ethical and prosodic assignment. Olson praises the syntactic eagerness of a projective verse that through sentence-fragment and denial of completed thoughts tries to represent 'the absolute condition of present things', while Robert Creeley is always against the sort of explanation which is 'anterior to instance', the usual habit of a description which 'wants to "accompany" the *real* but which assumes itself as "objectively" outside that context in some way. . . . Yet one is either there or not.' Dorn himself in his essay on Olson's *Maximus Poems* says:

> without ever having been there, I would be bored to sickness walking through [Olson's] Gloucester. . . . Description, letting

things lay, was reserved not necessarily for the doubtful, but the
slothful, or the merely busy.[4]

This Black Mountain ethos of stubborn anti-objectivity leads
to a distrust of examples, which manifests itself in an
unwillingness, typically in Dorn's *Maximus* essay, to give and
analyse quotations.

Politics

To build a scaffold from which we might construct an
adequate consideration of political writing in America, it is
best to delay emphasis on *political* till we first seek the non-
trivial meanings of the other, attached term, *poetry*. At this
level conservative and radical ideology meet in poetry, which
is by its nature in the era of late capitalism (a term Dorn does
not use) a rebellion against a time, against a form of con-
sciousness. In a business civilization where poetry is a
permitted activity, the types of poetry practised should help
define the contradictions of the historical moment. In the
capitalist countries poetry is tolerated because of its very
ability to comprehend, and resolve, complexities of attitude.
The ruling ideas—the ideas of the ruling class, however
defined—are mediated through poetry, inevitably, and to the
extent that they are poetry is supported by publishing
industries, university teaching, reviewing, and so on. (It is of
some interest that Dorn has not published with major
publishing-houses but rather, as he says in the Preface to
Collected Poems, 'with persons. . . . I have stayed with that care
because it is accurate and important.') But in American poetry
the ruling ideas are also in solution with counter-cultural ideas
and sometimes with radical ways of forming poems which are
themselves attenuated political statements. These emergent
and unincorporated ideas, utopian in their direction, diverse,
irrepressible, are a profoundly central element not only in
poetry as written since the Romantics but also in the myth of
poetry, of the bardic presence or solitary singer. Thus the poet
in a business civilization is at once on the furthest margins of his
or her society, and yet also central to the consciousness of
society. The imaginative, anti-technological, insurgent ideas

which have informed poetry since Wordsworth are, however, contained and softened by their presence in that escapist, ornamental institution: Poetry. Everything is permitted in poetry because its speech is by definition separate from the realm of action, which is the only realm which threatens capitalist enterprise. This situation, in which poetry is permitted but its complex indictment defined as irrelevant, constitutes a cycle from which in theory and practice one must break in order to defend political poetry, and thereby to describe and defend all poetry.

This didactic sketch helps us begin to see the difficulty of the position of Pound and Eliot, writers who wish in their social theories to negate consciousness, but who had to employ a literary form whose post-Romantic mission was to bring as much into consciousness as possible. Pound like Eliot was mistaken to think changes in his own material of literary language could budge anything in the fundamental base in economics and in the relations of classes, and yet Pound, of the two, especially believed in the social function of the poet and his art. Pound felt, even in the monstrous Rome radio talks which were meant with absolute sincerity, that the poet must affirm; this has made him more believable to such as Olson and Dorn, whose politics, so far as one can tell, are the opposite of authoritarian and élitist. Tracking some such line of thought Peter Ackroyd, in an accurate short review, argues Dorn's poetry of statement makes him 'the only plausible political poet in America', and then goes on to say political poetry 'has nothing whatever to do with the extent of the poet's political knowledge, his *savoir faire*, or even the "side" he takes; it has to do with the quality of his response to public situations, not whether that response is "right" or "wrong".'[5] The first reaction to Ackroyd, not my own, might well be the question: what, then, is so special about Dorn's response that makes it qualitatively superior to Lowell's, or Ginsberg's, or Bly's, or that of Adrienne Rich? One answer would be to show the nature of Dorn's analysis of the way things work, which moves very often on the level of world-systems and commodities as well as the level of personalities; to a greater extent he situates the psychological and individualist possibilities within a larger frame of reference. My own reaction to Ackroyd is to argue that his relativism of preferring quality to rightness of response is satisfactory at the level of our discussion of poetry as a counter-cultural form which is permitted in a business civilization, but begins to disintegrate when we get down to cases. Compare, for example, the extreme insistence of Lautréamont's 'Poetry must be made by everybody, not by one', on the one hand, and on the other the Rilke-Stevens cult of poetry as creating value when there was none before. As against the élitist theology of poetry, which is always in our century associated with reactionary politics, Dorn points in the direction of Lautréamont. It is not the first time (I think of Wordsworth, Whitman and Mayakovsky) that a populist poet had a certain degree of difficulty.

The people: not the masses, and certainly not the public. Thus Dorn's transfiguration of the genres of popular culture in his writing. The *Collected Poems* has fifty-nine songs listed in its contents, several Letters, a sixteen-page Sportscast on the subject of Colonialism, as well as an Oration, a History, a Notation, a Message, a Prayer, an Argument, a Pronouncement, an Explanation, a Chronicle, and an Obituary. *Slinger* as a metaphysical Western which is also a Quest, sets going a Talking Horse and a Talking Cracker Barrel, parodies the movies in its Literate Projector, includes a number of Songs and the THWANG THWANG punctuation of a guitar, and plays with the specialized lingos of philosophy and science, of the Newspaper and the Nightletter. Any survey of Dorn must also describe the rare item, *Bean News*, an Art Newspaper which associates with poetry because it gives all the news that *has been*, the news which because it is unparaphrasable and needs to be reproduced in exactly the same words *stays news*; more recently he has edited a three-times-a-year national newspaper of politics and the arts, *Rolling Stock* (Boulder, Colorado). There is also the fully characteristic publication, by Turtle Island press, of *Recollections of Gran Apachería* in a $12.00 art book and a $2.00 version dressed up exactly (with cartoon cover by Michael Myers) as a comic book. In addition to translating scorching guerrilla poems from Cuba and elsewhere in *Our Word* (1968), Dorn has (with Gordon Brotherston) done strong versions from Vallejo, the Peruvian who manages to be at once hermetic-surrealist and political, difficult and, in intention at least, nonetheless a people's poet.

The trouble with setting up as the people's poet in North America (Vallejo did so for Peru, finally, from Paris!) is, in one of Dorn's images, that so many of one's fellow citizens are complicit constabulary driving pickups with shotgun racks. Their America, of the Shale Contract, the Bloody Red Meat Habit, the railroad, the cash nexus, the Vietnam venture, is not the poet's America. Dorn's becomes a populist poetry for a people which does not yet exist, or exists in the quasi-tribal fellowship of writers and other craftsmen, or exists in the honorable part of the consciousness of those who are redeemable. This kind of utopian imagination is especially rare in America, doubtless for American reasons: related to the fact that we have had our revolution two centuries ago and the geographical frontier has been sealed off for a century.

An idea of the people may also be forged from our actively imagining and seeking the condition of America's victims: our failures, misfits, war-resisters, dead miners, the raped, and our Blacks and especially our Indians—those who are botched variously by the heavily mediated and mystified activities of the (for short) robber barons and pickup drivers. (Dorn is fascinated by the personalities of Daniel Drew, John Paul Getty and Howard Hughes.) Poems about and for this nomad élite of the oppressed always touch something centrally important in Dorn's politics, and I would list as exemplary 'Like a Message on Sunday', 'On the Debt My Mother Owed to Sears Roebuck', 'Los Mineros', 'The Land Below', 'The Problem of the Poem for my Daughter, Left Unsolved', 'For the New Union Dead in Alabama', 'The Sundering U. P. Tracks', all of *Recollections of Gran Apachería*, and 'Mourning Letter, March 29, 1963', whose lines to the starved miners of Hazard, Kentucky, end: 'Oh, go letter,/ keep my own misery close to theirs/ associate me with no other honor.' Beautiful in their writing and in their morality, the obligatory pages which describe Dorn's visit to the ancient Shoshoni Indian Willie Dorsey, in *The Shoshoneans* (his documentary study of 1966), derive from the same absolute identification with the dispossessed originals or strangers, 'the people who for one reason or another have compromised their allegiance to the thing that might destroy us all, including them.'[6]

This politics beyond the forms of politics is historical and racial, then, in its concerns; but also, in the fullest sweep of a writing 'theoretical in nature', global: political economy in the multinational era, a new movement when Hughes and Getty are themselves among the vanishing species of tycoons. *Collected Poems* includes a book of 1967, *The North Atlantic Turbine*, the most penetrating attempt any American poet has made at an inquiry, in and through imaginative thinking, into the world system of trade, control, and oppression. 'We are *all* in the sarcen circle./ We are *all* in the *da nang*.' It can only be asserted here that the six parts of the *Turbine* poem 'Oxford', enabled by a lyrical line of great prosodic interest and variety, move through paradox and humour to an analysis (idiosyncratic but highly searching) of multinational capitalism and of reasons why the American poet need not be overwhelmed by the weight of European culture.

> What they do in Freeborn County Minnesota is *more* my
> business.
> I grew up with death. I do not
> need to be reminded of anything
> by Europe, least of all do the easy
> >> corrections
> > of England
> >> instruct me. . . .

In the global context and in the American one, as Dorn writes in the first line of the first *Turbine* poem, 'Thesis', 'Only the Illegitimate are beautiful', only the nomad élite are 'Children/ of the Sun'; and yet 'only the Good/ proliferate'; hence the note of resignation that the bad Good will prevail because they control the means of production and thus the ruling ideas. That last phrasing is not Dorn's own way of speaking and doubtless too much compresses my own ideas of a materialist imagination, while it also over-specifies positions somewhat from Dorn's highly complex and qualified statement. But what I have said conveys Dorn's drift. So Ackroyd's notion of a value-neutral political poetry must be challenged. We may call this a socialist or populist poetry, but it tends in a certain direction and must freeze out a certain readership of those who are unnerved by any attempt to analyse and denounce. Yet those who are willing to follow an argument wherever it goes, who can accept that a political poetry can also move by zaniness, hesitation, wit, laconism, sudden bursts of speed, metaphorical leap, as well as by statement and denunciation, will find the arbitrariness justified.

If, as I believe, the subject of the political poem is the least adequately formulated of any in modern poetics, the reason for this state of affairs is itself political and has to do with unsolved and indeed unaddressed enigmas in the sociology of knowledge. In an otherwise splendid review of *Collected Poems* and *Slinger*, Marjorie Perloff calls Dorn's 'the lyric of geography, not of history. Accordingly, his overtly political poems are often simplistic and one-dimensional. "Whit Sunday" is invective rather than poetry'[7]: a typical dismissal, almost cheery in its complicity with a nodding editor and audience, and one index of the kind of difficulties any truly fine political poet will encounter when she or he tries to write for the people. To set the matter up as the binary opposition invective/poetry is to render it insoluble from the beginning, and that does seem to be the intention. That kind of critical sleight derives from schisms which go right through Anglo-American culture, dividing self from others, forestalling inquiry. It is our way of not really doing politics in our critical practice.

Slinger

Turbine includes 'An Idle Visitation', a strange and dazzling poem which does not fit with the others there, and which becomes the germ of *Gunslinger* (later called *Slinger* when Books I–IV were collected in the same volume in 1975). In his 1972 interview with Barry Alpert, Dorn says this poem's title is exact; the poem just arrived. To extend it into a narrative involved, we now see, pursuing to the fullest extent the themes and prosodies of his shorter poems. As he came out of the 1960s, his own several years' stay in England, and the analysis Vietnam forced upon all explainers of what there is of the American Mind, Dorn increasingly discovered another and more inward direction in *Slinger*. This long laughing anti-epic of the American Southwest is a kind of comedy of dogmatism, parodic and even self-parodic, the evanescence of space and

time relations and even of capitalism, and the entrance into the
new dimension of what he has called *intensity*. One's initial
response to it is a kind of excited apprenticeship, of the sort
which must have greeted the appearance of Williams's *Paterson*,
and the politics of the thing are so far under the surface that we
cannot even estimate the extent of the complexities before us.

   The area relation: South by West; Truth or Consequences
New Mexico, otherwise known as Universe City; Vegas. The
persons: Slinger, Semidíos and existential outlaw; the Stoned
Horse; Miss Lil, a whorehouse madam; Kool Everything, from
the drug culture; Dr. Flamboyant, a refugee from the
University; the literal-minded character 'I' whose questions
represent those of the puzzled reader, and who is killed off only
to be brought back; and Howard Hughes, who is present as a
determining absence: tracked by the others, who in their
journey become, as Dorn says to Alpert, 'a society in
trajectory'. The allusions: from Parmenides to Heidegger,
Lévi-Strauss, the drug culture, the oil industry, the Lone
Ranger, Delmore Schwartz, a heap of arcane and obvious
cultural clutter. The language: 'derives from a combination of
western soap opera, newspeak, rock-and-roll lyric, scientific
cybernetic argot, Shelleyan rhapsody, and comic strip
dialogue' (Michael Davidson's words from a fugitive article).
The allegory: finally, I suspect, this repeats in a finer tone
Turbine's interest in money's fundamental unreality as metal
and paper and trust, and the way this is combined with
absolute power by virtue of being *turned into* labour and
commodities, creating here a Hughes, there a 'Scarcity
Industry'. To suggest the range of the poem, I would offer a
passage which contains one of several lesser allegories, an
extended personification:

>   CO-KÁNG! is the way it begaine,
>   was a Girl from the montaine
>   raised on air and light
>   Erythralynn, painted with red clay
>   and dressed in leaves resembling myrtle
>   Erythra with a wig of roots
>   and she was vulgar and strong
>   as pure salt
>   and intuition came to her

like the red deer to a lick
to blow the bare words of insinuation
into human nature
the only nature to her,
because this Girl
is permanent Only in the air
Miss Americaine, was a mountain thaing
dressed in red bright calico
a long and tender radiating crystal
and like the knowledge in her nose
a lioness, intense
to the switching of the Inner Trail
which leads by hidden passage
to the Absolute Outside
yes, dressed in red bright calico
the sunne moves down
on the girl from Cuzco

Bright Erythra, the girl in calico
when the sunne comes up on Cuzco

She snaps her fingers
and they produce the numbers
never produced before, $C_{19} H_{21}$, then
five times more for the fugitive NO_4
five times more to lock it ON
the awful shyness of the NO_4

This, from Book IV, does for cocaine grown in South America
what Virgil or Dante would have done for it were they our
contemporaries: in an ample and ingenious metaphor sees the
drug's psychological effects and chemical makeup as the
attributes of a girl with a 'wig of roots'. In the vigour of its
concept and prosody—never mind the subject matter—such
an achievement makes natural, in free verse, gestures of genre
that are as old as poetry.

Slinger, though, tends to resist description. It is 'about' how
and why we spend money and words in this 'cosmological'
place, America; about, and enacting through puns, surreal
imagery, personifications, the texture of jokes, the paradoxical
aspects of thinking; about how a narrative line snares attention
despite or because of derangements; and about how a self or
voice can be differentiated into a cluster of other selves, which

228

then have a quasi-life of their own as voices-in-recitative. Barry
Alpert asked: 'Where's your personal presence in *Gunslinger?*'
Dorn: 'Omnipresent. It's omnipresent, absolutely omni-
present. . . . Actually, I'm absolutely uncommitted except to
what's happening.' So the first person singular, in an apotheosis
of the dramatic monologue, is first eliminated (the death of the
character 'I'), and then reintroduced as an omnipresence by a
poet who in the same interview says he believes in 'the shared
mind'. This is not, in our experience of the poem, in any way
contradictory, but it makes for a very high degree of opacity as
we struggle, in the absence of nearly all clues of punctuation or
quotation marks, to find which of the particular voices is speak-
ing at a given moment. That frustration is built in, intentional,
and one of the pleasures of the poem once you finally discover
the mechanism. Dorn in this poem followed the freedom of his
donnée, and that that was good and necessary should become
clearer the longer we live with and in the poem. Eventually an
account of *Slinger* will demonstrate how, without contradiction,
those complexities of matter and perspective, now so forbidding,
are really clarifying developments of a consistently populist
lifework.

The full reckoning will, I imagine, take as one ideological
marker the example of Hughes's reclusive weirdness ('they say
he moved to Vegas/ or BOUGHT VEGAS and/ moved it./ I can't
remember which'). That experience is so symbolic we would
have had to invent it (Clifford Irving tried) if it had not
happened (history continued Dorn's fiction in the isolate death
and verification of the body, the C.I.A. connections, the farce of
the wills): symbolic of the intense ingrown privacies of wealth,
the human incommensurability of 'the most crucial thing we
know, money' (Dorn to Alpert), the absolute perversion of
value. The other marker will be Willie Dorsey, in whom, Dorn
says in *The Shoshoneans*, 'we are honored to witness the total
exclusion of the private.'

Recent Work

After publication of the complete *Slinger* in 1975, Dorn
turned to epigram, aphorism, what he himself called 'dis-
patches' light and essential enough to be taken 'in the spirit/ of

the Pony Express'. In this Dorn seems to have been influenced in part by Robert Creeley's scorn of longer narrative forms, which reinforced Dorn's own need in the mid-'70s to find a speech more responsive to immediate social judgements than the long poem. The major volume between *Slinger* and the present day is *Hello, La Jolla* (1978), which consists (except for the five pages of 'Alaska') mainly of brief poems, some short enough to have been written while driving on California's route 101, one hand tied to the steering wheel. (Dorn: 'A rather open scrawl while one's eyes are fixed to the road is the only trick to be mastered.') Out of Dorn's notebooks from the late '70s Tom Clark has made another book from related materials, sparks tiny but brilliant, called *Yellow Lola, formerly titled Japanese Neon* (1981). From his base in Boulder, Colorado, Dorn is currently working on an extensive project concerning the American high plains, and once we have that we will be better able to estimate the place in his work of the brevities of the late '70s. Especially since the time of his stay in England for some years in the '60s, Dorn has been a reader of the great English satirists, for whom he feels an affinity. The Swiftian relationship to a select group of readers, the larger Augustan way of being political but not partisan, has already been explored for these two recent volumes by Alan Golding, and Kathryn Shevelow has argued that even the active readers of Dorn, the insiders, are now also subject to Dorn's ironies, implicated in the cultural analysis.[8]

Prosodies

In that free verse, which is, we have to remind ourselves, only relatively freer than the usual, technique as sincerity requires a way of constituting the poetic line which omits or distorts traditional metre and rhyme. In theory there are as many ways of doing this as there are free-verse poems; in practice there are a few major types. Dorn's writing partakes of the style of a school, and exploits and focuses a language similar to that of Olson, Creeley, Robert Duncan, Jonathan Williams. The loosely-collected group style known as Black Mountain may be generally indicated in its premises by Duncan's phrase 'mind is shapely', or William Carlos Williams's 'the poet thinks with his poem'. Despite Duncan's marvellous statements on such matters as the tone-leading of vowels, this kind of writing has always been more concerned with tracing a line of thinking than with euphony in the line of syllables. The response to one another of the sounds in Olson's lines is not often a matter of interest, and this is one way we might begin to distinguish Dorn's own from the group style. 'The Rick of Green Wood', from 1956 and the first item printed in *Collected Poems*, shows Dorn completely capable with free-verse techniques. I would also point to the variegation or scatter-page measures in Pound's later *Cantos* and in Olson's *Maximus Poems*, which are hardly carrying measures for a long unfolding utterance in the way of Dorn's medium-length lines in *Slinger*. Dorn's lines here are not anything like parcelled-out iambs in blank verse, or like Whitmanic one-line staves, and yet they do have an equality of length that is (despite other frustrations, and there are many) reassuring. The long poem's intent to develop a narrative, mostly by means of dialogue, meant retracting somewhat in prosodic format from the earlier, forbidding masterworks. In *Slinger*, the reader's difficulties are not primarily formal but in the hip metaphysics of point of view, voice, concept. Yet the poem's prosodies enact its play of ideas and wit, and so doing are a summation of many of Dorn's own achieved stylistic gestures as well as Black Mountain's.

In his shorter poems Dorn justifies the arbitrariness of his measures in a choral redundancy ('Thesis'), in witty social exploration (parts of 'Oxford'), nostalgia ('The Air of June Sings', 'Hemlocks'), tribute ('From Gloucester Out', 'Sousa', 'Mourning Letter'), and the love song, among other generic-prosodic types. Close inspection turns up a rich working of rhyme effects, almost always as instance rather than anterior-to-the-poem or line-end design. In one of the 'Love Songs', rhyme is an image for ecstatic consciousness:

> EYE high gloria
>   a fine europ ean morn ing
>   black coffee
> for Nick in the nick of time
> he gives me something for you
> and Otis Redd ing

with his feet up watching
infinity roll in and Nick
his time ing
and sudden lee the lid
comes off
            and we head straight for
the thing we could be in
cannabic warm
and rime ing

Typically, the attractiveness of the sounds in his 'Rick of Green Wood', or in a line like 'The banding of her slight-smiling lassitude', is always poised against the wryness of the thinking. Among Black Mountain writers he is the master of the singing line, and the use of that skill of prosodic speed and accuracy in the service of ambitious public concerns makes for his real distinctiveness. 'Theoretical in nature,' he says of the work, 'and poetic by virtue of its inherent tone': the free-verse writer can claim professional craft to the same extent as the rhyme-and-meter writer, yet is far less apt to fetishize his medium as order, with history and ordinary language as some miserable chaos. To the extent that this is so, free verse is perhaps less likely to be the vehicle of a reactionary politics.

Voice

The technical aspects of any poet's 'inherent tone' are diction, syntax and the devices of equivalence from metaphor to rhyme to the units of the chosen measure. But the moral aspect of tone, as the implied relation of writer to reader, involves the neglected category of voice. Voice is what the beginning writer needs to know and show in poems to recognize distinctiveness, and what the professional writer has to diversify and control to drive every intended effect home along the sequence of the reader's acts of attention. Dorn's own reading of *Slinger*, on tape now in various archives, is of an unexpected flatness, given the possibilities for hamming up the material. The many voices resolve into the one witty drone, and finally that seems right as a way of not specifying the relations of grammar, diction, person. Supercool lack of effect is the basic position, maintained by multiple perspective and by fending off or sending up every approach of cliché. And yet this resolves itself into a whole spread of more personal strategies of voice, all within range of the true, central voice (though more distant and indeterminate in the case of *Slinger*). This is, then, a political poetry which, in addition to being declarative with no diminishment of theory, is philosophical, affectionate, subtle, singing and humorous. Dorn writes in 'Idaho Out': 'My desire is to be/ a classical poet.' He is.

NOTES

1. The first comprehensive appraisal of the work, a focused collection of essays on Dorn's career by six readers, is *Internal Resistances: The Poetry of Edward Dorn*, edited by Donald Wesling (University of California Press, 1984).

   Thanks are due to Herbert Leibowitz, the editor of *Parnassus: Poetry in Review* (New York), for permission to use as the basis of the present essay my 'Bibliography on Edward Dorn for America', which appeared in the Spring–Summer issue, 1977.

   Passages longer than three lines from Edward Dorn's *Collected Poems 1956–1974* (Four Seasons Foundation) and from the poet's *Slinger* (Wingbow Press, 1975), are quoted by permission from the publishers, to whom grateful acknowledgement is made.

2. Charles Olson, *A Bibliography on America for Ed Dorn* (San Francisco: Four Seasons Foundation, 1964), especially p. 16.

3. 'An Interview with Barry Alpert', in Edward Dorn, *Interviews*, edited by Donald M. Allen (San Francisco: Four Seasons Foundation).

4. Passages from Olson, Creeley and Dorn from their respective essays as reprinted in Donald M. Allen and Warren Tallman (eds.), *The Poetics of the New American Poetry* (New York: Grove Press, 1973).

5. Peter Ackroyd, 'In Public', a review of *Collected Poems 1956–1974* in *The Spectator* (London), 10 January 1976.

6. Quoted from Edward Dorn, *The Poet, The People, The Spirit*, transcript of a lecture given 1 July 1965 at the Berkeley Poetry Conference (Vancouver, B.C.: Talonbooks, 1976), p. 29.

7. Marjorie Perloff, review of *Collected Poems 1956–1974* and *Slinger*, in *The New Republic* (New York), 24 April 1976.

8. Alan Golding writes on *Hello, La Jolla* and *Yellow Lola* in the last chapter of *Internal Resistances*, the book cited above in Note 1. Kathryn Shevelow has reviewed *Yellow Lola* in *Chicago Review* 33 (Summer 1981); and her article on 'Reading Edward Dorn's *Hello, La Jolla* and *Yellow Lola*' is published in *Sagetrieb* (Orono, Maine), 1984. Edward Dorn's most recent book is *Captain Jack's Chaps or Houston/MLA* (Madison, Wisconsin: Black Mesa Press, 1983).

Notes on Contributors

JOSEPH ALLARD is a lecturer in literature at the University of Essex. He has published a number of essays on American painting, prose and poetry, and on French music and art theory. He is co-editor of Ampersand (poetry) Press, has edited two anthologies of recent British poetry, and is a founder of the Essex Festival.

R. W. (HERBIE) BUTTERFIELD, the editor of this volume, is Reader in Literature at the University of Essex. He is the author of a book on Hart Crane, a monograph on Robinson Jeffers, and numerous essays and shorter pieces on American poets and prose-writers, including Poe, Hawthorne, Melville, James, Cather and Hemingway.

GRAHAM CLARKE is a lecturer in English and American literature at the University of Kent and the current chairman of its American Studies programme. His publications include pieces on Hawthorne, Hemingway and Black American writing. He has an especial interest in the literature of American landscape and in American painting.

ANDREW CROZIER was a graduate student in the Department of Literature at the University of Essex from 1965 to 1967. He now teaches at the University of Sussex.

MICHAEL EDWARDS has published several collections of poetry, and translations from French, Italian and Spanish. His critical works include books on Racine, T. S. Eliot and Christian Poetics, and he has edited volumes on Raymond Queneau, contemporary French poetry, and the relation of words and music. For a number of years he was a joint editor of *Prospice*. He is Reader in Literature at the University of Essex.

RICHARD GRAY is Reader in Literature at the University of Essex. He has edited two anthologies of American Poetry, a collection of essays on Robert Penn Warren, and (in the Critical Studies series) a collection of essays on American Fiction. He is also the author of *The Literature of Memory: Modern Writers of the American South* as well as essays on American poetry and fiction.

JACK HILL is a lecturer in literature at the University of Essex, with particular reference to the Literature and Art of the English and Italian Renaissance. He also teaches a course in Classical Latin Poetry. He was co-editor and translator of the *Everyman Book of Baroque Poetry*, and is a poet, whose published volumes include *An Eagle Each* (with David Pownall), *Passport to Walk*, and *The Turns of Time*, a sequence of memorial poems.

JACQUELINE KAYE is a lecturer in literature at the University of Essex. She has written articles on Melville, Naipaul, St. Omer and Marti and several comparative studies of United States, Caribbean and Latin American literature.

CLIVE MEACHEN teaches American literature at the University College of Wales, Aberystwyth. He is the author of a study of Charles Olson.

ERIC MOTTRAM is Professor of English and American Literature at King's College, University of London. He is author of books on Faulkner, Ginsberg, Rexroth, Burroughs, Paul Bowles, and the theory of poetry; of numerous essays on such writers as Poe, Melville, Hawthorne, Pound, Dahlberg, Douglas Woolf and Hemingway, as well as on technology and science fiction; and of a dozen books of poetry, the latest being *A Book of Herne* and *Interrogation Rooms*.

GABRIEL PEARSON is Professor of Literature at the University of Essex. He was founder-editor of *New Left Review*. With John Gross he edited *Dickens and the Twentieth Century*. He has published essays on Thomas Mann, Iris Murdoch, Henry James, Dickens, Arnold, Berryman, Lowell, Winters, Malamud and Bellow, and, with Eric Rhode, on 'New Wave' French cinema and Antonioni. He has been a frequent contributor to a number of journals and a regular reviewer for *The Guardian*. He has just completed an essay for a collection on Geoffrey Hill.

JIM PHILIP is a lecturer in American and modern English literature at the University of Essex. He has also been a visiting fellow at the University of Pennsylvania. His doctoral thesis was on the poetry of William Carlos Williams and Charles Olson, and he has published essays on, amongst others, Theodore Dreiser and John Middleton Murry.

235

JEREMY REED is a poet whose published volumes include *Bleecker Street* (Carcanet Press), *By the Fisheries* (Jonathan Cape, 1984), and a novel, *The Lipstick Boys* (Enitharmion Press, 1984). He is writing a doctoral thesis on Hart Crane for the University of Essex.

DONALD WESLING is Professor of English Literature at the University of California, San Diego. He is the author of books on Wordsworth, John Muir the California naturalist, and the phenomenon of poetic rhyme; and the editor of *Internal Resistances*, a collection of essays on Edward Dorn's poetry.

Index

237

Index

238

Index

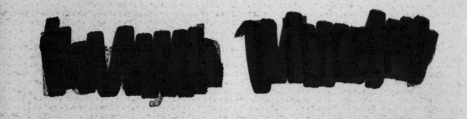